# Prisoners of Hope?

Aspects of Evangelical Millennialism
in Britain and Ireland, 1800-1880

STUDIES IN EVANGELICAL HISTORY AND THOUGHT

STUDIES IN EVANGELICAL HISTORY AND THOUGHT

# Prisoners of Hope?

Aspects of Evangelical Millennialism
in Britain and Ireland, 1800-1880

Edited by
Crawford Gribben and
Timothy C. F. Stunt

Foreword by David Bebbington

**PATERNOSTER**

Copyright© Crawford Gribben and Timothy C. F. Stunt
and the contributors 2004

First published 2004 by Paternoster

Paternoster is an imprint of Authentic Media,
9 Holdom Avenue, Bletchley, Milton Keynes, MK1 1QR, U.K.
and
P.O.Box 1047, Waynesboro, GA 30830-2047, U.S.A.

10 09 08 07 06 05 04 1 2 3 4 5 6 7

The right of Crawford Gribben and Timothy C. F. Stunt to be identified
as the Editors of this Work has been asserted by them in accordance
with the Copyright, Designs and Patents Act 1988.

*All rights reserved. No part of this publication may be reproduced, stored in a
retrieval system, or transmitted, in any form or by any means, electronic,
mechanical, photocopying, recording or otherwise, without the prior permission
of the publisher or a license permitting restricted copying. In the UK such
licenses are issued by the Copyright Licensing Agency, 90 Tottenham Court
Road, London W1P 9HE.*

**British Library Cataloguing in Publication Data**
A catalogue record for this book is available from the British Library

ISBN 1-84227-224-1

Typeset by Crawford Gribben
Printed and bound in Great Britain
for Paternoster

# Series Preface

The Evangelical movement has been marked by its union of four emphases: on the Bible, on the cross of Christ, on conversion as the entry to the Christian life and on the responsibility of the believer to be active. The present series is designed to publish scholarly studies of any aspect of this movement in Britain or overseas. Its volumes include social analysis as well as exploration of Evangelical ideas. The books in the series consider aspects of the movement shaped by the Evangelical Revival of the eighteenth century, when the impetus to mission began to turn the popular Protestantism of the British Isles and North America into a global phenomenon. The series aims to reap some of the rich harvest of academic research about those who, over the centuries, have believed that they had a gospel to tell to the nations.

# Series Editors

David Bebbington, Professor of History, University of Stirling, Stirling, Scotland, UK

John H.Y. Briggs, Senior Research Fellow in Ecclesiastical History and Director of the Centre for Baptist History and Heritage, Regent's Park College, Oxford, UK

Timothy Larsen, Associate Professor of Theology, Wheaton College, Illinois, USA

Mark A. Noll, McManis Professor of Christian Thought, Wheaton College, Wheaton, Illinois, USA

Ian M. Randall, Deputy Principal and Lecturer in Church History and Spirituality, Spurgeon's College, London, UK, and a Senior Research Fellow, International Baptist Theological Seminary, Prague, Czech Republic

# Contents

# Contributors

Dr Tim Grass is an associate lecturer at Spurgeon's College, London and teaches occasionally in seminaries in Eastern Europe. He has edited *Evangelicalism and the Orthodox Church* (2001) and has written numerous articles on nineteenth-century church history, hymnody and Eastern Orthodoxy. He is currently writing a history of the Brethren movement in Britain and Ireland.

Dr Crawford Gribben is Research Fellow in the Centre for Irish-Scottish Studies at Trinity College, Dublin. In autumn 2004 he will take up a new appointment in English and American Studies at the University of Manchester. He is the author of *The Puritan Millennium* (2000) and a number of articles on puritan, evangelical and millennial studies.

Dr Andrew Holmes is Research Associate at the Academy for Irish Cultural Heritages, Magee College, University of Ulster. He was awarded a Ph.D. from Queen's University, Belfast, in 2002 for a thesis entitled 'Ulster Presbyterian belief and practice, 1770-1840'.

Professor Gary L. Nebeker is Associate Professor of Theology at Grace University in Omaha, Nebraska. He has recently published a number of articles in *Bibliotheca Sacra, Trinity Journal, Journal of Biblical Counseling, Fides et Historia,* and *The Evangelical Review of Theology,* and currently serves on the steering committee of the Dispensational Study Group of the Evangelical Theological Society in North America.

Professor Douglas Shantz holds the Endowed Chair of Christian Thought in the Department of Religious Studies at the University of Calgary, Alberta, Canada. His fields of research are the radical Reformation and radical German Pietism, including Pietist millennialism, spiritual autobiography and Pietist forms of community. His first book was *Crautwald and Erasmus: A Study in Humanism and Radical Reform in 16th Century Silesia* (1992); at press is a study of the Reformed Pietist Court Preacher Konrad Broske (1660-1713).

Professor Ken Stewart, a Canadian, is Professor of Theological Studies in Covenant College, Lookout Mountain, Georgia. A graduate of Westminster Theological Seminary and the University of Waterloo, he gained the Edinburgh Ph.D. for a dissertation on British evangelical involvement in post-Napoleonic Europe. His recent publications include 'Evangelicals and the Apocrypha', in *Books and Culture* (May-June 2003), and 'William J. Abraham's *Canon and Criterion:* An Historical-Theological Reflection', in *Didaskalia* (Winter 2003).

Dr Timothy C. F. Stunt has been a teacher of History, Literature and Latin in secondary schools in England, Switzerland and the United States. His *From Awakening to Secession: Radical Evangelicals in Switzerland and Britain 1815-35* (2000) earned him a Ph.D. from Cambridge University. He has written numerous articles on early nineteenth-century church history and is currently working on a biography of the textual scholar Samuel Prideaux Tregelles.

# Foreword

'Household franchise and lodgers' franchise are fulfilling prophecy', it was said in 1880, 'and causing us to hear the chariot-wheels of the coming King.'[1] In the year that marks the end-point of the coverage of this volume, it was believed that the granting of the vote to a wider public in Britain was a sign of the imminence of the second coming. A mass electorate would wield power irresponsibly and in antagonism to the laws of the Almighty. Only the return of Christ would set matters right. Prophecy was conceived as having a direct bearing on the political developments of the day. The journal from which the quotation is taken, the *Christian,* was particularly fond of dwelling on such themes, but it was by no means alone in looking at the secular world through the prism of millennia! expectations. Evangelicals as a whole, the dominant sector in global English-speaking Christianity, regarded events in church and state alike as the fulfilment of prophecy. Here were the roots of the enthusiasm for prophetic studies that marked late twentieth-century America. The best-selling book of the 1970s was Hal Lindsey's *The Late Great Planet Earth,* a vivid synopsis of the dispensationalism that originated in the British Isles in the early nineteenth century. The rise of new forms of millennialism in that period has a major bearing on the subsequent evolution of Protestant Christianity.

Few aspects of the history of the faith have been so subject to misapprehension as the field covered by the current book. It is often supposed that by the nineteenth century, millennialism, whatever its earlier history, was the preserve of wild fanatics and confined to obscure sects. In reality, however, distinctive forms of millennia! expectation were upheld by politicians, scholars and men of culture. Lord Shaftesbury, the greatest social reformer of the nineteenth century, for example, was a committed adherent of premillennial teaching. Again, it is commonly thought that prophetic studies, by whomsoever held, constituted a form of private hobby and so were of

---

[1] *Christian,* 22 April 1880, 12.

marginal significance. On the contrary, the various types of millennia!belief were intimately bound up with central themes of Christian thought and practice. The postmillennial party, holding that Christ would return only after the millennium, looked confidently for the spread of vital Christianity over the whole earth before that time and so participated actively in the rising Protestant world missions. The premillennial school, expecting an imminent second advent, eventually decided in the early twentieth century that social reform was a worthless way of propping up structures destined to destruction and so turned against what they denigrated as the 'social gospel'. Millennialism contributed a great deal to forming the worldview of its adherents and so impinged on most other attitudes of Evangelical believers.

For these reasons a set of studies of millennia!beliefs during the nineteenth century is a particularly welcome addition to the historical literature. In these essays the existing scholarship in the area is appraised and many of the important developments in the period are identified. J. N. Darby and Edward Irving, two of the giants in the interpretation of prophecy, loom appropriately large, but the opinions of ordinary occupants of pews are not neglected. The contribution of Ireland is properly highlighted, but the role of thinkers in England and Scotland is not undervalued. So millennia! hope in the British Isles has been given more of its due. The differing ways in which Christians looked at prophecy have been newly explored. If some Evangelicals were imprisoned in particular expectations, many were liberated by their views of the future to attempt great things for God.


David Bebbington
University of Stirling
*May2004*

# Abbreviations

| | |
|---|---|
| AHR | *American Historical Review* |
| ANB | *American National Biography* |
| BAHNR | *Brethren Archivists and Historians Network Review* |
| BS | *Bibliotheca Sacra* |
| BR | *Biblical Research* |
| BTB | *Biblical Theology Bulletin* |
| CH | *Church History* |
| CT | *Christianity Today* |
| DNB | *Dictionary of National Biography* |
| DSCHT | *Dictionary of Scottish Church History and Theology* |
| EQ | *Evangelical Quarterly* |
| ER | *Epworth Review* |
| FH | *Fides et Historia* |
| HTR | *Harvard Theological Review* |
| JEH | *Journal of Ecclesiastical History* |
| JEPTA | *Journal of the European Pentecostal Theological Association* |

| | |
|---|---|
| *JETS* | *Journal of the Evangelical Theological Society* |
| *JHI* | *Journal for the History of Ideas* |
| *JPHSE* | *Journal of the Presbyterian Historical Society of England* |
| *JRH* | *Journal of Religious History* |
| *JRHealth* | *Journal of Religion and Health* |
| *JSNT* | *Journal for the Study of the New Testament* |
| *JURCHS* | *Journal of the United Reformed Church Historical Society* |
| *LQHR* | *London Quarterly and Holborn Review* |
| *LT* | *Literature and Theology* |
| *OED* | *Oxford English Dictionary* |
| *pp* | *Past and Present* |
| *RL RR* | *Religion in Life* |
| *RSCHS* | *Reformed Review* |
| | *Records of the Scottish Church History Society* |
| *RSR* | *Religious Studies Review* |
| *SBET* | *Scottish Bulletin of Evangelical Theology* |
| *SCJ* | *Sixteenth Century Journal* |
| *SJT* | *Scottish Journal of Theology* |
| *SSR* | *Scottish Studies Review* |
| *TB* | *Tyndale Bulletin* |
| *TS* | *Theological Studies* |
| *USQR* | *Union Seminary Quarterly Review* |

CHAPTER **1**

# Introduction

Crawford Gribben and Timothy C. F. Stunt

'Historical understanding of millenarianism does not come easily these days,' J. F. C. Harrison complained in 1979 – and, certainly with regard to the intellectual world, he was right.[1] Outside medieval studies, the significance of millennialism has been consistently underestimated in the scholarly analysis of human thought and society. And yet it is surprising that this should be so. In the mid-twentieth century, Biblical scholars agreed that eschatological themes were central to the early Christian writings.[2] Rudolf Bultmann's reading of the *Theology of the New Testament* (1955) was inherently eschatological, and Jürgen Moltmann's *Theology of Hope* (1967) initiated a revolution in theological studies by calling attention to the teleology of all Biblical thinking about God. But these studies, and the conclusions they popularised, were deeply rooted in their own historical moment, and despite a brief flurry of interest among historians in the 1970s, they made little impact on the wider scholarly community. The 'theologians of hope' enjoyed the initial momentum and suffered the ultimate decline of the utopian protest movements of the 1960s.[3] Contemporary theologians write in their shadow; but the theologians of hope are themselves in eclipse.

Harrison's comment still rings true, and the enthusiastic work of the small number of 'historians of hope' has done little to challenge

---

[1] J. F. C. Harrison, The *Second Coming: Popular Millenarianism, 1780-1850* (London, 1979), 3.
[2] For a general survey of contemporary Christian eschatology see Stephen Williams, 'Thirty years of hope: A generation of writing on eschatology,' in K. E. Brower and M. W. Elliot (eds), *The reader must understand:· Eschatology in Bible and Theology* (Leicester, 1997), 243-62.
[3] Richard Bauckham, 'Moltmann's *Theology of Hope* revisited,' *SJT* 42 (1989), 201.

wider scholarly inactivity. Eschatology is still pushed to the 'sidelines of scholarly concerns';[4] it is still the 'missing link in much contemporary theology'.[5] And if Moltmann is correct – if 'Christian eschatology...is millenarian eschatology'[6] – then a reassertion of the importance of millennialism is central to the larger project of re-establishing the importance of eschatology in the agenda of scholarly enquiry.

Paradoxically, with its lack of interest in millennialism, contemporary scholarly activity seems not to reflect the interests of contemporary popular culture. If either the Y2K scare or the reception of a number of recent books and movies is a reliable indicator, millennialism's place in popular culture seems assured. Nowhere is this more obvious than in a recent series of evangelical novels, whose description of the apocalyptic impact of the 'rapture', the rise of an Iraq-based Antichrist, the collapse of the United Nations and the ensuing 'tribulation' has propelled millennialism back into the mainstream of popular concern.[7] These *Left Behind* novels have achieved outstanding marketability, with sales increasing by some 60% in the aftermath of the terrorist attack on the World Trade Centre on 11 September 2001. Between 1995 and January 2003, the franchise sold 32 million novels and 18 million associated products, generating a $17.4 million movie and vast wealth for the series' authors. The new century is witnessing a boom in doom.

Despite their often-ambivalent reception, however, these novels are much more than merely 'a dramatic expression of...foolishness'.[8] Whatever scholars may think of the exegetical foundation and political implications of the novels' narratives, the apocalyptic tenor they represent is a fundamental expression of popular Protestantism throughout North America, with roots deep in the continent's religious history. Philip Jenkins, surveying North American cults and messiahs, has noted that 'perhaps the largest component of the religious spectrum in contemporary America remains what it has been since colonial times: a fundamentalist evangelicalism with

---

[4] Christopher Rowland, 'Mterword,' *JSNT* 25:2 (2002), 256.
[5] Dermot Lane, *Keeping Hope Alive: Stirrings in Christian Theology* (Dublin, 1996), 5.
[6] Jurgen Moltmann, *The Coming of God: Christian Eschatology* (London, 1996), 202.
[7] Crawford Gribben, 'Rapture fictions and the changing evangelical condition', *LT* 18:1 (2004), 77-94.
[8] Daniel Hertzler, 'Assessing the "Left Behind" Phenomenon', in Loren L. Johns (ed.), *Apocalypticism and Millennialism: Shaping a Believers' Church Eschatology for the Twenty-First Century* (Kitchener, Ontario, 2000), 363.

powerful millenarian strands.' Describing the history of such radical religion, he argues that 'the doomsday theme has never been far from the centre of American religious thought.'[9] But Europeans should not dismiss the centrality of eschatology as a typically American aberration. Apocalypticism and millennialism, though often consigned to the lunatic fringe of the Christian mainstream, are much closer to its heart than many historians have suspected.[10] Christian millennialism is not only central to Christian eschatology, as Moltmann has claimed; according to Paul A. Cohen, it is also one of the 'quintessential attitudes of Western civilisation'. Recent research has confirmed the extent to which the Christian faith was born with notions of apocalypse, and has never left them behind.[11]

## A Note on Terminology

Part of the problem noted by Harrison may be related to taxonomy. Many of the difficulties of millennial studies may be explained by 'the theological complexities of the subject' and the lack of an agreed vocabulary of inquiry.[12] Throughout the twentieth century, historians developed their analyses of millennialism with often little recourse to a theological terminology that had been designed specifically to describe the phenomenon. There may be sound reasons for this. The familiar terms – 'premillennial', 'postmillennial' and 'amillennial' – are not ideally suited to describe the eschatological flexibility of earlier exegetes. The terms themselves were popularised only in the nineteenth century and seem insufficiently fluid to describe an immense variety of millennial beliefs in a range of historical periods.[13] The most basic assumption of each of these terms – that the several 'thousand years' mentioned in Revelation 20 refer to only one period of time – would not be shared by every important commentator on the passage. Even in the period in which the terms were being established, 'the categories...hardly seem applicable to most of the early-nineteenth-century British works on

---

[9] Philip Jenkins, *Mystics and Messiahs: Cults and New Religions* m *American History* (Oxford, 2000), 5.
[10] Harrison, *The Second Coming* (1979), 3.
[11] Paul A. Cohen, 'Time, Culture, and Christian Eschatology: The Year 2000 in the West and the World', *AHR* 104:5 (1999), 1628.
[12] D. H. Hempton, 'Evangelicalism and eschatology', *JEH* 31(1980), 180.
[13] *OED*, s.v. For their limitations in seventeenth century and confessional contexts, see Crawford Gribben, 'The eschatology of the puritan confessions', *SBET 20:1* (2002), 51-78.

biblical prophecies.'[14] That is not to say the terms have no use – many nineteenth-century writers, such as David Brown, author of *Christ's Second Coming: Will it be Premillennial?* (1846), evidently thought they did. The essays in this volume will therefore use the established pre-, post-, and amillennial categories as terms of reference familiar to many nineteenth-century and contemporary readers.

There are similar difficulties with the distinction between 'millennialism' and 'millenarianism'. One school has argued, with Ernest Lee Tuveson, that 'millenarianism' should be identified with premillennialism, and 'millennialism' with postmillennialism. [15] But this distinction is not made with sufficient clarity or regularity to be tenable, is not supported by standard dictionaries, and if it were to be exported into the primary material, where it is rarely made at all, the effect would be confusion. The categories do overlap, but for clarity the essays in this volume will prefer to use the vocabulary of 'millennialism', if only for reasons of uniformity.

However precisely the theological terms reflect the fluidity of their subject, this focus on ideological categories should not eclipse another range of descriptive possibilities based on the implications of each eschatological position. The pre-, post- and amillennial categories are insufficient as descriptive terms in that they do not address the range of social and cultural meanings that students of prophecy derive from their millennial systems. Perhaps in an effort to address this problem, a number of historians and theologians have abandoned strictly theological terminology in favour of sociological or political categories. Bryan R. Wilson led the way with his attempt to describe millennialists (rather than the systems of thought to which they adhered) as objectivists, subjectivists or relationists. Objectivists, he argued, might believe that God would overturn the current world order (revolutionists), that the believer should abandon the current world order (introversionists), that the believer should attempt to change the current world order (reformists), or that the believer should entirely reconstruct the current world order (utopians). Subjectivists, he continued, might believe that it is not so much the world that God is interested in changing as individuals within it (conversionists). Relationists, on the other hand, might

---

[14] Sandra L. Zimdars-Swartz and Paul F. Zimdars-Swartz, 'Apocalypticism in Modern Western Europe', in Bernard McGinn, John J. Collins, and Stephen J. Stein (eds), *The Encyclopedia of Apocalypticism* (New York, 1998), ii. 269.

[15] Ernest Lee Tuveson, *Redeemer Nation: The Idea of America's Millennial Role* (Chicago, 1968), 33-4.

believe that it is not the world they are expected to change but rather their perception of it (manipulationists), or that millennia! beliefs urge little more than a conviction that God will intervene in the current world order to effect specific miracles (thaumaturgists).[16] Moltmann, in *The Coming of God* (1996), has developed another taxonomy, suggesting that 'political millenarianism' (the identification of the reign of God with an individual political system), 'ecclesiastical millenarianism' (the identification of the reign of God with the institutional church), and 'epochal millenarianism' (the identification of the reign of God with one historical period, e.g. the Enlightenment) exist in tension with the this-worldly millennia! hope of Scripture.[17]

The advantage of Moltmann's taxonomy is that it emphasises the this-worldly implications of other-worldly hopes; the advantage of Wilson's approach is that it recognises the inadequacy of a merely theological analysis, realising that the structures of formal doctrine could be shared while the implications of these shared doctrines could vary enormously. Both emphasise the flexibility of millennia! rhetoric. As Harrison has noted, millennialism 'provided a common language and set of images and concepts in which people could express both individual and collective needs...but it remained a mode of expression, a means of communication, rather than an end with an agreed meaning and programme.'[18] This practical flexibility explains, for example, why the pessimistic premillennialism of the Seventh-Day Adventists has tended to foster social liberalism, while the pessimistic premillennialism of other Protestant fundamentalists has tended to promote right-wing cultural withdrawal.[19]

Recent analysis of millennialism has recognised that both kinds of analysis- the exegetical and the ethical- must be used. End-of-the-world discourses offer a totalising worldview and tend to blur belief

---

[16] Bryan R. Wilson, *Magic and the Millennium: A Sociological Study of Religious Movements of Protest among Tribal and Third-world Peoples* (London, 1973), 491.

[17] Moltmann, *Coming of God* (1996), 159-92. Note that Moltmann does not deny the importance of the traditional terminology of pre- and post-millennialism, e.g. 153.

[18] Harrison, The *Second Coming* (1979), 6-7.

[19] Douglas Morgan, 'Adventism, apocalyptic, and the cause of liberty,' *CH* 63:2 (1994), 235-6. The disadvantage of Wilson's approach, however, was that it tended to support the latent suspicion that millennialism should be studied as a psychological or social disorder, rather than as a serious exegetical concern; see E. P. Thompson, The *Making of the English Working Class* (London, 1963), 53, and Pedro Lima Vasconcellos, 'Apocalypses in the history of Brazil,' *JSNT* 25:2 (2002), 245.

and the believer, theology and its practical consequences; varieties of millennialism are 'ways of looking at the world, rather than specific doctrines'.[20] This is evidenced in any overview of the evangelical millennial tradition. The history of evangelical millennialism is a good lens through which to view wider changes in evangelicalism- and beyond.[21]

## The Historical Lineage of Evangelical Millennialism

The sixteenth-century Reformation is in many respects a paradoxical place to begin a description of the historical lineage of evangelical millennialism, for the reforming movement was far from being millennialist. The first reformers were faced with the twin dangers of Rome's institutional monolith and the uncontrolled ferment of the Anabaptists. Both movements were characterised by eschatological speculation. While Anabaptists – such as those at Munster in the 1530s – immersed themselves in millennial aspirations and sought to establish the social patterns they believed would characterise the new world order, the Catholic hierarchy refused to abandon the eschatological innovations they had elaborated throughout the medieval period – purgatory and the limbos.[22] The leaders of magisterial reform therefore sought to open up a critical distance from their enemies on left and right by condemning millennialism and by refusing to entertain any detailed investigation into the prophetic passages of Scripture. It was obvious that the Pope was the Antichrist, they contended; 'anyone who has learned from Scripture what are the things that belong particularly to God, and who on the other hand considers well what the Pope usurps for himself, will not have much difficulty in recognizing Antichrist, even though he were a ten year old boy', Calvin wrote.[23] Beyond that, the Reformed commentaries and creeds moved with caution. The Lutheran Confession of Augsburg (1530), transcribed by Melanchthon and published with Luther's consent, explicitly condemned millennialism as a 'Jewish opinion'; the second Helvetian confession (1566), prepared by the pastors of Zurich but approved by the Churches of Geneva, Savoy, Poland, Hungary and Scotland, similarly condemned ideas of a 'golden world' before the judgement

---

20 Harrison, The *Second Coming* (1979), 6.
21 Hempton, 'Evangelicalism and eschatology' (1980), 181.
22 Gribben, 'The eschatology of the puritan confessions' (2002), 56-7.
23 John Calvin, *Calvin's Commentaries:* The *Epistles of Paul the Apostle to the Romans and to the Thessalonians,* trans. Ross Mackenzie (Edinburgh, 1972), 401.

as a 'Jewish dream'.[24] Calvin's Scriptural commentaries followed suit, covering almost every New Testament book except Revelation. For some time, a neglect of eschatological concern was thought to characterise the movement for reform: Catholic polemicists noted their belief that a wholesale rejection of the canonicity of Revelation was typical of the Protestant movement.[25]

Simultaneously, however, the sheer polemical utility of the Biblical genre of apocalyptic meant that its literature could not be neglected, and as the sixteenth century moved into the seventeenth, the popularity of eschatological study became almost inversely proportional to its earlier neglect. Nothing was now so familiar, James Ussher complained, than to 'father upon Antichrist, whatsoever in church matters we do not find to suit with our own humours'.[26] Suddenly, the Antichrist was everywhere.

In the puritan cultures of Britain and Ireland, these eschatological interests climaxed during the civil wars of the mid-seventeenth century. A series of publications throughout the 1630s and 1640s had created a flourishing market for prophetic speculation. Although their conclusions were diverse, puritan commentators and theologians established the basic contours of the prophetic thought of later evangelicalism. Discussing the millennium, puritan commentators generally abandoned the conservative Augustinian readings of their reformed heritage, no longer adhering to the idea that the millennium was a metaphor for the entire period of church history (an interpretative position now known as 'amillennialism'). Instead, they tended to project the millennium into the future, identifying it with a future revival- the eschatological conversion of the Jews to Christianity and an extended period of worldwide adherence to the gospel. Opinions differed as to the relationship between this millennium and the second coming of Christ. Some polemicists, like John Milton, imagined the millennium to be initiated by the second coming of Christ (a position now known as 'premillennialism').[27] Others, like John Owen, imagined that the millennium would precede the second coming of Christ (a position now known as

24 Peter Hall (ed.), *Harmony of the Protestant Confessions* (London, 1842), 88, 106.
25 Irena Backus, 'The Church Fathers and the Canonicity of the Apocalypse in the Sixteenth Century: Erasmus, Frans Titelmans, and Theodore Beza', *SCJ* 29 (1998), 662; see also Irena Backus, *Reformation Readings of the Apocalypse: Geneva, Zurich, and Wittenberg* (Oxford, 2000).
26 James Ussher, *The Whole Works of James Ussher,* eds C. R. Elrington and J. R. Todd (Dublin, 1847-64), vii. 45.
27 Crawford Gribben, *The Puritan Millennium: Literature and Theology, 1550-1682* (Dublin, 2000), *passim*.

'postmillennialism').28 Almost all were certain that the millennium had not yet begun.29 Many understood their own movement- and their own nation – to be at the centre of the outworking of providence. In 1653, according to Oliver Cromwell, England was a nation 'at the edge of the promises'. 'What is the Lord a-doing?' the Protector would ask; 'what prophecies are now fulfilling?'30 Biblical prophecy had become the lens through which to read contemporary history, and England, sometimes Scotland, was the nation at the centre of God's plan. In 1653, standing tiptoe on the brink of a bright eschatological future, Cromwell could hardly have anticipated the political failure – and the millennia! disappointment – that lay ahead for the English puritans.

Mter the Restoration of Charles in 1660, puritanism slipped into dissent and its commitment to millennialism lost something of its earlier political vigour. Scholars of this period agree that the 'quietism' that characterises later seventeenth and early eighteenth century nonconformity had moved a long way from the political engagement of civil war puritans.31 Occasional voices were raised in defence of earlier expectations- Charles Wesley and John Gill, the doughty Calvinistic Baptist, were both vocal in their premillennial-ism32 -but the more moderate postmillennialism of Daniel Whitby held sway.33 In North America, Whitby's postmillennialism was invested with evangelical hope by Jonathan Edwards' experience of revival. In the midst of the Great Awakening, Edwards speculated, the millennium was beginning on American soil.34 There was nothing

---

28 Christopher R. Smith, "Up and be doing': The pragmatic puritan eschatology of John Owen', *EQ* 61:4 (1989), 340. While there has been a recent flurry of interest in Owen, scholars have been slow to demonstrate interest in his eschatological convictions.

29 Gribben, *The Puritan Millennium* (2000), *passim.*

30 Oliver Cromwell, *The Writings and Speeches of Oliver Cromwell: With an Introduction, Notes and an Account of his Life,* ed. W. C. Abbott (1939; rpr. Oxford, 1988), iii. 64, ii. 482.

31 See, for example, Neil H. Keeble, *The Literary Culture of Nonconformity in Later Seventeenth Century England* (Leicester, 1987).

32 Crawford Gribben, 'John Gill and puritan eschatology', *EQ* 73:4 (2001), 311-326; Kenneth Newport, *Apocalypse and millennium: Studies in Biblical Eisegesis* (Cambridge, 2000), 55-62, 119-49.

33 James H. Moorhead, 'Apocalypticism in Mainstream Protestantism, 1800 to the Present', in McGinn *et al.* (eds), *The Encyclopedia of Apocalypticism* (1998), ii. 74.

34 Jonathan Edwards, *Apocalyptic Writings,* ed. Stephen J. Stein (New Haven, 1977), 17-21, 26-29; George M. Marsden, *Jonathan Edwards: A Life* (New Haven, 2003), 264-67, 335-37.

new in this prioritisation of the North American experience; Edwards' innovation was to build his eschatology on the fashionable philosophical presuppositions that were contouring his commitment to New England Calvinism. The same epistemological confidence that fostered Edwards' belief in the assurance of salvation also fostered a 'uniformly postmillennial' optimism.[35] Postmillennialism, one historian has noted, 'provided a means whereby Protestants accommodated the apocalyptic hope to Enlightenment ideals of rational order and benevolence'.[36] But throughout the period millennia!hopes and fears extended far beyond the intellectual elite. Eighteenth-century chapbook culture capitalised on prophetic concerns, republishing 'godly works' from the previous century such as *Christ in the Clouds* (1635), thereby contributing to a wide range of popular millennia! expectations. [37] Throughout the eighteenth century, therefore, British evangelicalism retained its millennia! hope. But the hope was shared- even developed- by many on the Continent.

In the years following the dispersal of the Camisards by the forces of Louis XIV, millennia!expectations had often been couched in terms of the hope of a faithful remnant for whom the Lord's return would be a critical moment of intervention but among whom there had been vouchsafed the gift of prophecy.[38] Such had been the view of John Lacy, a leading follower of the 'French Prophets' in London, and it became an increasingly familiar perspective as the eighteenth century drew to an end. In the early 1790s Pierre Pontard, Bishop of the Dordogne, and others, inspired by the prophecies of Suzette Labrousse, welcomed the French Revolution as the herald of spiritual renewal and purification associated with an unfolding millennium.[39] By way of contrast in 1795, an English Protestant, Richard Brothers, saw the Revolution as a sign of God's wrath and insisted that the British government's support for the French monarchy, rejected by God, had made London a latter-day Babylon

---

[35] D. W. Bebbington, *Evangelicalism in Modern Britain: A History from the 1730s to the 1980s* (London, 1989), 62; Christopher Burdon, *The Apocalypse in England: Revelation Unravelling, 1700-1834* (London, 1997).

[36] Moorhead, 'Apocalypticism in Mainstream Protestantism, 1800 to the Present' (1998), 75.

[37] Deborah M. Valenze, 'Prophecy and popular literature in eighteenth-century England,' *JEH* 29:1 (1978), 78-82.

[38] Hillel Schwartz, *The French Prophets: The History of a Millenarian Group in Eighteenth-century England* (Los Angeles, 1980), 90.

[39] C. Garrett, *Respectable Folly: Millenarians and the French Revolution in France and England* (Baltimore, MD, 1975), 29-30.

ripe for judgement with George III playing the part of Belshazzar.[40] This was nearer to the position adopted by many Jansenists, one of whom, according to Stunt's essay later in the present volume, was a significant influence in the early development of J. N. Darby. For the Jansenists, the Revolution was the scourge of God and therefore but one more sign that the end was nigh.[41] With all these writers, Pontard, the Jansenists and Brothers, there was a pressing interest in plans for the restoration of the Jews to Jerusalem, a national hope that would become a recurring feature of much apocalypticism in the next century. The numerous editions of Brothers' book published in the United States as well as in London, Dublin, and Paris are an indication of the sympathetic reception given to such ideas at the height of the revolutionary crisis.

On the other hand, as the anti-Christian dimensions of Jacobinism became more defined, prophetic discourse became increasingly premillennial. Beleaguered or isolated Christians reverted to the Camisard hope of deliverance by the returning Saviour. A variety of figures were identified as Elias, the forerunner described by Malachi, and the imminence of the Lord's return was the fervent hope of Joanna Southcott's followers when they sang:

CHRIST'S SECOND COMING is at hand
In MIGHT and *POWR* 'twill be;
For CHRIST will *Renovate* the land
And set the captive free.[42]

Although much Southcottian piety was very conservative and far from revolutionary, a significant minority was associated with reformers who had plans for ushering in a radical millennium without waiting for Christ's return. From this wing there emerged a succession of charismatic leaders such as 'Zion' Ward, John Wroe, and James Elishama Smith, but such figures were always viewed with deep suspicion by the more conventional evangelicals.[43] Indeed

---

[40] Richard Brothers, *A Revealed Knowledge of the Prophecies and Times*, parts I and II (London, 1794, 1795). For the editions of Brothers's works see Harrison, *The Second Coming* (1979), 241 n. 8.

[41] Garrett, *Respectable Folly* (1975), 22-23.

[42] J. K. Hopkins, *A Woman to Deliver her People: Joanna Southcott and English Millenarianism in an Era of Revolution* (Austin, TX, 1982), 148.

[43] See Timothy C. F. Stunt's articles on Richard Brothers (1757-1824), John "Zion" Ward (1781-1837), John Wroe (1782-1863), James Elishama Smith (1801-57), Henry James Prince (1811-1899), Thomas Lake Harris (1823-1906), and James Jershom Jezreel (1849-1885) in the *Oxford Dictionary of National Biography* (forthcoming).

these maverick characters were an important factor in the widespread disapproval among many orthodox Christians of anything that could be described as millennialism. Despite their disapproval, evangelicalism had certainly not lost its millennia! hope. Its continuity with the Camisards is well illustrated in Edward Irving's republication in 1834 of John Lacy's *General Delusion of Christians touching the ways of God's revealing himself* (original edition, 1712). Continental hopes fed into the development of British and Irish expectations.

Nevertheless, it was not until the nineteenth century that the prophetic parameters shared by many modern evangelicals were finally established. The period upon which this collection focuses – described by Moltmann as 'the Christian era'[44] – witnessed a prophetic renaissance. Paradoxically, as Moltmann's taxonomy suggests, premillennial pessimism seemed to capture the imagination of evangelicalism at precisely its most culturally persuasive moment. Between 1800 and 1840, for example, at least one hundred books were published on the signs of the times, ten prophetic periodicals were established, and a number of societies and conferences were organised for the study of Biblical prophecy.[45] But this fascination with eschatology transcended the evangelical movement. In Ireland, during the 1820s, Pastorini's prophecies – predicting the imminent final collapse of the Protestant establishment – remained popular among Catholics despite their clergy's disparagement of them.[46] Missionaries promoting Mormon apocalyptic entered Britain in 1837, and, by 1851, had gained some 50,000 convertsY In England, radical political activism was suffused in the rhetoric ofmillennial belief.[48] Evangelicalism did not maintain a monopoly on millennia!expectation, but it was in evangelicalism, and especially in its smaller groupings, that eschatology provided a fully over-arching worldview for the reconstruction of Christian life and thought.[49]

---

[44] Moltmann, *Coming of God* (1996), 3.

[45] Ronald R. Nelson, 'Apocalyptic speculation and the French revolution,' *EQ* 53 (1981), 205.

[46] Patrick O'Farrell, 'Millennialism, Messianism and Utopianism in Irish history', *Anglo-Irish Studies* 2 (1976), 52.

[47] Harrison, *The Second Coming* (1979), 188-89.

[48] Harrison, *The Second Coming* (1979), 224.

[49] For the importance of millennialism in the ecclesiology of nineteenth-century Brethren and Presbyterians, see Crawford Gribben, '"The worst sect a Christian man can meet": Opposition to the Plymouth Brethren in Ireland and Scotland, 1859-1900', *SSR* 3:2 (2002), 34-53.

## The Papers

This collection of essays, representing the work of both established and junior scholars, is able to offer a series of new perspectives on the reception and development of evangelical millennialism in the nineteenth century. The essays are arranged chronologically, describing the appropriation and development of evangelical millennial concepts in the early nineteenth century before moving on to illustrate their impact in Britain and Ireland. The papers reflect the 'third generation' scholarship described by Douglas Shantz in his bibliographical overview. His paper sketches the evolution of millennial studies across disciplines and provides a useful survey of trends within recent millennial scholarship. According to Shantz, the most salient trends in contemporary millennial scholarship emerge from the immediacy and social relevance of such study. With varieties of millennialism moving closer to the centre of popular culture, third-generation scholars are well able to refute older notions that the development of millennialism was somehow linked to mental or social disease. One of the main emphases of his paper is to provide a corrective to the frequently cited 'deprivation theory' – popularised by Norman Cohn's *The Pursuit of the Millennium* (1957) and echoed by countless theorists- which contends that millennial ideas fester on the margins, either as the prerogative of an outcast class or as the result of a combination of unusual social and cultural pressures. Instead, Shantz maintains, third-generation scholars have fused historical, literary, Biblical and theological interests to demonstrate the plasticity of millennial motifs, proving that millennial ideas can emerge from a variety of environments, and can be used for a variety of ends, either promoting the reform of society, the subversion of society, or withdrawal from society. Subsequent papers demonstrate the validity of his thesis for nineteenth-century evangelicals, whose millennial interests grew within social elites, sponsored by aristocratic patrons, responding to the revolutionary threats of Europe in the late eighteenth century.

The first of the historical studies, Timothy Stunt's paper, offers a challenging reading of the way in which one influential millennial scholar, John Nelson Darby (1800-1882), responded to Ireland's revolutionary threat in the period between his initial conversion in 1822 and his 1827-28 decision to adhere to evangelicalism. Stunt suggests that Darby was already engaged in millennial studies in the mid-1820s, while still adhering to Anglo-Catholicism and denying that Luther and Calvin were within the scope of God's covenanted mercy. Darby's readings in Catholic theology, in the three years between his leaving the legal profession in 1822 and his

ordination in 1825, would have been buttressed by his visit to Paris
in the early part of 1830. There, Darby probably encountered a
Jansenist community that had been engaged in a vigorous debate
about the timing of the rapture and its relation to the millennium.
One member of the community, Pierre-Jean Agier, had republished
the conclusions of Lacunza, the Jesuit commentator who espoused
futurism, premillennialism, and a one-stage coming of Christ. But
Lacunza's discussion of the one-stage rapture had been contested by
the Jansenist and Dominican writer, Bernard Lambert, who argued
that Christ's coming must occur in two stages, with an initial
gathering of believers preceding Christ's coming to inaugurate the
millennium. Stunt shows that Darby was not unhesitatingly
committed to premillennialism before 1830, but that his visit to
Paris probably committed him to the concept of the two-stage coming
that would later characterise his ministry. Despite the claims of a
series of recent polemicists, Stunt concludes that Darby was clearly
familiar with the two-stage rapture paradigm before he witnessed
the controversial prophecy of Margaret Macdonald in Scotland later
that year.

In the next chapter, Gary L. Nebeker develops Stunt's argument
for Darby's conservative context by arguing that his eschatological
interests developed within one of the mainstream traditions of
spirituality in the medieval church. Adopting a more theological
approach, Nebeker interprets Darby's 'eschatological mysticism' and
compares its nuptial imagery to that of various ecclesiastical
traditions. The use of bridal imagery to express the relationship
between believers (individually and collectively) and God is common
throughout church history – indeed, it is a salient feature of
mainstream Christian spirituality. Nebeker therefore minimises the
links between Darby's spirituality and the prevailing tenor of
European Romanticism, and finds that Darby's mystical thought
corresponds most closely with that of the English puritans and
Continental Pietists of the seventeenth century. Nebeker further
argues that Darby's millennialism was much less radical than was
that of many of his contemporaries. As Darby's eschatological
mysticism developed within an overtly Augustinian paradigm of
heaven, his millennialism refused to divert Christians from their
heavenly hope of nuptial union with Christ. In Darby's thought, the
Church would not be on earth during the millennium, nor would it
be on earth after the millennium. Nebeker's conclusion is teasingly
paradoxical. Darby, it appears, was a staunch premillennialist who
had no millennial object of hope either for himself or for the Church.
The enjoyment of the millennium would be restricted to Israelites
and those Gentiles who would come to faith after the rapture and

during the tribulation. Thus Darby's presentation of the pre-tribulation rapture was radically orientated towards heaven, and the two-stage rapture that he advanced was introduced, in part, to realise the traditional Augustinian motif of heavenly union with Christ. Unlike later dispensational scholasticism, Nebeker contends, Darby's focus was not on the rapture *per se* but rather on the goal that it would accomplish- the believer's heavenly communion with God. Only in the twentieth century, Nebeker argues, with the rise of dispensational scholasticism, did this 'eschatological mysticism' cease to be a distinguishing feature of the mainstream dispensational tradition.

It is by now a commonplace that Darby's interest in premillennialism and Roman Catholicism was contoured by his study of Lacunza's text. Its importance had previously been established by Edward Irving (1792-1834), who had translated it into English under the influence of the Romantic pessimism of S. T. Coleridge. Irving's own developing eschatological interests are documented by Tim Grass, who argues that a radical millennialism underlay Irving's emerging ideas of church government, denominational secession and the restoration of charismatic gifts. Irving came from a conservative Scottish Presbyterian background. Holding firmly to the establishment principle, he believed in the importance of a nation baptised into covenant with God. But with his developing eschatological speculation and Christological heresy, Irving found himself out of step with the Church of Scotland's governing authorities. His unease was confirmed by the passing of the Catholic Emancipation Act in 1829 and by the General Assembly's judgement on the John McLeod Campbell case in 1831. Believing the professing church to be in the final stages of decay, Irving abandoned his adherence to the idea of the church as an established entity that defined the spiritual life of the nation, adopting instead the idea of the church as a faithful remnant, called to separation in the face of impending apocalyptic judgement. Grass notes that Irving's evolving ecclesiology related to his eschatologically-driven concept of the judgement of the Gentile churches and the necessity of a new order – a charismatic ecclesiology – through which it might be replaced. Irving believed that the restoration of charismatic gifts and apostolic church government was evidence that the second coming of Christ was at hand. Only when the millennium began would the church return to its rightful position at the centre of a truly Christian society.

The focus on Irving is continued in Kenneth Stewart's paper, which charts the rise and fall of the Continental Society for the Diffusion of Religious Knowledge. The Continental Society was an important second-generation evangelical missionary society, whose non-sectarian stance was demanded by its pan-evangelical membership. The Society emerged in the aftermath of visits to Geneva by Robert Haldane and Henry Drummond. Under their guidance, a number of Genevan theological students had openly identified themselves with the evangelical cause, and so found their path barred to ecclesiastical preferment. Haldane and Drummond combined their resources to consolidate the Swiss evangelical advance by organising funding to support these students in missionary outreach throughout French-speaking Europe. With the promotion of the gospel as the Society's over-riding concern, and with its goal of not exporting the divisions within British evangelicalism, it soon attracted wide support from the domestic evangelical constituency – Stewart notes the involvement and support of Anglicans, Presbyterians, Independents, Baptists and Methodists. This pan-denominational agenda was supported by the Society's choice only to use indigenous preachers, and by its guarantee that each of these preachers adhered to the Thirty-Nine Articles and the Westminster Shorter Catechism. Despite these assurances, the Society was challenged by a series of conflicts, disputes about the proper subjects of baptism, the propriety of distributing Bibles containing the apocrypha, the personality and theology of Edward Irving, and, most vitally, the premillennialism that Irving and Henry Drummond were promoting among the Society's leadership. Stewart reports that the crisis over premillennialism involved questions of wider importance than eschatology, questions that struck at the heart of the unity the Society aimed to promote. The millennial question drove a wedge between members of the established and dissenting churches by contesting whether, in the aftermath of the eighteenth century's evangelical revivals, the revolutions of the 1780s and 1790s should be read as evidence of coming glory and greater liberties for the dissenting population, or coming judgment, with an end to hierarchical society, traditional morality and an established church. The increasingly premillennial tenor of the Society's proceedings brought dismay to the majority of the Society's supporters, who still adhered to the older postmillennial optimism, and it was this conflict, more than any other, that crippled the rapid progress of the Society's missionary interests.

The contested reception of radical millennialism is further explored in Andrew Holmes' analysis of Ulster Presbyterianism. His chapter is a sustained challenge to the deprivation theory. Ireland, with its large Catholic majority and Anglican apparatus of state, provided ideal conditions for the growth of radical premillennialism, but such radical eschatologies failed to take root in Ulster's apocalyptic landscape. As Holmes notes, studies of Irish Presbyterian millennialism have concentrated upon the political radicalism of the 1798 rebellion, which was fuelled by millennial rhetoric. With a long legacy of disaffection from the Anglican establishment, and with a tradition of political liberalism, many Ulster Presbyterians supported the rebellion. Its failure, Holmes argues, and the disappointment of the many Presbyterian clergy and laypeople who had been involved in it, led to the decline of 'prophetic Calvinism' and propelled evangelicalism into the ascendancy within Ulster Presbyterianism. The increasing popularity of evangelicalism was linked to a growing interest in world mission, an interest that was often underpinned by explicitly postmillennial assumptions. These assumptions argued that the expected millennium would not be inaugurated by the return of Christ, but would be effected by the spread of education, and, as its consequence, the faithful use of the means of grace. Ulster Presbyterianism therefore adopted explicitly 'worldly' means of pursuing the millennium. This consensus was shared across the Presbyterian denominations, but was increasingly challenged by the discouraging state of Christendom – throughout the 1830s and 1840s, epidemics, wars, Catholic emancipation and the Irish famine were all regarded as signs of the times. But premillennialism failed to take root among Ulster Presbyterians. With its close association with the discredited Edward Irving, it was easy to dismiss. In any case, when revival came in 1859, it seemed to many Ulster Presbyterians that their expectation of a millennium brought about by preaching had, at last, been finally confirmed.

But revival, too, brought division. Just as evangelicals divided over the proper exegesis of Revelation 20, so they divided over the best interpretation of the events of 1859. Crawford Gribben's paper begins with the strange ambivalence of Andrew Bonar's 1859 commentary on the Psalms, and sketches the background to Bonar's concern for the future of British Protestantism in the midst of evangelicalism's most spectacular success since the Reformation. Like Darby, Bonar was interested in premillennialism before his conversion to evangelical faith. Its rapid development exercised a powerful appeal upon his imagination and coloured his sense of call to ministry. Gribben's study charts Bonar's increasing fascination with premillennialism, and notes Bonar's own concern that his eschatological interests – shared by so few in the Church of Scotland –were blocking his path into parish ministry. Personal crisis fused with national ecclesiastical crisis as Bonar departed on the Church's 'Mission of Inquiry' to Israel. He and his colleagues discovered strong messianic expectations among Jews throughout Europe. As news filtered through to Israel of sporadic revival in the Church's evangelical congregations, Bonar and McCheyne linked God's blessing upon the Church with its recovery of its duty to send the gospel 'to the Jew first', in expectation of the latter-day conversion of the Jews so fundamental to Scottish Presbyterian apocalyptic. With the Disruption of the Scottish Church in 1843, the emerging Free Church aligned itself with a radical evangelicalism and a populist appeal. Bonar's continued study of millennialism led him to challenge the traditional identification of the Antichrist – it could not be the Pope, he argued, for his position was already declining. Bonar's conclusions challenged the ideal of confessional subscription, and linked his doctrine of Antichrist with his interest in defending inerrancy. Scotland's postmillennial consensus, he believed, could be maintained only by appealing to the very rationalistic hermeneutic that was destroying evangelicalism in Germany. Bonar's conservative negotiation with the Westminster consensus therefore paved the way for later, more radical, dismissals of the Confession's authority, but he withdrew from the confrontation, speaking at Moody's Northfield Conference and charting a similarly pan-denominational premillennial unity in Scotland. Bonar's eschatological interests had challenged the orthodox consensus and laid the foundation for an emerging fundamentalism.

## Conclusion

What this collection demonstrates, then, is that a sustained interest in millennialism characterised British and Irish evangelicals throughout the nineteenth century. It is therefore less than accurate to state that 'by the 1860s millenarian speculation was going out of fashion.'[50] Students of prophecy were committed to the belief that it was the 'fashion of this world' that was passing away (1 Corinthians 7:31), that the events in church and nation proved 'it is high time to awake out of sleep: for now is our salvation nearer than when we believed' (Romans 13:11). Harrison may still have cause to complain that 'historical understanding of millenarianism does not come easily these days'; but these essays will, it is hoped, offer something of substance to the history of the 'blessed hope'.

---

[50] Desmond Bowen, *The Protestant Crusade in Ireland, 1800-1870: A Study of Protestant-Catholic Relations between the Act of Union and Disestablishment* (Dublin, 1978), 248.

# CHAPTER 2

# Millennialism and Apocalypticism in Recent Historical Scholarship

Douglas H. Shantz

The *Apocalypse* of St. John has exercised a continuing fascination throughout the Christian past. In Protestant history, especially, a lively interest in the book has characterised not only sectarian groups but major thinkers and denominations as well. [1] This interest and fascination have significantly impacted the way western history has unfolded. Frank Kermode observed, 'Religious and political history would have been unimaginably different if the prophecies of *Daniel* had been excluded from the Old Testament or those of *Revelation* from the New.'[2] Scholars continue to be alternately shocked and intrigued by these apocalyptic traditions. In this chapter we shall examine recent historical scholarship in the area of Christian apocalypticism and millennialism. The main argument is that the revisionist bent of recent historical interpretations of apocalyptic and millennial movements and ideas is more noteworthy than the quantity of recent scholarship in this area. Three key themes emerge from a survey of recent studies: apocalyptic and millennial ideas are far more central to western historical consciousness than was previously recognized; apocalypticism and millennialism arise in a wide variety of social contexts and encompass a broad range of emphases and perspectives; and certain periods of Christian millennialism still suffer from relative scholarly neglect, notably late seventeenth-century German Pietist millennialism, and

---

[1] Gottfried SeebaB, 'The Importance of Apocalyptic for the History of Protestantism', *Colloquium: The Australian and New Zealand Theological Review* 13:1 (1980), 24, 35. He notes that 'apocalyptic texts are deeply interwoven with the history of Protestantism.'
[2] Frank Kermode, 'The Canon', in Robert Alter and Frank Kermode (eds), *The Literary Guide to the Bible* (London, 1987), 605.

the millennialism of evangelical Protestantism in nineteenth-century Britain and Ireland. We begin by defining some terms; then we observe the recent proliferation of studies in this field, provide a brief overview of three generations of millennia! scholarship, highlight new directions, and summarize the growing consensus.

The terms 'apocalypticism' and 'millennialism' require definition and clarification. For Bernard McGinn, apocalypticism refers to 'the complex of ideas associated with [John's] *Apocalypse*, and especially the imminent end of history and the catastrophic events that it entails'.[3] While the terms apocalypticism, eschatology, chiliasm,[4] millennialism and messianism overlap and are often used interchangeably,[5] more precise definitions are needed to indicate aspects of nuance and difference. McGinn offers the following helpful distinctions:

> Eschatology covers any type of belief that looks forward to the end of history as that which gives structure and meaning to the whole. What sets off apocalypticism from general eschatology is the sense of the proximity of the end. What makes the apocalypticist a particular kind of prophet is not only the specification of his message, but also the way in which he proclaims it, especially its learned, written or scribal character...Millenarianism refers to beliefs in a coming more perfect terrestrial form of society...Such expectations do not exhaust the content of the apocalyptic message, but concentrate on its optimistic pole.[6]

Millennialism, then, represents a particular instance of apocalypticism that focuses on earthly utopias.[7] Scholars in disciplines other than history define these concepts somewhat differently from McGinn. Social scientists, for example, often treat millennialism and apocalypticism as 'roughly equivalent'.[8] This reflects the fact that the

---

[3] It includes the belief that 'God has revealed the imminent end of the ongoing struggle between good and evil in history'; Bernard McGinn, John J. Collins, and Stephen J. Stein (eds), The *Encyclopedia of Apocalypticism* (New York, 1998), ii. ix. Seebal3 has defined 'apocalyptic' more broadly as 'all that which is directly or indirectly considered to be an exposition of the relevant [prophetic] texts' of the Hebrew and Christian scriptures and the Apocrypha; see Seebal3, 'The Importance of Apocalyptic' (1980), 24.

[4] This word has a Greek etymology and, like 'millennium', also refers to a period of one thousand years.

[5] McGinn *et al.* (eds), The *Encyclopedia of Apocalypticism* (1998), ii. x, xi.

[6] Bernard McGinn (ed.), *Apocalyptic Spirituality* (Mahwah, 1979), 5.

[7] McGinn *et al.* (eds), The *Encyclopedia of Apocalypticism* (1998), ii. x, xi.

[8] See Dennis C. Duling, 'BTB Readers Guide: Millennialism', *BTB* (1994), 134.

apocalyptic groups that they study are generally millennial groups.

## The Proliferation of Scholarship on Apocalyptic Themes

The last three decades have witnessed an explosion of scholarly writing on apocalyptic themes, especially in North America.[9] This is evident from the books that have appeared on the subject and the scholarly conferences that have been organised. The volume of scholarly writing on apocalyptic themes has been amazing:

> Over the past thirty years, more scholarship has been devoted to apocalypticism than in the previous three hundred. This is true not only regarding [scholarship into] the origins of apocalypticism in Judaism and early Christianity, but also [into] the development of Christian apocalyptic traditions in Europe down to the modern era.[10]

Another scholar observes in a similar vein:

> Over the last two decades, the study of millenarian movements has moved from the periphery to the center. No longer the exclusive domain of small coteries of specialists, it has come to be seen as a major category of social analysis.[11]

It is increasingly difficult for scholars to keep up with the latest publications in this burgeoning field. [12]

The three-volume *Encyclopedia of Apocalypticism* (1998) [13] reflects some of the best of this recent historical scholarship, providing a comprehensive and collective treatment of the apocalyptic traditions of the three Western monotheistic faiths, Judaism, Christianity and

---

[9] Ted Daniels indicates that 'America seems to be a particularly lavish source of millennialism'; see Ted Daniels, *Millennialism: An International Bibliography* (New York, 1992), x.

[10] John J. Collins, Bernard McGinn, Stephen J. Stein, 'General Introduction', in McGinn *et al.* (eds), *Encyclopedia of Apocalypticism* (1998), ii. xi.

[11] Michael Barkun, *Millennialism and Violence* (London, 1996), 1.

[12] Richard Landes observed that historians face the difficult challenge of 'absorbing the extensive literature on eschatology...and its various manifestations'; Landes, 'On Owls, Roosters, and Apocalyptic Time: A Historical Method for Reading a Refractory Documentation', *USQR* 49:1-2 (1995), 49.

[13] The three volumes are arranged as follows: volume one: John J. Collins (ed.), *The Origins of Apocalypticism in Judaism and Christianity;* volume two: Bernard McGinn (ed.), *Apocalypticism in Western History and Culture;* volume three: Stephen J. Stein (ed.), *Apocalypticism in the Modern Period and the Contemporary Age.*

Islam.[14] The work is intended as a tool for investigating the role of apocalypticism over the last two thousand years and beyond.[15] The editors noted that their endeavour was made possible by the 'explosion of scholarship over the past generation' and by the 'growing interest in ends and beginnings that is gaining momentum as we approach the new millennium'.[16]

Similar interests have been displayed in a series of recent conferences. On 17-18 March 1994, an important conference on apocalyptic-millennial themes was sponsored by the Mid-Atlantic Regional Meeting of the American Academy of Religion (AAR) and Society of Biblical Literature (SBL). The conference was held at Union Theological Seminary in New York City and eo-hosted by the General Theological Seminary, Hebrew Union College, the Jewish Theological Seminary of America, Princeton Theological Seminary, and St. John's University. The meeting's purpose was to take a fresh look at the type of religious worldview which looks for 'the imminent, cataclysmic end of the cosmos and of the forces of evil and the dawn of a new, paradisiacal age'.[17] Coming just a year after the deaths of eighty members of the 'Branch Davidians' outside Waco, Texas, the conference included papers that considered recent outbreaks of apocalypticism. Papers also discussed the current state of scholarly opinion about apocalypticism, and future directions for research into this type of religion.[18] Since 1996 the Center for Millennia!Studies at Boston University has sponsored annual conferences on millennialism. Conference themes have included: 'The Apocalyptic Year 1000: History and Historiography' (1996), 'Millenarian Views of Unbelievers Among Jews, Christians and Muslims' (1997), 'Knowing of a Time, Knowing the Time: A Multidisciplinary Inquiry into Historical and Contemporary Practices of Dating the End' (1998), 'New World Orders: Millennialism in the Western Hemisphere' (1999), 'Swords into Ploughshares: Mass Enthusiasm, Peace

---

14 Collins, McGinn and Stein, 'General Introduction', in McGinn *et al.* (eds), *Encyclopedia of Apocalypticism* (1998), ii. ixf.
15 Collins, McGinn and Stein, 'General Introduction,' in McGinn *et al.* (eds), *Encyclopedia of Apocalypticism* (1998), ii. xi, xii: 'this multivolume effort looks beyond 2000-2001 in an attempt to provide an indispensable resource for the study of apocalypticism as an ongoing religious and cultural movement.'
16 Collins, McGinn and Stein, 'General Introduction,' in McGinn *et al.* (eds), *Encyclopedia of Apocalypticism* (1998), ii. xi. This work will be discussed in more detail below.
17 Stephen L. Cook, 'Reflections on Apocalypticism at the Approach of the Year 2000', *USQR* 49:1-2 (1995), 3.
18 Cook, 'Reflections on Apocalypticism' (1995), 3.

Movements and Transformational Millennialism' (2000), 'Unbinding Prometheus to Build the New Jerusalem: Millennialism, Power and Technology' (2001), and 'Sweet in the Mouth, Bitter in the Stomach: Apocalyptic Disappointment and its Millennia!Mutations' (2002). Finally, on 10-13 April 2000 the Oxford Millennium Conference was held at St. Catherine's College, Oxford, England, as an interdisciplinary conference on apocalyptic. Featured speakers included John Collins, Frank Kermode, and Bryan Wilson.[19] These conferences and books provide clear evidence that interest in this academic field has grown dramatically in recent years.

## Accounting for the Growing Academic Interest in Apocalypticism

Several factors help to account for this increased academic interest. First, there is a growing fascination with the subject of the millennium and the world's end in American culture generally. In 1979 historian Leonard Sweet suggested that, 'even more than baseball', America's favorite pastime is 'watching, waiting, and working for the millennium'.[20] A survey conducted in 1992 by *Time* and CNN found that '20 percent of [American] adults believed that the end-times would begin sometime around the year 2000. Another 31 percent responded that they thought this was possible but were not sure about it.'[21] More recently, a *Time/CNN* poll indicated that 'fully 59% [of Americans] say they believe the events in Revelation are going to come true, and nearly one-quarter think the Bible predicted the Sept. 11 attack' on the World Trade Center in New York.[22]

Second, millennialism has moved to the centre of religious

---

[19] Another noteworthy conference was the twelfth annual Klutznick Symposium, Omaha, Nebraska, 'The End of Days? Millennialism from the Hebrew Bible to the Present', 10-11 October 1999. It was sponsored and organized by the Klutznick Chair in Jewish Civilization, Creighton University, Omaha, Nebraska.

[20] Leonard I. Sweet, 'Millennialism in America: Recent Studies', *TS* 40:3 (1979), 531. Randall Balmer shows in a fine study that 'throughout American history there has always been a symbiotic relationship between apocalypticism and popular culture'; see Randall Balmer, "Thy Kingdom Come': Apocalypticism in American Culture', *USQR* 49 (1995), 27.

[21] Cook, 'Reflections on Apocalypticism' (1995), 4.

[22] Nancy Gibbs, 'The Bible and the Apocalypse', *Time.com* (Sunday, June 23, 2002). The poll also found that 'more than one-third of Americans say they are paying more attention now to how the news might relate to the end of the world, and have talked about what the Bible has to say on the subject.'

consciousness in North America as fundamentalism has grown in numbers and influence.[23] In the early 1970s Christian evangelists discovered cable television as a vehicle for their apocalyptic message.[24] Hal Lindsey's *The Late Great Planet Earth* (1970) was the best selling non-fiction book of the 1970s, reaching millions with his detailed end-time scenarios.[25] For *Time* magazine, Lindsey was 'the Jeremiah of our generation' with his forecasts of the approaching end. During the administration of Ronald Reagan, Lindsey served as a consultant to the Pentagon and to the Israeli government.[26]

More recent are the dispensational Bible expositions of Grant Jeffrey[27] and the *Left Behind* series by Tim LaHaye and Jerry B. Jenkins, promoted as 'the most fascinating Christian fiction serial ever to be published'. The authors envision twelve novels to be published between 1995 and spring 2003. The first four titles enjoyed 'phenomenal success', with over three million copies in print.[28] Book nine, published in October 2001, was the best-selling fictional work of 2001. The series has sold 32 million copies, with sales jumping by 60% after the events of September 11. The tenth book, *The Remnant*, was released on 2 July 2002 with 2.75 million hardcover copies in print. The *Left Behind* books were featured as the cover story of the 1 July 2002 issue of *Time* magazine.[29] *Christianity Today* described the series as a 'post-Rapture dispensational soap opera'.[30] The *Left Behind* industry includes a

---

[23] Barkun, *Millennialism and Violence* (1996), 1.

[24] Barkun, *Millennialism and Violence* (1996), 2.

[25] Hal Lindsey, The *Late Great Planet Earth* (Grand Rapids, 1970). Balmer notes that the book sold over twenty-eight million copies; see Balmer, 'Apocalypticism in American Culture' (1995), 24.

[26] Nancy Gibbs, 'The Bible and the Apocalypse,' *Time.com* (Sunday, June 23, 2002).

[27] Jeffrey's early books included *Armageddon: Appointment with Destiny* (Toronto, 1988) and *Apocalypse: The Coming Judgment of the Nations* (New York, 1992). In the 1990s Jeffrey published a book a year on apocalyptic themes, claiming to offer 'a uniquely authoritative interpretation' of the book of Revelation.

[28] Robert Clouse, Robert Hosack, and Richard Pierard, The *New Millennium Manual: A Once and Future Guide* (Grand Rapids, 1999), 135.

[29] Nancy Gibbs, 'The Bible and the Apocalypse,' *Time.com* (Sunday, June 23, 2002). Gibbs suggests that the books' success indicates that 'interest in End Times is no fringe phenomenon'. She observes that 'only about half of Left Behind readers are Evangelicals, which suggests there is a broader audience of people who are having this conversation.'

[30] Michael G. Maudlin, 'Inside CT', *CT* (5 October 1998), 6. Gibbs observes that some evangelical pastors 'promote the books as devotional reading'.

children's series, a video and a $17.4 million motion picture, *Left Behind*, which appeared in February 2001. The movie plot features the experiences of two family members who are 'left behind' when Christ returns to rapture the church and take believers back to heaven. Amidst mass confusion and hysteria on earth, these two people gradually come to understand what has happened and God's plan for the future. They then prepare for the revealing of the Antichrist and for their appointed task as the 'tribulation force'. In line with the influence of Hal Lindsey's books, scholars believe these latest fictional scenarios represent a 'potent political force', capable of shaping public attitudes on American policy in the Middle East.[31]

A third factor behind this academic interest can be found in the way even secular social commentators now portray an 'apocalyptic future' for the world. Francis Fukuyama and Robert Heilbroner offer 'end-of-the-world scenarios' as the inevitable result of nuclear war, famine or economic collapse. Like a dying patient, the world does not have much time left.[32] Scholars point to a world-wide sense of apocalyptic expectation.[33]

Fourth, popular media have nurtured interest in some 'unusual religious groups, often of a distinctly millenarian sort'. These include the People's Temple in Guyana (1978), the Branch Davidians of Waco, Texas (1993), and the Solar Temple in Canada and Switzerland (1994). Ted Daniels has identified by name some 1,100 apocalyptic groups. In 'Millennium Prophecy Report', a newsletter published out of Philadelphia, Pennsylvania, Daniels reviews the mailings and books these groups produce.[34]

## Three Generations of Scholarly Study of Millennialism

In order to provide some perspective on this scholarly proliferation, it is useful to identify several 'generations' of millennial scholarship in the twentieth century. The first generation corresponds to the first half of the twentieth century, up to the late 1960s. Inspired by sociologists and Marxists, it promoted the deprivation theory, the idea that millennialism was 'a function of social frustration', and therefore the 'preserve of peasants and the oppressed, of assorted

---

[31] Barkun, *Millennialism and Violence* (1996), 2.

[32] Barkun, *Millennialism and Violence* (1996), 2.

[33] Cook, 'Reflections on Apocalypticism' (1995), 4. In 1995, Cook observed that 'a deepening sense of apocalyptic expectation is currently making itself apparent in various parts of the globe.'

[34] Cook, 'Reflections on Apocalypticism' (1995), 14 n.2.

cranks and crackpots'.[35] The second generation extends from 1969 to the early 1990s, and was characterized by scholars' efforts to understand millennialism as 'a natural, rational, and sometimes normative force that can exert formative influence over all strata of society'.[36] The third generation can be dated from the mid-1990s as scholars respond to the dawning millennium and the time thereafter. The third generation seeks to further extend second-generation revisionism through cooperative and inter-disciplinary study of millennialism, and through revision of earlier scholarship. These three generations can be further illustrated and explained.

### *First-Generation Scholarship: Before 1970*

In the social sciences one observes an interest in millennialism among sociologists and anthropologists going back to the late nineteenth- and early twentieth-century theories of Max Weber and Ernst Troeltsch.[37] Under Weber's influence, Troeltsch developed the contrast between the *church* as an objective dominating institution in society into which one is born, and the *sect* as 'a voluntary community whose members join it of their own free will'. Sectarian religion was also marked by an affinity for 'eschatological views'. As a select group of the elect standing in opposition to the world, Troeltsch noted that, 'Insofar as the sect-type maintains Christian universalism at all...the only form it knows is that of eschatology.'[38]

In the sect Jesus is still the Herald of the Kingdom of God which

---

[35] Sweet, 'Millennialism in America' (1979), 512-13. Sweet noted that 'many recent scholars present sophisticated revisions of the Marxist socioeconomic interpretation and its variant forms of revitalization and deprivation theories' (512).

[36] Sweet, 'Millennialism in America' (1979), 513. Sweet credited Hillel Schwartz with introducing the notion of 'second generation' study of millennialism: 'Hillel Schwartz, whose illuminating bibliographical essay reveals that he has as firm a grasp of millennial scholarship as anyone in the country, contends that in 1969 the study of millennialism entered a new phase with a 'second generation' of scholarship'; see Hillel Schwartz, 'The End of the Beginning: Millenarian Studies, 1969-1975', *RSR* 2 (1976), 1-15. Moreover, Schwartz's perceptive and sympathetic works on the eighteenth-century French Prophets demonstrated that he was no mere theoretician of millennial studies.

[37] Cook, 'Reflections on Apocalypticism' (1995), 5.

[38] Ernst Troeltsch, *The Social Teaching of the Christian Churches*, trans. Olive Wyon (London, 1931), i. 337-339. In the end, the whole world will be transformed not by the church or by human effort, but by God and 'purely moral principles of love'.

He ushers in Himself; thus the sect is inclined to chiliasm. By contrast, for the *mystic* and the mystical type of religion, the dominion of Christ means the dominion of the Divine Spirit; therefore, from this point of view, the Kingdom of God is only within us.[39] 'From the 1930s through the present, social scientists [and historians] have been amassing data on millennialism, at the same time reintroducing and refining many of Weber's views.'[40]

These early scholars were marked by certain 'first generation notions': the 'madness' hypothesis and the 'deprivation' hypothesis. Sweet observed,

> There are still quite a few defenders of the first-generation notion that the serious study of prophecy either found a man crazy or left him so, or, as Walter Rauschenbusch phrased it...'eschatology is usually loved in inverse proportion to the square of the mental diameter of those who do the loving.' Bryan Wilson and Michael Barkun...hark back to [this] thesis and stress the pathological or deviant character of the millennia! mindY

Closely related to the madness hypothesis is the deprivation theory, which argued that millennialists were generally socially frustrated people. 'Their 'legitimate expectations' of the world are not fulfilled... and they turn to religion for salvation from this situation.'[42] This latter view is exemplified by Norman Cohn's widely read and cited book, *The Pursuit of the Millennium* (1957). [43]

Using Max Weber's theories, Cohn sought to find 'the social and economic causes of millennia! movements' during the Middle Ages and in the early modern period.[44] Cohn suggested that the apocalyptic outlook was generally part of a reaction to social crisis (over-population, rapid social and economic change), persecution and oppression, or the inevitable expression of impotence and anxiety.[45] Cohn observed that,

> The areas in which the age-old prophecies about the Last Days took on a new, revolutionary meaning and a new, explosive force were the areas in Europe which experienced similar circumstances: they were becoming seriously over-populated and were involved in rapid

[39] Troeltsch, *Social Teaching of the Christian Churches* (1931), ii. 995.

[40] Cook, 'Reflections on Apocalypticism' (1995), 5.

[41] Sweet, 'Millennialism in America' (1979), 512.

[42] Daniels, *Millennialism: An International Bibliography* (1992), xxxi.

[43] Norman Cohn, *The Pursuit of the Millennium: Revolutionary Millenarians and Mystical Anarchists of the Middle Ages* (New York, 1957; 1970).

[44] Cook, 'Reflections on Apocalypticism' (1995), 5, 7.

[45] Cohn, *Pursuit of the Millennium* (1970), 53, 60.

economic and social change...with traditional social bonds being weakened and the gap between rich and poor becoming a chasm...In these areas a collective sense of impotence and anxiety and envy suddenly [expressed] itself in a frantic urge to smite the ungodly...and to bring into being the final kingdom.[46]

Cohn defined millennial groups as those expecting change that was 'collective, this-worldly, imminent, total and supernatural'.

Political historians noted the implications of Cohn's book for understanding violent political behaviour:

In successive editions, Cohn linked the millenarian movements of late medieval Europe first with the rise of Communism and Nazism, then with protest movements in the Third World and the youth movements of the 1960s...Latter-day millennialism took its most politically significant forms in movements that used or threatened violence.[47]

Cohn's book served, more than any other, to '[sensitize] social scientists to millennialism's political implications'.[48]

Today, however, scholars see Cohn as part of a generation 'horrified by the effects of radical ideologies'. Writing in the ruins of World War II, he read apocalypses 'in their sinister key' and emphasized their ability to 'spark bloodshed on a vast scale'.[49] He so focussed his attention on the radical revolutionary side of various medieval and early modern groups and movements that he missed their rich variety.[50]

A short time after Cohn's book was published, alternative understandings of millennialism began to appear, notably Sylvia L. Thrupp's book of edited conference papers entitled *Millennial Dreams in Action: A Comparative Study* (1962).[51] The 1960 conference aimed to 'draw together certain findings of historical work and of recent work by anthropologists and sociologists on religious movements that have been animated by the idea of a

---

[46] Cohn, *Pursuit of the Millennium* (1970), 53, 60.

[47] Barkun, *Millennialism and Violence* (1996), 1, 4. Later editions of Cohn's book were much more cautious in drawing links between millennialism and Communism and Nazism.

[48] Barkun, *Millennialism and Violence* (1996), 1.

[49] Anthony Grafton, 'The Varieties of Millennial Experience: The latest trends in apocalyptic thought', The *New Republic* (8 November 1999), 77, 85.

[50] Grafton, 'The Varieties of Millennial Experience' (1999), 78.

[51] Sylvia L. Thrupp (ed.), *Millennial Dreams in Action: A Comparative Study* (The Hague, 1962). The conference was held on 8-9 April 1960 at the University of Chicago under the auspices of the Editorial Committee of *Comparative Studies in Society and History*.

perfect age or a perfect land'. 'It was agreed that enquiry should ideally cover the nature and history of the ideas involved, the circumstances in which these excited action, the character of leadership and recruiting, and the career of the movement.'[52] Thrupp noted the difficulties that the documentary sources of millennia! groups present to historians.[53] Thrupp further highlighted the lack of knowledge of quieter movements with less extremist leaders. She showed that many visions of the future were far from revolutionary, serving rather to reinforce the existing order of things.[54] Hillel Schwartz used Thrupp's work to illustrate that 'seminal works of the first generation remain valuable and may share some of the best qualities of the second generation.'[55]

## *Second-Generation Scholarship: The 1970s and 1980s*

A 'veritable blizzard' of scholarly and popular writing on millennialism appeared in the sixties and seventies,[56] precisely the time when the millennium returned to prominence in western culture.[57] In his review essay, 'The End of the Beginning: Millenarian Studies, 1969-1975', Hillel Schwartz argued that in 1969 'millennia!scholarship entered a new phase with a 'second generation' of scholarship.'[58] A shift in theory and emphasis occurred in the late sixties, evidenced by 'seminal studies' by historians such as J. F. C. Harrison, William

---

[52] Sylvia L. Thrupp, 'Millennia! Dreams in Action: A Report on the Conference Discussion,' in Thrupp (ed.), *Millennial Dreams in Action* (1962), 11, 13. The 1960 conference called for establishing 'better communication between those who work on the history of millennia!thought and those who work on the analysis of situations in which this thought has incited action' (26).

[53] Thrupp, 'Millennia!Dreams in Action' (1962), 13. 'The text of a prophet's orations cannot communicate the nuances that rest on the cadence of speech and on facial expression...we do not know who read them nor how readers responded.' The conference frankly drew attention to the inadequacies of scholarship up to that point. It was recognized, for example, that scholarship into millennia!movements 'is heavily biased towards the more dramatic types of movement, those that alarm civil and religious authorities or openly clash with them'.

[54] Grafton, 'The Varieties ofMillennial Experience' (1999), 85.

[55] Schwartz, 'The End of the Beginning' (1976), 7.

[56] Sweet, 'Millennialism in America' (1979), 511.

[57] Grafton, 'The Varieties ofMillennial Experience' (1999), 80.

[58] Schwartz, 'The End of the Beginning' (1976), 1-15. Also see Sweet, 'Millennialism in America' (1979), 511.

Lamont, Marjorie Reeves, and Peter Toon.[59]

> What the first generation...had originally found to be sporadic frontier phenomena, the second generation has found to be the constant center of religious life. Anthropologists, historians, social psychologists, political analysts and literary critics are now prone to stress the continuity and strength of millennial expectations. The first generation had regarded end-of-the-world hopes and movements as symptomatic of social or personal illness. The second generation describes millenarian beliefs and actions less often as the products of disease, more often as an arsenal of world-sustaining forces.[60]

Schwartz moved chronologically through key periods in the history of western millennialism, noting how innovative studies have changed our understanding of millennial groups. Reeves and McGinn found 'a backbone of millenarianism in the body of medieval Christianity'.[61] Weinstein highlighted complex millennial hopes and a civic identification with the New Jerusalem in Savonarola's Florence. James Stayer and others have shown a continuous and vital apocalyptic outlook from the late middle ages to Luther to the Anabaptists. Scholars observe a spectrum of understanding 'between peaceful and revolutionary millenarianism'. Studies of seventeenth-century English sectarians have indicated 'the centrality of

---

[59] J. F. C. Harrison, *Robert Owen and the Owenites in Britain and America: The Quest for the New Moral World* (London, 1969), and *The Second Coming: Popular Millenarianism 1780-1850* (London 1979); William L. Lamont, *Godly Rule: Politics and Religion, 1603-1660* (London, 1969); Marjorie Reeves, *The Influence of Prophecy in the Later Middle Ages: A Study of Joachimism* (Oxford, 1969); Peter Toon (ed.), *Puritans, the Millennium and the Future of Israel* (Cambridge, 1970). See also Robert G. Clause, 'Johann Heinrich Alsted and English Millennialism', *HTR* 62 (1969), 189-207; Christopher Hill, *Antichrist in Seventeenth-Century England* (London, 1971); Bernard McGinn, 'Apocalypticism in the Middle Ages: An Historiographical Sketch', *Mediaeval Studies* 37 (1975), 252-286; and Donald Weinstein, *Savonarola and Florence: Prophecy and Patriotism in the Renaissance* (Princeton, NJ, 1970).

[60] Schwartz, 'The End of the Beginning' (1976), 1.

[61] Schwartz, 'The End of the Beginning' (1976), 4. Reeves observed that, 'Because Christian apocalyptic writings set the life of the human soul in the context of a time process begun, and to be ended, by God, they speak to both individuals and societies in terms of watchful duty and patient waiting'; see Marjorie Reeves, 'Preface', in McGinn (ed.), *Apocalyptic Spirituality* (1979), xlv.

millenarian thinking to all streams of Protestantism'.[62] American historians have become impressed with 'the millenarian core within colonial theology'.[63] Schwartz pointed to 'the continuity of a complex millenarianism in Western culture', and to 'the most profound eschatological elements [that] inform the modern perspective'. He concluded that 'one can no longer type apocalyptic feelings as premodern or dysfunctional.'[64] He called for scholars of millennialism to move beyond moral judgementalism, and to recognize millennial movements as 'works of art'.[65]

In 1979 Sweet observed that the work of second-generation scholars 'slices deeply into assumptions held by their forebears'. Some of the revisionist themes promoted by this second generation of scholars include the following:

> They stress the ambiguity and ambivalence of millennial thought. They are sensitive to the importance of eschatological symbols and apocalyptic rhetoric...Finally, the paranoid and polarizing tendencies in millennialism are confronted without the conclusion that millennialism is the product of mental aberration and psychosocial disorder.[66]

Sweet pointed optimistically to 'the growing preoccupation of serious scholars with the subject of the future in general and millennialism in particular'.[67] Sweet concluded:

> The yield from millennial scholarship has been great, and its prospects are even more promising. It has promoted cross-cultural, comparative research, encouraged conversations between social scientists, historians, theologians, and anthropologists, and necessitated improvisation and improvement of social theories. Through its lens one is able to see clearly the social consequences of religious ideology, and the dissemination of theology among folk audiences and mass movements. These are not bad dividends from a subject that is mentioned only once in the Bible in *Revelation* 21:1-15 [sic].[68]

Bernard McGinn argued in the 1970s that apocalyptic thought was rooted in a perennial human concern – the desire to understand

---

[62] Weinstein, *Savonarola and Florence* (1970), *passim;* Schwartz, 'The End of the Beginning' (1976), 4.

[63] Schwartz, 'The End of the Beginning' (1976), 5.

[64] Schwartz, 'The End of the Beginning' (1976), 6.

[65] Schwartz, 'The End of the Beginning' (1976), 7.

[66] Sweet, 'Millennialism in America' (1979), 512.

[67] Sweet, 'Millennialism in America' (1979), 511.

[68] Sweet, 'Millennialism in America' (1979), 531. The reference should be to Revelation 20:1-15.

history, its unity, structure, and goal: 'A sense of belonging in time, as well as the need to understand the special significance of the present, is the anthropological root of apocalyptic systems of thought.'[69] McGinn showed how apocalyptic writings address 'permanent and pressing human anxieties' that cannot simply be set aside: 'The special strength of apocalyptic beliefs is the way in which they answer the desire for knowledge of past, present and future that is certain and detailed, not merely tentative and general.'[70]

While Cohn's account of sixteenth century apocalypticism focussed upon Thomas Miintzer and the Munster Anabaptists, second generation Reformation scholars observed that the apocalyptic mindset is 'deeply interwoven with the history of Protestantism' and is not merely the domain of heretical sects.[71] Of special note is the example of Martin Luther,[72] who among the major reformers demonstrates 'the most consistently pronounced apocalyptic outlook'.[73] For Lutherans, Anglicans, and puritans, apocalyptic traditions drew attention to 'an actual or an alleged confrontation between the true and false church, or between enemies and the people of God'.[74]

The second generation is represented in Biblical scholarship by two issues of the journal *Semeia* devoted to apocalypse as a genre and apocalyptic literature in general.[75] The 1979 issue reflected the work of the Apocalypse Group of the Society of Biblical Literature Genres Project which sought to provide 'a comprehensive survey of all the texts which might be or have been classified as apocalypses and can be dated...in the period 250 BCE – 250 CE, to establish how

---

[69] Bernard McGinn, *Visions of the End: Apocalyptic Traditions in the Middle Ages* (New York, 1979), 30.

[70] McGinn (ed.), *Apocalyptic Spirituality* (1979), 13.

[71] Seebal3, 'The Importance of Apocalyptic for the History of Protestantism' (1980), 24, 35.

[72] Luther's apocalyptic mindset is emphasized in Heiko Oberman, *Luther: Man between God and the Devil* (New Haven, 1989).

[73] Robin Barnes, 'Images of Hope and Despair: Western Apocalypticism ea. 1500-1800,' in McGinn *et al.* (eds), *Encyclopedia of Apocalypticism* (1998), ii. 151. 'In general, Protestant piety directed the focus of religious attention away from traditional rituals, turning it toward prophecy and prayer. This shift concentrated the outlook of believers on the promise of future salvation, the threat of the coming last judgment.'

[74] Seebal3, 'The Importance of Apocalyptic for the History of Protestantism' (1980), 24.

[75] See John J. Collins, 'Introduction: Towards the Morphology of a Genre', *Semeia* 14 (1979), and Adela Yarbro Collins, 'Introduction', *Semeia* 36 (1986).

far they can be regarded as members of one genre'.[76] The group
concluded that 'there is a phenomenon which may be called
'apocalyptic' and that it is expressed in an ill-defined list of writings
which includes the Jewish works Daniel, chap. 7-12, I Enoch, 4 Ezra,
2 Baruch and the Christian book of Revelation.'[77] They also offered a
concise but comprehensive definition of the literary genre.[78] In 1986
the social function of the genre was clarified. Apocalyptic literature
is 'intended to interpret present, earthly circumstances in light of the
supernatural world and of the future, and to influence both the
understanding and the behaviour of the audience by means of divine
authority'.[79]

In 1992 Ted Daniels published an annotated bibliography of
millennial studies and reviews that contained 3,762 entries. Most of
these had been pursued since the late 1960s, representing primarily
'second-generation' scholarship.[80] He sought to explain the interest:

> The millennium fascinates everyone. Whether we respond with horror,
> ridicule, delight, disgust or any combination of these or other emotions,
> it is almost impossible not to feel some thrill at the idea of the ultimate
> revolution, when God will finally roll up history's scroll and cleanse the
> wicked earth.[81]

Daniels' work serves nicely to sum up and epitomize the transition
from second- to third-generation scholarship.

---

[76] John J. Collins, 'Preface', *Semeia* 14 (1979), iii.
[77] Collins, 'Introduction: Towards the Morphology of a Genre' (1979), 3.
[78] "Apocalypse' is a genre of revelatory literature with a narrative framework
in which a revelation is mediated by an otherworldly being to a human
recipient, disclosing a transcendent reality which is both temporal, insofar
as it envisages eschatological salvation, and spatial insofar as it involves
another, supernatural world.' Collins, 'Introduction: Towards the Morphology of a Genre' (1979), 9.
[79] Collins, 'Introduction' (1986), 7. John Collins wrote in 1974, 'The effect of
apocalyptic is a perspective on human life. Physical death is not an ultimate
disaster. There is a life, and there are values which go beyond, or transcend,
death. The purpose of apocalyptic is to foster the cherishing of values which
transcend death and thereby the experience of transcendent life.' See John J.
Collins, 'The Symbolism of Transcendence in Jewish Apocalyptic,' *BR* 19
(1974), 7.
[80] Daniels, *Millennialism: An International Bibliography* (1992). Daniels
writes that, 'This book refers you to some of the 7,500 references of more or
less direct relevance that I know of, but while I believe that I have a fairly
complete listing from sociology and anthropology, I have only begun to
scratch the surface in the other disciplines' (x).
[81] Daniels, *Millennialism: An International Bibliography* (1992), xv.

### Third-Generation Scholarship: The 1990s and Beyond

Since the late 1990s a third generation of scholarship has become evident. These scholarly works respond to late twentieth-century *angst* at the cusp of the new millennium, and the rise and violent suppression of apocalyptic sects, as witnessed in the deaths of eighty members of the Branch Davidians outside Waco, Texas in 1993. This research is noteworthy, therefore, for the immediacy and social relevance that characterize it. This third-generation scholarship is also marked by an effort to consolidate second-generation gains, and to resist the ongoing tendency towards reductionism and the citation of the deprivation theory as a means to millennia!understanding.

Stephen Cook recently reflected on issues raised by the conference papers from the 1994 regional AAR/SBL meeting at Union Theological Seminary in New York. He discussed the current relevance of apocalypticism, contemporary cross-disciplinary study, current issues in the field, variety within millennialism, and the contribution apocalyptic biblical texts can make to Christian theology.[82] His comments serve well to indicate trends that mark third-generation scholarship at the turn of the new millennium.

Cook pointed to the significant cross-disciplinary study of apocalyptic groups that now exists. Thanks in part to the greater availability of the Dead Sea Scrolls, Biblical scholars have become increasingly interested in apocalyptic religion and writings. At the same time, social scientists have been focussing recently on apocalypticism 'as a social phenomenon', represented in the form of various millennia!groups. Not surprisingly, biblical scholars are availing themselves of the insights and data discovered by the social scientists, while social historians and sociologists are turning their attention to work on apocalypticism by biblical scholars.[83]

Cook argued that work still must be done to break down the

---

[82] Cook, 'Reflections on Apocalypticism' (1995), 3, 12. This article is Cook's introduction to a special issue of the *USQR* devoted to papers from the 1994 regional AAR/SBL meeting. Also see Cook's 'Introduction' to his book, Stephen L. Cook, *Prophecy and Apocalypticism: The Postexilic Social Setting* (Minneapolis, 1995), where he criticizes use of deprivation theory by Hebrew Bible scholars and calls for a new cross-disciplinary approach.

[83] Cook, 'Reflections on Apocalypticism' (1995), 5. As an example of how fascination with apocalypticism in the biblical world has spread to scholars outside the biblical disciplines, Cook cites Norman Cohn, *Cosmos, Chaos and the World to Come: The Ancient Roots of Apocalyptic Faith* (New Haven, 1993).

persistent notion that deprivation is 'the cause of millennialism'.[84]
Indeed, 'this approach...was certainly well represented at the Union
conference.'[85] But for Cook, this approach is misguided; deprivation
'may or may not be present in any given instance ofmillennialism'.[86]

> Millennia!groups, the social setting of apocalyptic writings, cannot be
> explained at this level of causation. Such groups form when an
> apocalyptic worldview is focused, a cognitive process that may take
> place under a variety of larger social conditions. This cognitive process
> involves the eschatologizing of mythic paradigms, that is, the
> integration and fusing of group myth into future-oriented, linear-time
> thinking. Definite factors, such as a catalyzing visionary-leader or
> influential writing, often motivate this process, but the process itself is
> creative and positive, not best viewed as reactive and compensatory.[87]

Cook cited a catalogue of historical cases to illustrate that millennia!
groups are, often, neither deprived nor from the social margins.
Some examples include the city of Florence in the time of
Savonarola, the Franciscan Spirituals of the late middle ages, and
the wealthy members of the nineteenth-century Irvingite movement
in England.

Cook also pointed to increasing recognition of the variety in and
among millennia!groups, demonstrating that they 'do not share an
essential, intrinsic nature'.[88] Group differences could include social
withdrawal versus social engagement, rigid moral discipline versus
antinomianism and licentious behaviour, pacifism versus violence,
and finally, supporting social values and institutions versus undermining majority values in service to a minority voice.[89] The final
trend observed by Cook is the new appreciation for the positive role
that apocalyptic scriptures can play in theology. These Biblical
themes keep the horizon of history prominent in Christian thinking;
they are a corrective for the na'ive hope for human progress and
evolution; and they give prominence to the global future of the world,
one that includes all peoples.[90]

Third-generation scholars have been critical of previous study.

---

[84]   Cook, 'Reflections on Apocalypticism' (1995), 8. 'The association of
apocalypticism with alienation and disenfranchisement is now so prevalent
that it is familiar even among students and laypeople.'
[85] Cook, 'Reflections on Apocalypticism' (1995), 7-8.
[86] Cook, 'Reflections on Apocalypticism' (1995), 9.
[87] Cook, 'Reflections on Apocalypticism' (1995), 8.
[88] Cook, 'Reflections on Apocalypticism' (1995), 9.
[89] Cook, 'Reflections on Apocalypticism' (1995), 11.
[90] Cook, 'Reflections on Apocalypticism' (1995), 13-14.

Anthony Grafton recently drew attention to ongoing problems and challenges in the scholarly study of millennial movements. [91] First, he observed that 'the language of millennialism...has become foreign' to the educated elite in our culture. When federal agents at Waco heard David Koresh refer to the seven seals (Revelation 6:1-8:6), they thought he was talking about performing animals:

> [For] members of the educated elite...the apocalypse is decidedly not now, not for us, not really. It is [rather] a curiosity, a script idea, a marketing strategy, something to generate magazine theme issues... Members of the educated elite, even if they practice a mainline religion, often have no exposure in childhood to the millennium, any more than they do to other unpleasant aspects of Christian tradition.[92]

It remains a challenge, therefore, to explain millennialism to educated people who desire a deeper understanding of the phenomenon.[93]

Secondly, Grafton suggested that historians currently working on millennialism 'share a common problem': despite their best intentions, they regularly give in to the 'deadly temptation' to mock these eschatological groups and their beliefs.[94] Such an attitude hinders historians in their effort to discover deep and important realities in apocalyptic thinking: 'Deep dimensions of apocalyptic thought, serious problems about the way it functions and the sources of its appeal, remain unexplored.'[95] Finally, Grafton highlighted the great challenge that faces the historian of apocalyptic diversity, the problem of how 'the visions of John precipitated such sharply different kinds of mental weather in different cultural micro-climates'.[96]

It is with the aim of addressing these kinds of concerns that the Center for Millennial Studies at Boston University presents itself as a forum for a 'new kind of scholarship'.[97] The Center seeks to

---

[91] Grafton, 'The Varieties of Millennial Experience' (1999), 76-88.
[92] Grafton, 'The Varieties of Millennial Experience' (1999), 82.
[93] Grafton, 'The Varieties of Millennial Experience' (1999), 83.
[94] Grafton, 'The Varieties of Millennial Experience' (1999), 84.
[95] Grafton, 'The Varieties of Millennial Experience' (1999), 85.
[96] Grafton, 'The Varieties of Millennial Experience' (1999), 83.
[97] The Center's literature is quite optimistic compared to the concerns expressed by Grafton: 'Previous generations of scholars were either drawn in to the maelstrom of apocalyptic passions, or were repelled by them, contemptuous of raving madmen and fools.' The Center for Millennial Studies Newsletter (September 1997) states that 'this millennium is unique: there is, at last, enough maturity about the study of religious phenomena

promote a wide intellectual discourse among scholars and the larger public through its website, conferences and publications, including the online academic journal, *Journal of Millennial Studies,* edited by Richard Landes. The Center's logo features the owl and the rooster, the owl representing the anti-apocalyptic believer who prefers caution and quiet and believes the dawn is far off, the rooster representing the apocalyptic believer who heralds the dawn of a new day, and wakens the barnyard.[98]

The benefits of this kind of approach are epitomized in *The Encyclopedia of Apocalypticism.* The stated purpose of the *Encyclopedia* nicely captures the approach of this third-generation scholarship:

> These essays seek neither to apologize for the extravagances of apocalyptic thinkers nor to excuse the perverse actions of their followers. Rather, they strive to understand a powerful, perhaps even indispensable, element in the history of Western religions that has been the source of both good and evil.[99]

Several innovative themes are presented. First, apocalypticism is represented as 'a major element in the three Western monotheistic faiths of Judaism, Christianity and Islam' and, it is claimed, there are 'genetic and historical links in the apocalyptic traditions of these three faiths'.[100] Second, 'A psychological sense of the imminence of a final division of good from evil, both personal and general, was of importance in the formation and development of Western Christendom.'[101] Third, these thinkers and movements from the distant past are not only fascinating and antiquarian; they are 'an important part of the development of Western religious traditions' and we can 'still draw food for thought from their faith'.[102] Fourth, apocalyptic beliefs can be used by various social groups 'for a variety of purposes,' both to reform society and to subvert it.[103] These themes have been the source of both great good and great evil in western

---

that we have a generation of scholars prepared to take seriously beliefs they do not share, to record, archive, and interpret currents that have always run deep, but now begin to surface in this new world disorder we currently inhabit.'

[98] *Millennial Stew: A Publication of the Center for Millennial Studies* 1:1 (1998), 5.

[99] McGinn *et al.* (eds), *Encyclopedia of Apocalypticism* (1998), ii. xii.

[100] McGinn *et al.* (eds), *Encyclopedia of Apocalypticism* (1998), ii. ix.

[101] McGinn *et al.* (eds), *Encyclopedia of Apocalypticism* (1998), ii. xviii.

[102] McGinn *et al.* (eds), *Encyclopedia of Apocalypticism* (1998), ii. xix.

[103] McGinn *et al.* (eds), *Encyclopedia of Apocalypticism* (1998), ii. 103.

history.[104] Fifth, McGinn finds at least four different models in the middle ages for relating apocalyptic hopes to practical reform.[105] He finds that the majority of twelfth-century apocalyptic thinkers were situated in 'high echelons of intellectual and political power'.[106]

## New Directions

Third-generation scholarly approaches are gradually impacting the study of German Pietist millennialism as well as recent work on British and Irish evangelicalism. German scholars have tended to neglect the subject of millennialism in German history. Richard Kyle recently suggested that by the late seventeenth and early eighteenth centuries end-time thinking in Europe 'was less intense and not as far-flung'.[107] Hans Schneider deserves credit for drawing attention to the importance of eschatological thinking as an interpretative key to understanding the radical Pietists of the late seventeenth century:

> the great significance that eschatology attained in Pietism appears to have increased even further among its radical representatives. For many figures and groups it became simply the central focus of their theology and piety.[108]

Thanks to Schneider's writings and his academic influence, careful investigation of these late seventeenth-century German chiliasts and their conflicts is now being pursued as never before.[109]

---

[104] 'Apocalyptic beliefs may be judged...dangerous because of their innate power to foster self-righteousness among the elect and at times violent opposition to, even persecution of, those identified as belonging to Satan's party...a source of intransigence and savagery on the part of some oppressors'; 'Apocalypticism has been the source of hope and courage for the oppressed'; McGinn *et al.* (eds), *Encyclopedia of Apocalypticism* (1998), ii. xii.

[105] McGinn *et al.* (eds), *Encyclopedia of Apocalypticism* (1998), ii. 102.

[106] McGinn *et al.* (eds), *Encyclopedia of Apocalypticism* (1998), ii. 85-86. McGinn argues, against Landes, that 'the still-current belief that expectation of the end was more widespread around the year 1000 CE than at other times in the Middle Ages must be abandoned'; see McGinn *et al.* (eds), *Encyclopedia of Apocalypticism* (1998), ii. xi.

[107] Richard Kyle, *The Last Days are Here Again: A History of the End-Times* (Grand Rapids, 1998), 66, 68.

[108] Hans Schneider, 'Der radikale Pietismus im 17. Jahrhundert', in Martin Brecht (ed.), *Geschichte des Pietismus* (Gottingen, 1993), i. 394f.

[109] Three of Schneider's graduate students have published doctoral dissertations on Pietist figures for whom eschatology was a central concern: Markus Matthias, *Johann Wilhelm und Johanna Eleonora Petersen* (Gottingen, 1993); Willi Temme, *Krise der Leiblichkeit: Die Sozietit der*

In a recent article, Schneider sketched the landscape of radical Pietist eschatology in Germany during the late seventeenth and early eighteenth centuries, drawing on recent research in this field.[110] Schneider's work highlights key figures in late seventeenth century German eschatological speculation, suggests factors that account for the attractiveness of a millennia! eschatological worldview at this time, and shows how people responded when turn-of-the-century millennia! hopes went unfulfilled. The millennia! expectations of Philipp Jakob Spener, whose hopes for better times for the church represented a dramatic shift from the idea in Augustine and Luther of a soon-coming final judgment, set off an 'explosion' of chiliastic thinking in early German Pietism.[111] A series of publications by Spener's radical followers predicted the coming conversion of the heathen, provided 'keys' to Daniel and Revelation, showed how prophecies were fulfilled in current events, predicted the dawning of the millennium in their lifetime, and attacked church authorities. Especially influential were the writings of English Philadelphians such as Jane Leade, whose works became available in German translation in the mid 1690s. Schneider noted that Pietist activities in Hessen and Westfalia are better researched than those in other regions of the German Empire.[112]

Schneider pointed to several factors that help to explain the increasing apocalyptic excitement among the Pietists as the year 1700 approached. Schneider suggested a social-psychological explan-

---

*Mutter Eva (Buttlarsche Rotte) und der Radikale Pietismus um 1700* (Gottingen, 1998); Stephan Goldschmidt, *Johann Konrad Dippel (1673-1734): Seine Radikalpietistische Theologie* (Gottingen: Vandenhoeck & Ruprecht, 2001). The present author's investigation of Pietism and eschatology began during a sabbatical year in Marburg in 1992-1993 under Professor Schneider's mentorship; see Douglas H. Shantz, 'The Master Work of a Minor Prophet: The Literary Career of the Radical Pietist Court Preacher Conrad Broske', in Wolfgang Breul-Kunkel and Lothar Vogel (eds), *Rezeption und Reform: Festschrift für Hans Schneider zu seinem 60. Geburtstag* (Darmstadt und Kassel, 2001); and Shantz, 'The Millennia! Study Bible of Heinrich Horch (1652-1729): A Case Study in Early Modern Reformed Hermeneutics', in Peter Lillback (ed.), *The Practical Calvinist: A Festschrift for Claire Davis* (Fearn, Scotland, 2002).
[110] Hans Schneider, 'Die unerfüllte Zukunft: Apokalyptische Erwartungen im radikalen Pietismus um 1700', in Manfred Jakubowski-Tiessen *et al.* (eds), *Jahrhundertwenden: Endzeit- und Zukunftsvorstellungen vom 15. bis zum 20. Jahrhundert* (Gottingen, 1999), 187-212.
[111] Schneider cites Martin Greschat, 'Die 'Hoffnung besserer Zeiten' für die Kirche,' *Zur neueren Pietismusforschung* (Darmstadt, 1977), 238.
[112] Schneider, 'Die unerfüllte Zukunft' (1999), 187-200.

ation that seems similar to the deprivation theories of first generation millennia! theorists. The ongoing crises that the seventeenth century experienced over several generations, starting with the Thirty Years' War, produced a sense of anxiety and threat that found expression in an 'end of the age' mentality. Social-economic changes should also be considered. Radical separatist Pietism seemed to attract people from social groups that were affected by changing economic conditions, such as members of craft guilds and impoverished nobility. Large numbers of theologians and preachers were also among the Pietists, often due to disillusionment with the moral failings of the churches. Finally, the impact of early Enlightenment doubt and the historical-critical method within Protestant orthodoxy may account for figures such as Heinrich Horch and Johann Konrad Dippel turning to a more spiritualistic path of private prophetic revelations.[113] In the end, Schneider joins second- and third-generation millennia!theorists in pointing to the great variety represented among Pietist millennialists in terms of their social background, motivations and ideological expressions – a pattern that will be repeated in any study of nineteenth century evangelicalism in Britain and Ireland.

A recognition of this kind of millennia!variety is at the heart of recent work in the British and Irish contexts. Scholarly interest began to bloom in the late 1970s, and the parameters of debate were established by a series of publications that continue to dominate the field. Ernest Sandeen's survey of *The Roots of Fundamentalism: British and American Millenarianism 1800-1930* (1978) and J. F. C. Harrison's *The Second Coming: Popular Millenarianism 1780-1850* (1979) focused, respectively, on the institutions of the 'Anglo-American' millennia!revival and the popular culture it generated. In 1980, David Hempton focused more narrowly on the British and Irish contexts in his *Journal of Ecclesiastical History* article on 'Evangelicals and eschatology'. The article asserted that evangelical millennialism in the nineteenth century was generally characterised by 'biblical literalism, social and ecclesiastical pessimism, Calvinism, anti-Catholicism, anti-radicalism, anti-rationalism and support for the Established Churches'.[114] His analysis was complicated by the competing ecclesiologies of nineteenth-century dissent, and qualified

---

[113] Schneider, 'Die unerfiillte Zukunft' (1999), 201-208. As members of the educated elite within German society, Pietist figures such as Horch, Dippel, the Petersens and Conrad Broske serve to illustrate Cook's point that millennia!groups are not always deprived nor are they always from the social margins.

[114] D. H. Hempton, 'Evangelicalism and eschatology', *JEH* 31(1980), 191.

by his admission that we lack a 'coherent picture of what was happening to British evangelicalism' in the period, but his insistence that millennialism was the cause and consequence of an 'ultra-simplistic' view of the Bible was unmissable.[115]

These publications provoked scholars into investigating the variety of millennial experiences in nineteenth-century evangelicalism, and acted as the catalyst for a surge of interest in the subject. In 1980 Hempton described the secondary literature as 'scant'; by 1998, the *Encyclopedia of Apocalypticism* described it as 'considerable'.[116] Although most scholarly research on the period has been carried out on millennialism's American contexts, a growing number of studies have begun to address the scholarly lacuna Hempton noted.[117] Hempton's article called for more research into the intellectual culture of Trinity College Dublin in the early part of the nineteenth century; without this, he claimed, it would be 'difficult to be certain about the relationship between anti-Catholicism and pre-millennialism' in Britain and Ireland.[118] His appeal was answered by a series of dissertations, including Joseph Liechty's 'Irish evangelicalism, Trinity College Dublin, and the mission of the Church of Ireland at the end of the eighteenth century' (NUI Maynooth, 1987). A recent series of doctoral dissertations, monographs and articles has focused attention upon narrower denominational and individual millennial concerns.[119] None

---

[115] Hempton, 'Evangelicalism and eschatology' (1980), 187.

[116] Hempton, 'Evangelicalism and eschatology' (1980), 180; Sandra L. Zimdars-Swartz and Paul F. Zimdars-Swartz, 'Apocalypticism in Modern Western Europe', in McGinn *et al.* (eds), *Encyclopedia of Apocalypticism* (1998), ii. 267.

[117] Hempton, 'Evangelicalism and eschatology' (1980), 180.

[118] Hempton, 'Evangelicalism and eschatology' (1980), 185; cf. Desmond Bowen, *The Protestant Crusade in Ireland, 1800-1870: A Study of Protestant-Catholic Relations between the Act of Union and Disestablishment* (Dublin, 1978), 65.

[119] These theses and monographs would include Timothy Grass' 'The Church's ruin and restoration: The development of ecclesiology in the Plymouth Brethren and the Catholic Apostolic Church, c. 1825-c. 1866' (King's College London, 1997), Kenneth Newport's *Apocalypse and Millennium: Studies in Biblical eisegesis* (Cambridge, 2000), Timothy Stunt's *From Awakening to Secession: Radical Evangelicals in Switzerland and Britain, 1815-35* (Edinburgh, 2000), Grayson Carter's *Anglican Evangelicals: Protestant Secessions from the via media, c. 1800-1850* (Oxford, 2001), Tom Kelley's 'Trapped between two worlds: Edward Nangle, Achill Island, and Protestant evangelicalism in Ireland, 1800-1862' (Trinity College Dublin, 2002), Gary Nebeker's 'John Nelson Darby and Trinity College Dublin: A study in eschatological contrasts', *FH* 34 (2002), 87-108, and Jonathan D.

of these studies matches the immense breadth of LeRoy Edwin Froom's *The Prophetic Faith of our Fathers: The Historical Development of Prophetic Interpretation* (1946-54), but all of them are more objective in their study of nineteenth-century millennialism in Britain and Ireland. Increasingly, scholars of British and Irish evangelicalism are challenging the utility of the deprivation theory, and illuminating something of the rich variety of evangelicalism's millennial experiences.

The extent of this variety has, however, been underplayed by an unfortunate scholarly tendency. In a volume of essays devoted to evangelical millennialism we should address the fact that many evangelicals, in seeking to establish their distinct identity, have been wary of acknowledging the possibility of connections with heterodox or marginalized groups. Harrison and others established the existence of an extensive subculture of Swedenborgian millennial enthusiasm but little has been done, with the notable exception of Jackie Latham's study of James Pierrepont Greaves, to determine its links with evangelicals who, at the time, vehemently dissociated themselves from the likes of Joanna Southcott and 'Zion' Ward.[120] Similarly, in spite of the ever-burgeoning interest in the mind and work of William Blake, millennial studies have neglected the impact of his thinking on John Linnell and Frederick Tatham, a Plymouth Brother and an Irvingite respectively.[121]

There has also been a tendency to ignore the wider North Atlantic dimension of Anglo-Irish millennialism. Here again, it could be argued that the evangelical fear of guilt by association has contributed to the problem. Valuable studies by Edwin Gaustad, James Moorhead, Charles Lippy, David Rowe, Michael Barkun, Ronald Numbers, and Grant Underwood have suggested a more coherent *Sitz im Leben* for the origins of such movements as the Mormons, the Seventh-Day Adventists and the Christadelphians,

---

Burnham's *A Story of Conflict: The Controversial Relationship between Benjamin Wills Newton and John Nelson Darby,* Studies in Evangelical History and Thought (Carlisle, 2004).

[120] J. E. M. Latham, *Search for a New Eden: James Pierrepont Greaves (1777-1842): The Sacred Socialist and his Followers* (Madison, NJ, 1999).

[121] See E. P. Thompson, *Witness against the Beast: William Blake and the Moral Law* (New York, 1993), and the wider discussion in M. H. Abrams, 'Apocalypse: Theme and variations', in C. A. Patrides and Joseph Wittreich (eds), The *Apocalypse in English Renaissance Thought and Literature* (Ithaca, N.Y., 1984). For Linnell, see D. Linnell, *Blake, Palmer, Linnell & Co: The Life of John Linnell* (Lewes, 1994). It is to be hoped that the recent acquisition of the Linnell Archive by the Fitzwilliam Museum, Cambridge will stimulate enquiry on this front.

but little comparable attention has been given to the British followers of Joseph Smith, William Miller and John Thomas.[122] These sects and their eschatological hopes, with other marginal groups like the British Israelites and such maverick figures as Henry Prince and James Jezreel, need to be related to the millennial mainstream of the nineteenth century. Only when these ecclesiastical 'outsiders' have been integrated with the wider context will we be in a position to appreciate the thinking and careers of such diverse characters as John Ruskin, W. B. Yeats, Lord Kelvin, and many a military man like General Gordon, Lord Allenby (of Armageddon) and Orde Wingate. We have nothing comparable on the European-British front to the well-researched overviews of the prophetic dimension in North America for the more recent period by Timothy Weber and Paul Boyer. [123]

## Conclusion

A brief summary of the growing scholarly consensus, as outlined above, should therefore include the following ten themes. First, apocalyptic and millennial ideas are far more central to western historical consciousness than was previously recognized. Scholars observe the 'continuity and strength' of millennial expectations in past western cultural experience. Modern western thought is still profoundly influenced by millennial-infused historical assumptions

---

[122] E. S. Gaustad (ed.), *The Rise of Adventism: Religion and Society in mid-Nineteenth Century America* (New York, [1974]); J. H. Moorhead, *American Apocalypse: Yankee Protestants and the Civil War, 1860-1869* (New Haven, CT, 1978); J. H. Moorhead, *World Without End: Mainstream American Protestant Visions of the Last Things, 1880-1925* (Bloomington, IN, 1999); C. H. Lippy, 'Waiting for the End: The Social Context of American Apocalyptic Religion' in L. P. Zamora (ed.), *The Apocalyptic Vision in America: Interdisciplinary Essays on Myth and Culture* (Bowling Green, OH, 1982), 37-63; D. L. Rowe, *Thunder and Trumpets: Millerites and Dissenting Religion in Upstate New York, 1800-1850* (Chico, CA, 1985); M. Barkun, *Crucible of the Millennium: The Burned-Over District of New York in the 1840s* (Syracuse, NY, 1986); M. Barkun, *Disaster and the Millennium* (New Haven, 1974); R. L. Numbers and J. M. Butler (eds), *The Disappointed: Millerism and Millenarianism in the Nineteenth Century* (Knoxville, TN, [1993]); G. Underwood, *The Millenarian World of Early Mormonism* (Urbana, IL, 1993).

[123] Paul Boyer, *When Time Shall Be No More: Prophecy Belief in Modern American Culture* (Cambridge, MA, 1992); T. P. Weber, *Living in the Shadow of the Second Coming: American Premillennialism, 1875-1925* (New York, 1979; second ed., 1987).

and perspectives. Second, millennial thinking is central to all the main branches of Protestantism in Britain, the European Continent and North America. Third, this mindset reflects the perennial western need for a sense of meaning and direction in history: 'Christian apocalyptic writings set the life of the human soul in the context of a time process begun, and to be ended, by God.'[124] Fourth, apocalypticism and millennialism arise in a wide variety of social contexts and encompass a broad range of emphases and perspectives. These beliefs can be used by various social groups 'for a variety of purposes', both to reform society and to subvert it. Fifth, millennial beliefs and actions most often arise as a creative, world-sustaining response to these various contexts; reductionist efforts to attribute them to personal or social disease are misplaced. Sixth, scholars in the social sciences and humanities are now taking seriously the centrality and impact of millennial views of the world. More and more of this scholarship is being pursued in co-operative cross-disciplinary fashion. Seventh, third-generation scholarship has the continuing task of building on second-generation challenges to deprivation theory, and responding to current social needs and anxieties. Eighth, scholars face the continuing challenge of nurturing an understanding and respect for the apocalyptic mindset. The key word for future research must be one of 'balance' – a balanced understanding that reflects both critique and respect for millennial movements and groups, and a balanced judgement that is aware of both the legacy of good and the legacy of evil that apocalypticism has engendered. Ninth, apocalyptic themes have a positive theological value. They keep the horizon of history prominent in Christian thinking; they are a corrective for the naïve hope for human progress and evolution; they give prominence to the global future of the world, one that includes all peoples; and they may keep Protestantism from falling into an unhealthy individualism. Finally, previously neglected fields of millennial research are slowly being addressed, especially late seventeenth-century German Pietist millennialism, and its nineteenth century evangelical descendant. As the essays in this volume attest, such study highlights the need for humility among both the scholars and the advocates of Christian millennial ideas.

---

[124] Reeves, 'Preface' (1979), xiv.

# CHAPTER 3

# Influences in the Early
# Development of J. N. Darby

Timothy C. F. Stunt

To consider the early career and teaching of John Nelson Darby is to walk into a minefield of current controversy. For many evangelical Christians today the millennia!timetable is a burning issue of huge importance and it is unlikely that their interest in 'the last days' will have been reduced by the quasi-apocalyptic events of September 2001. The importance of Darby's influence in such eschatological thinking (and more particularly in the development of the dispensationalist hermeneutic) is generally acknowledged, but the controversy, which occupies so many evangelical web sites, is concerned with whether his influence has been the bane or the benison of the evangelical world. [1] The following study is not a contribution to that debate. We shall be concerned with Darby's early intellectual and spiritual development, and some of the influences that contributed to his eschatological thinking. But we should first consider a significant shift in the eschatological outlook of the evangelical world, which was occurring at a crucial stage in Darby's development.

Although the early evangelicals had frequently found themselves in conflict with the values and assumptions of the world of the rational Enlightenment, there was a significant element of eighteenth-century optimism in their worldview. Soon after the cataclysmic developments in France of the 1790s, a violent massacre of Europeans in Southern India had confirmed the *Edinburgh Review* (as well as many others) in its opinion of the 'complete

---

[1] It is an indication of the extent of his influence that his portrait appeared in *Time's* cover feature, 1 July 2002, 'The Bible and the Apocalypse: Why more Americans are reading and talking about the End of the World.'

hopelessness' of Christian missions in India.[2] In striking contrast was William Carey's assurance for the future:

> He who raised the Scottish and brutalised Britons to sit in heavenly places in Christ Jesus, can raise these slaves of superstition. The promises...make us anticipate that not very distant period when He will famish all the gods of India, and cause these idolaters to cast their idols to the moles and bats, and renounce for ever the work of their own hands.[3]

In this older perspective the millennium was to be ushered in by the faithful diligence of believers and would conclude with Christ's return, the 'restoration of all things', and the last judgment. In a somewhat self-congratulatory but not untypical letter to the *Evangelical Magazine* it was claimed in 1820 that instead of 'calculating prophetic dates' for the commencement of the millennium, the Bible, Missionary and Tract Societies are introducing it'.[4] Such a millennium might be more literal than Augustine's symbolic thousand years but Christ's return was clearly envisaged as postmillennial and for many years only a marginal minority took seriously the suggestion of Joseph Mede that Christ's return could be expected before the millennium. These 'millennialists' were easily dismissed by the established evangelical journals as a product of the fanatic fringe and labelled as chiliasts or antinomians, reminiscent of the Diggers, the Fifth Monarchists and other wild men of the seventeenth-century interregnum. Indeed, in the 1820s, Edward Irving's histrionic tendencies and his eccentricities of language contributed further to the image of a pre-millennialism

> whose poverty and puerility in theological science, and whose lamentable deficiency in the very rudiments of biblical learning...are united with a startling wildness of imagination, [whose] thoughts [are] governed by no law of logic, and exhibiting a strange caricature of genius, a mode of writing which is the very panorama of affectation,

---

[2] *Edinburgh Review* xii (April 1808), 169.

[3] Quoted Iain H. Murray, The *Puritan Hope: Revival and the Interpretation of Prophecy* (Edinburgh, 1971), 153.

[4] *Evangelical Magazine* xxviii (1820), 280. See also this passage from Bogue's *Discourses:* 'By the preaching of the Gospel, the reading of the Bible, and the zeal of Christians in every station...will the glory of the latter days be brought about'; *EM* (new series) v (1827), 68.

and a haughtiness of dogmatism which is no symptom of the calm
perception of evidence and the firmness of conviction.[5]

The first two decades of the century had seen a proliferation of
strange writing on prophetic subjects and even though there were
sober and thoughtful men among those invited to Albury, the home
of Henry Drummond, for the purpose of prophetic study, enthusiasts
like J. H. Frere and Lewis Way, who founded the Society for the
Investigation of Prophecy in 1826, were widely regarded as eccentric
or peculiar.[6] Nevertheless, with some reluctance, the *Evangelical
Magazine* had to recognise in 1828 that not all premillennialists
could be reduced to this caricature. In a lengthy review of Gerard
Noefs *Brief Inquiry into the Prospects of the Church of Christ in
connexion with the Second Advent,* a contributor systematically
rejected 'the radical [premillennial] errors running through his whole
system' but was constrained to recognise that Noefs *Inquiry* was the
work 'of a holy and devout Christian and it manifests a constant
anxiety to promote the interests of practical godliness'. That the
reviewer was somewhat disconcerted by the unexpected phenomenon
of responsible and reasonable premillennialism is apparent in his
references to 'the incongruities in reasoning, and the great
misunderstanding of Scripture passages, which we lament to find in
any writing, from such an excellent man, and valuable servant of
Christ, as Mr Gerard Noef. While emphasising his 'alarm and
apprehension of the *baneful practical effect* of the revived millennary
doctrine', the reviewer was nonetheless relieved that 'Mr Noefs
better feelings and holy benevolence have prevented him from being
quite carried away by the narrow and absorbing influence of the
system in which he is entangled' and concluded with an extract
'which breathes the amiable, holy and conciliatory spirit of its
author'.[7]

This is a development that has to be born in mind when we

---

[5] *EM* (new series) vi (1828), 348.
[6] The phenomenal outpouring of prophetic interpretation in the wake of the
French Revolution is well illustrated in L. E. Froom, The *Prophetic Faith of
Our Fathers:* The *Historical Development of Prophetic Interpretation*
(Washington, DC, 1946), iii. 263-65. But Froom is far from exhaustive as he
omits any reference to the more extreme characters like Richard Brothers or
Joanna Southcote, or even to the less celebrated interpreters of Napoleon's
place in the prophetic scheme like Lewis Mayer whose works went through
several editions between 1803 and 1809.
[7] *EM* (new series) vi (1828), 351, 348, 390-1.

examine the early spiritual development of John Nelson Darby.[8] His conversion, as we shall see, dated from several years earlier but it was to his experience of spiritual renewal, late in 1827, that he looked back repeatedly in subsequent years as a time of deliverance and assurance.[9] This experience, which effectively served to identify him as an evangelical, came, therefore, at a time when a little of the stigma that had previously attached to premillennialism was beginning to diminish. Admittedly this eschatological perspective was particularly associated with the colourful preaching of Edward Irving, but even the uncompromising rigorists for whom Irving was something of a standard bearer could still be considered as an integral element in the evangelical movement.[10] Mter all, Irving's followers were as yet untainted with charges of Christological heresy, and although the possibility of Pentecostal manifestations had been mooted there had not yet been any tongue speaking or miraculous healings. So, for a churchman to be identified with the evangelical movement did not preclude his showing public sympathy for millennialism. However we must be careful not to confuse Darby's experience of 1827 with his conversion which had occurred 'six or seven years' before, in late 1820 or early 1821.[11] These previous years require closer attention for reasons that will become

---

[8] For a basic outline of Darby's career see *The Blackwell Dictionary of Evangelical Biography*, s.v. (article by Timothy C. F. Stunt); Timothy Larson (ed.), *Biographical Dictionary of Evangelicals* (Leicester, 2003), s.v. (article by Neil Dickson); and the *Oxford Dictionary of National Biography* (forthcoming), s.v. (article by Timothy C. F. Stunt).

[9] Although some have insisted that this experience occurred in 1826, the evidence for late 1827 is overwhelming. **If** the accompanying convalescence had occurred in the previous year, Frank Newman would not have been able to recall seeing Darby's 'crippled limbs resting on crutches...in a drawing room'; F.W. Newman, *Phases of Faith or Passages from the History of my Creed*, 6th edition (1860), 17, but see also below, nn. 40 and 44.

[10] For the rigorist wing of evangelicalism see T. C. F. Stunt, *From Awakening to Secession: Radical Evangelicals in Switzerland and Britain, 1815-1835* (Edinburgh, 2000), 95-102, 114.

[11] For repeated references to 'six or seven years', see J. N. Darby, *Collected Writings*, ed. William Kelly (n.d.), i. 36; J. N. Darby, *Notes and Jottings from various meetings* (Lancing, [1978]), 304; [J. N. Darby], *Letters of J.N.D* (London, n.d.), ii. 310, 433; iii. 298. M. S. Weremchuk has published a transcription of some autobiographical marginal notes in Darby's Greek New Testament, which is now in the JRULM, CBA, Darby Sibthorp Collection, Box 157. The text is carelessly written with hardly any punctuation but includes the extraordinarily imprecise statement, '[I] loved Christ, I have no doubt sincerely and growingly since June or July 1820 or 21, I forget which'; Weremchuk, *John Nelson Darby: A Biography* (Neptune, NJ, 1992), 204.

apparent later.

In his early fifties Darby observed, 'I think I am intellectual enough, and my mind – though my education was in my judgment not well *directed,* save by God – cultivated enough to enjoy cultivated society.'[12] We can only speculate whether Darby's later reservations were concerned with the predominantly classical system of his day or with the way it was applied at Westminster School, London, and Trinity College Dublin. Whatever the perceived shortcomings of his teachers, his later publications and correspondence suggest that they did nothing to quench his spirit of almost universal enquiry – a spirit that was fascinated by a wealth of ideas ranging from such subjects as language or philosophy to geology or politics.[13] More than one writer has wondered, not unreasonably, what part the teaching faculty of Trinity College Dublin may have played in the spread of premillennialist thinking among Irish evangelicals, but such an enquiry can shed only minimal light on Darby's early development.[14] His studies at Trinity (1815-19) were classical as opposed to theological, and they were finished some time before his conversion. The eschatology of lecturers at Trinity may help to explain how Darby's ideas were later received, but to look for the roots of his own prophetic thinking in the theological publications of his classical teachers is of questionable value.[15] Such a line of enquiry may be likened to looking for the origins of Luther's teaching on justification in the Nominalism of the reformer's early teachers. It is improbable that Darby's thinking at Trinity was focused on theology, let alone prophecy.

Although he certainly met some earnest evangelicals like John Bellett, when he was at Trinity, Darby's spiritual enquiries at that stage appear to have been more concerned with broader philosophical issues.[16] One specific moment in his education recurred

---

[12] [Darby], *Letters of J.N.D* (n.d.), i. 205.
[13] Some examples of this range will be found in my 'John Nelson Darby: The Scholarly Enigma', *BAHNR* 2:2 (2003), 70-74.
[14] For example, Ernest R. Sandeen, *The Roots of Fundamentalism: British and American Millenarianism 1800-1930* (Chicago, 1970), 90.
[15] This is G. L. Nebeker's elusive objective in 'John Nelson Darby and Trinity College, Dublin: A study in Eschatological Contrasts,' *FH* 34 (2002), 87-108. The essay is further impaired by the author's reluctance to identify the gradual development of his subject's thinking. Darby's eschatological thinking in the 1820s is repeatedly illustrated with quotations from his writings from a much later period.
[16] This statement may have to be revised in the light of a very recent discovery made at the time of proofreading. A copy of *The Character of a Primitive Bishop in a letter to a non-juror* by a Presbyter of the Church of

in his thoughts repeatedly for the rest of his life. This was when reading a passage in Cicero's *De Officiis* (On *Duty)* which referred to truth as being the material under the control *('materia...subjecta)* of the philosopher.[17] In his early thirties Darby recalled that this was before his conversion 'when I was a poor dark creature,' but that even then he had been struck by the realization that such an idea implied the impossibility of any rational knowledge of God, as this would deny divine supremacy.[18] Such a recollection tallies with other statements, which suggest that in his youth Darby was of a serious-minded inclination. He had been 'brought up to know the Scriptures' and 'believed that there was a Christ as much as I do now'.[19] He also tells us that his 'sense of beauty' had awakened him to the possibility of a relationship with God beyond that of merely a creature.[20] In the absence of any more specific details of his conversion we may perhaps reasonably conclude that it was an experience in which submission to God and a decision to follow the Saviour were the principal elements. To accept such an account, however, is to be totally dependent on the subject's recollections and perceptions after – often long after – the event. To make sense of his experience and of subsequent developments we need to digress somewhat into the family environment in which he found himself prior to going to Trinity.

Darby was descended from gentry who had profited from commerce. On his father's side his ancestors had settled in Ireland

---

England (London, 1709) has the MS endorsement 'J. N. Darby 1819'. This suggests that *even before his conversion* Darby was exercised about Episcopal succession and the authenticity of Anglican orders.

[17] 'Quo circa huic, quasi materia quam tractet et in qua versetur subiecta est veritas'; Cicero, *De Officiis* i. 16. Curiously in Walter Miller's Loeb Classical Library translation (New York, 1913), the weight of the word *subiecta* is lost: 'So, then, it is truth that is, as it were, the stuff with which this virtue has to deal and on which it employs itself.'

[18] [Darby], *Letters of J.N.D* (n.d.), i. 20 (August 1833). His later accounts of this episode include Darby, *Collected Writings* (n.d.), vi. 27-8 (1853); xxxii. 339 (c.1870?); J.N. Darby, *Notes and Comments* (n.d.), i. 293; ii. 174 (c. 1872). Although Darby was very familiar with the patristic writings he makes no reference, as far as I know, to the not dissimilar reservations (about knowing God rationally) entertained by Ambrose in his *De Officiis Ministrorum*, i. 26 – a work which was consciously modelled on Cicero's work.

[19] Darby, *Notes and Jottings* (1978), 379; Darby, *Collected Writings* (n.d.), xxvii. 368. Compare this with his remark in 1853, 'I always regarded with indignant contempt Mr. Hume's argument against miracles'; Darby, *Collected Writings* (n.d.), vi. 47

[20] Darby, *Notes and Comments* (n.d.), ii. 174.

and owned Leap Castle in County Offaly, but his father as a younger son had pursued a mercantile career. Resident in London,[21] John Darby senior profited from the Napoleonic Wars by securing lucrative government contracts.[22] Earlier, when he was a young man, it was probably through business that he came into contact with Samuel Vaughan (1720-1801), a wealthy businessman with sugar-plantations in Jamaica. Vaughan owned large estates in Maine at Hallowell which he founded with a Boston merchant, Benjamin Hallowell, whose daughter he had married in 1747. Naturally Vaughan's sympathies were with the colonists in the War of Independence and as the war drew to a close he went, with his family, to live in Philadelphia. When John Darby senior wed Samuel Vaughan's daughter, Ann, in 1784, he was marrying into a family widely respected for its learning and philanthropy, 'lovers of science, humanity and America'.[23] We do not know much about John Nelson Darby's father other than his commercial activity, but the background of Ann Darby gives us a good idea of the world into which our subject was born.

John Nelson Darby's mother was half-American and as a young woman in her mid-twenties, before she married, had lived with her parents in Philadelphia where her father, a respected naturalist, was entrusted with the landscaping of Independence Square.[24] George Washington had visited their home and for some years corresponded with her father.[25] Forgotten today, the members of Ann Darby's family represent a galaxy of late eighteenth-century achievement. Like their father, her brothers were active in a wide

---

[21] His business was in Milk Street, Cheapside, and his home was first in Hackney and later in Westminster where John Nelson Darby was born. Weremchuk, *John Nelson Darby* (1995), 21.

[22] According to the recollections of B. W. Newton, the contracts (to supply victuals to the navy) were obtained through Lord Nelson, presumably with Darby's naval brother Horatio as an intermediary; JRULM, CBA 7060, Small MS Book vi, 38.

[23] *ANB*, xxii. 294. Dr Max Weremchuk has kindly informed me that the marriage was solemnized in Trinity Church Parish, New York, on 21 July 1784 (letter, 15 December 2003).

[24] William Darlington, *Memorials of John Bartram and Humphry Marshall* (Philadelphia, 1849), 556-7.

[25] One of the earliest plans of Mount Vernon was prepared for Washington by Samuel Vaughan; see the letter from Washington to Vaughan, 12 November 1787; John C. Fitzpatrick (ed.), *The Writings of George Washington from the Original Manuscript Sources,* xxix. The text is available at the Electronic Text Center of the library of the University of Virginia (http://etext.lib.virginia.edu/washington/fitzpatrick).

range of fields outside their own business life. William Vaughan (1752-1850), a London merchant and Fellow of the Royal Society, was an advocate of canal construction, a pioneer in the development of the London docks and the establishment of the first savings bank in 1815.[26] Samuel Vaughan, junior (1762-1802), watched with interest (and reported on) the earliest stages in the development of the American constitution,[27] proposed an ambitious plan of mineral exploration to support the coinage of the recently established U.S. Mint,[28] and later provided details of breadfruit cultivation for Sir Joseph Banks.[29] Another brother, John Vaughan (1756-1841), a wine merchant, served the American Philosophical Society as Treasurer and Librarian for some forty years.[30] The most distinguished of the brothers was the eldest, Benjamin Vaughan (1751-1835), whose friendship with Lord Shelburne and with Benjamin Franklin resulted in his giving crucial assistance in the negotiation of the peace at the end of the War of Independence in 1782-3.[31]

For John Nelson Darby, to have grown up in the shadow of such activity may well have been intimidating, but the significance of this influence becomes clearer when we bear in mind that the members of the Vaughan family were Unitarians. *Par excellence,* they were a product of the eighteenth-century Enlightenment. Their circle included radical thinkers like Benjamin Franklin, Jeremy Bentham and Joseph Priestley, whose Warrington Academy the older Vaughan brothers had attended. Priestley's Unitarianism was very much a product of the deist rationalism of the day and although John Darby's family were Anglicans we may reasonably surmise that a man who married into the Vaughan family shared some of their rationalist self-confidence and optimistic faith in humanity. John

---

[26] *DNB* (1885-1900) xx. s.v.

[27] For his interest in the Constitutional Congress see his letter to James Bowdoin, 30 November 1787, in Merrill Jensen (ed.), The *Documentary History of the Ratification of the Constitution, Vol. 11 Ratification of the Constitution by the States, Pennsylvania* (Madison WI, 1976), 262-263.

[28] J. J. Lloyd, 'A Link that failed', *Journal of the History of Earth Sciences Society* 5 (1986).

[29] William Vaughan to J. Banks, 16 July 1794, with extract from letter by Samuel Vaughan; State Library of New South Wales, Sir Joseph Banks Archive, Series 72.191 (www.sl.nsw.gov.au). In 1790 William and Samuel had provided Thomas Jefferson with seeds of mountain rice; see Jefferson to S. Vaughan, 27 November 1790, in *Letters of Thomas Jefferson,* available online at www.ai.mit.edu/people/hqm/writings/jefferson.

[30] *ANB* xxii. 294-6.

[31] See *DNB* (1885-1900) xx; *Dictionary of American Biography* (New York, 1936), xix. 233-34; *ANB* xxii, 289-90.

Nelson Darby's conversion may therefore be seen as a possibly (but not necessarily) unconscious rejection of this aspect of his family's tradition. The attraction of the 'vitaf and spiritual Christianity he had encountered at Trinity outweighed the self-confident and manifestly 'human' good works of his family. It is in this context therefore that we should see Darby's decision to submit to God and follow the Saviour. At this stage such a decision could equally well lead in a catholic or evangelical direction.

It was soon after his conversion that Darby was called to the bar in January 1822 and many writers say that he never practised.

I was a lawyer; but feeling that, if the Son of God gave Himself for me I owed myself entirely to Him, and that the so-called christian world was characterised by deep ingratitude towards Him, I longed for complete devotedness to the work of the Lord, my chief thought was to get round amongst the poor Catholics of Ireland. I was induced to be ordained. I did not feel drawn to take up a regular post, but being young in the faith and not yet knowing deliverance, I was governed by the feeling of duty towards Christ, rather than by the consciousness that *He* had done *all* and that I was redeemed and saved; consequently it was easy to follow the advice of those who were more advanced than myself in the christian world.

As soon as I was ordained [in August 1825], I went amongst the poor Irish mountaineers, in a wild and uncultivated district, where I remained two years and three months, working as best I could.[32]

If Darby never practised as a barrister there are some three years to be accounted for between the completion of his legal studies and ordination. In view of his remarkable familiarity in later years with the patristic writings (not to mention numerous other works of divinity) we may reasonably conclude that a significant part of this time was spent in theological reading. Such studies had had no place in his earlier classical curriculum and he would have had no apparent reason to engage in them before his conversion.

On various occasions in later life he drew attention to his far from evangelical outlook at this time and how near he was to becoming a Roman Catholic.[33] Comparing the perspective of John Henry

---

[32] [Darby], *Letters of J.N.D* (n.d.), iii. 297, to Professor F. A. G. Tholuck of Halle University, c. 1855.

[33] Writing to a French Catholic journalist in 1878, 'Rome, at the beginning of my conversion, had not failed to attract me. But the tenth chapter of the Epistle to the Hebrews had made that impossible for me'; [Darby], *Letters of*

Newman's *Apologia pro Vita Sua* (1866) with his own earlier lack of assurance he recalled:

> I too, governed by a morbid imagination, thought much of Rome, and its professed sanctity, and catholicity, and antiquity... Protestantism met none of these feelings, and I was rather a bore to my clergyman by acting on the rubrics. I looked out for something more like reverend antiquity...

> [Y]ears before Dr Newman...I fasted in Lent so as to be weak in body at the end of it; ate no meat on week days – nothing till evening on Wednesdays, Fridays, and Saturdays, then a little bread or nothing; observed strictly the weekly fasts, too. I went to my clergyman always if I wished to take the sacrament that he might judge of the matter. I held apostolic succession fully, and the channels of grace to be there only. I held thus Luther and Calvin and their followers to be outside. I was not their judge, but I left them to the uncovenanted mercies of God. I searched with earnest diligence into the evidences of apostolic succession in England, and just saved their validity for myself and my conscience.[34]

**It** is important to bear in mind that though Darby's devotions may have been unusually meticulous they were part of a well-established tradition of exact churchmanship in Ireland to which the confident

---

*J.N.D* (n.d.), ii. 434. He likens 'the hopeless effort of Romans 7' to 'an honest monks' [sic] labour, which I have tried'; [Darby], *Letters of J.N.D* (n.d.), iii. 90. Darby's account written in his Greek New Testament includes the following: 'my mind had passed, after its own repentance, under the dark cloud of the popish system...I used to hold up Christ to my brother as availing against the claim of men on their points yet it prevailed so far as to prevent my mind from finding comfort in the truths I honestly urged on him which I had found in what poor reading of Scripture I had'; cited by Weremchuk, *John Nelson Darby* (1995), 205. For Darby's older brother, William Henry (at one time a Roman Catholic, later with the Brethren), see B. W. Newton's recollections in JRULM, CBA 7061, 131; 7064, 25. W. H. Darby's fifth son (born 1864) was named John Nelson Darby.

[34] Darby, *Collected Writings* (n.d.), xviii. 146, 156. This may be compared with another account (1878): 'I gave way to it at the beginning of my conversion. I said to myself, **If** I fast two days, three would be better, seven better still. Then that would not do to go on, but **I** pursued the system long enough. **It** led to nothing, except the discovery of one's own powerlessness'; [Darby], *Letters of J.N.D* (n.d.), ii. 429. See also Darby, *Collected Writings* (n.d.), xxvii. 91, where he notes the parallels with the Gnostic teaching that 'matter was an evil thing'.

assurance of the evangelicals was quite alien. Henry Woodward, the Rector of Fethard, who was married to one of Darby's cousins, observed that there had developed in the diocese in which he found himself 'a disposition to preserve a cautious distance from, what had begun for some time to be called the Evangelical clergy', though in due course he began to co-operate with them.[35]

When Darby was ordained in 1825 he was sent to work in what was not yet the separate parish of Calary not far from the Delgany home of his brother-in-law Edward Pennefather and Robert Daly's parish of Powerscourt. It is clear that like Henry Woodward he began to work with his evangelical fellow clergy but by his own account the next two and half years were still part of the eight years during which 'universal sorrow and sin pressed upon my spirit'.[36]

> I was troubled in the same way when [I was] a clergyman...going from cabin to cabin to speak of Christ, and with souls, these thoughts sprang up, and if I sought to quote a text to myself it seemed a shadow and not real. I ought never to have been there, but do not think that this was the cause, but simply that I was not set free according to Romans viii.[37]

Commenting in 1863 on how often converted Christians 'are as if outside God's house and circle, and desiring, hoping, praying that it may be well with them, and that they may be found within',[38] he is far from scornful, adding, 'I was a good while so myself...The only safe state, so to speak then, is rigid legality and devotedness on that ground – a kind of Thomas à Kempis life.'[39] Only in December 1827, after a serious riding accident, when Darby underwent a time of enforced convalescence on crutches in the home of his sister, Susannah Pennefather, did the assurance of his being 'risen with Christ' bring him experimentally (i.e. in terms of spiritual

---

[35] H. Woodward, *Essays, Thoughts and reflections, and Letters, with a Memoir by his Son Thomas Woodward* (1864), 451. I have expanded on this tradition of exact churchmanship in Stunt, *From Awakening to Secession* (2000), 151-5.

[36] [Darby], *Letters of J.N.D* (n.d.), i. 345.

[37] [Darby], *Letters of J.N.D* (n.d.), iii. 453-4

[38] [Darby], *Letters of J.N.D* (n.d.), i. 354; cf. 'I remember when I was converted all the Christians I met, were like people outside, and trusting they would be right when they got in, instead of being already inside'; Darby, *Notes and Jottings* (1978), 219.

[39] It was this sort of austerity that gave rise to Frank Newman's much quoted references to Darby's 'severe deprivation' and his eating 'food unpalatable and often indigestible'; 'his whole frame might have vied in emaciation with a monk of La Trappe'; Newman, *Phases of Faith* (1860), 17-18.

experience) into the evangelical ranks.[40]

However we must resist the temptation of making the 1827-28 episode so decisive that we ignore the continuities which extended from the earlier period into his later life. For example the rigorous anti-Erastian note that characterised his *Considerations addressed to the Archbishop of Dublin* (written in 1827 *before his accident*) was to remain a characteristic emphasis in his approach to ecclesiastical issuesY Even more significant for our purposes is the fact that his interest in eschatology had clearly begun in the earlier period. Years later he observed:

> A man may not know much about the rapture of the church, and yet be waiting for someone to come and take him out of this scene. Before ever I knew about the Lord's coming, I think I loved His appearing. I knew nothing about the doctrine, but the principle of loving His appearing was in my mind, though I could not define it. I do not talk now of the rapture, though it is most blessed to get that, too. What I delight in, is Christ's coming and setting aside the whole thing I am in.[42]

In 1874 when Charles Eynard referred to the need for tranquility in a time of political agitation, Darby replied:

> Nearly fifty years ago I remarked that, when speaking of shaking the heavens and the earth (Heb. 12:26), Paul says, "he [God] hath promised [saying, Yet once more I shake not the earth only but also heaven]." I, a conservative by birth, by education and by mind; a Protestant in Ireland into the bargain; I had been moved to the very depths of my soul on seeing that everything was going to be shaken. The testimony of God made me see and feel that all should be shaken, but...that we have a kingdom that cannot be shaken.[43]

There can be little doubt that this apocalyptic realisation that the earth was destined for destruction also predates his experience of deliverance. Indeed it probably goes back to the growing confrontation between Catholics and Protestants that gave rise to Archbishop Magee's Charge of 1826 and the Petition to the House of

[40] See Stunt, *From Awakening to Secession* (2000), 171 n. 86, where I have summarised the reasons for believing that J. G. Bellett miswrote the year in his letter, which should have been dated 31 January 1828 and not 1827. His statement in January that Darby had been 'laid up for nearly two months from a hurt in his knee' enables us to place the date of the accident fairly precisely.

[41] Darby, *Collected Writings* (n.d.), i. 1-19.

[42] Darby, *Notes and Jottings* (1978), 99-100.

[43] [Darby], *Letters of J.N.D* (n.d.), ii. 254.

Commons for Protection in February 1827. Frank Newman arrived
in the Pennefather household in September 1827, some two months
before Darby's accident, and yet one of his first letters (8 October
1827) is an indication of the impact Darby's apocalyptic thinking had
already made on him.

> I think I now fully feel that this world is not only horribly disordered
> but that God proposes no remedy for its disorder...but he proposes to
> gather to himself *out* of the world a peculiar people to *suffer* with
> Christ here, that they may reign with him hereafter.[44]

The realisation that Darby's eschatology had already taken a
millennia! direction *before* his experience of assurance and
deliverance – i.e. before he could be identified as an evangelical – is
of considerable importance. An enquirer after truth who, on his own
admission, had regarded 'Luther and Calvin and their followers to be
outside' the covenanted mercies of God would have been studying
patristic and catholic theology in those early formative years. What
these works were is hard to establish from his early writings where
he makes no reference to them. It is nevertheless apparent from
some of his later works of controversy that, at an earlier stage, he
had made himself familiar with the Fathers and with many Roman
Catholic writers.[45]

Looking in Darby's publications for the sources of his ideas is, on
the whole, a fruitless task. In the vast bulk of his writing, Darby
tended only to quote from the works of other writers when he was
disagreeing with them in controversy or when he was giving a source
of information rather than an opinion.[46] In his very earliest works
the names of a few older churchmen like Archbishop John Tillotson

---

[44] The letter is quoted more fully in Stunt, *From Awakening to Secession*
(2000), 207-8. I dissent from Weremchuk's claim that Newman's first
encounter with Darby was after Darby's accident. His account was written
more than twenty years later. The reference to Darby 'on crutches in a
drawing-room' need not have been his first impression. If Darby was already
incapacitated on Newman's arrival, when would the latter have seen the
devoted austerities that so impressed his parishioners?

[45] See Stunt, 'John Nelson Darby: The Scholarly Enigma' (2003), 71-72.

[46] For example, in his autobiographical marginal notes, Darby says 'Scott's
essays gave a strong determination to my thought at one time'; Weremchuk,
*John Nelson Darby* (1995), 204. I have not observed a single quotation from
Scott in Darby's writing.

(1630-94),[47] Bishop Humphrey Prideaux (1648-1724) and William Lowth the elder (1660-1732) are occasionally cited with approval but these are exceptions.[48] There is no doubt however that at some stage in 1827 or 1828 he read Irving's translation of *La Venida del Mesias en gloria y magestad,* the celebrated work of the Jesuit, Manuel Lacunza.[49]

The extraordinary influence of this work on other writers was meticulously outlined by Alfred-Felix Vaucher in 1941, and his wry comment that 'if the Plymouth Brethren had been in the habit of citing their sources, Lacunza's name would have frequently recurred in their writings' is perhaps justified.[50] However in Darby's first published work on prophecy he specifically referred to Irving's translation and went so far as to say that, although he disagreed with the translator on many things, he considered some of Irving's work as 'profitable and timely'.[51] In the same article he mentions Thomas Erskine's *Freedom of the Gospel* observing that he found the work 'in many respects useful and that *extensively'.[52]* These positive references are striking because by 1829 both Irving and Erskine were beginning to be regarded as *enfants terribles* and their doctrinal

---

[47] Referred to by Darby as Dean Tillotson as he was Dean of St. Paul's at the time of his protest against Erastianism; Darby, *Collected Writings* (n.d.), i. 11.

[48] We must distinguish between the older William Lowth (1660-1732) and his son Robert Lowth, Bishop of London (1710-87). William's *Commentary on the Prophets* led Darby in 1829 to call him 'the calm and judicious Lowth'; Darby, *Collected Writings* (n.d.), ii. 26. This Lowth was later cited by Darby against B. W. Newton (c. 1848) when arguing that 'chief prince' in Ezekiel 38 should be translated 'prince of Rash'; Darby, *Collected Writings* (n.d.), i. 295-6. In contrast he allows (1834) that Robert Lowth may have been a useful grammarian and scholar but insists that he cannot be trusted for interpretation; Darby, *Collected Writings* (n.d.), xiii. 9. Later he dismissed the Bishop's work on Isaiah as 'never to be trusted'; Darby, *Notes and Comments* (n.d.), iv. 31.

[49] J. J. Ben-Ezra [M. de Lacunza y Diaz], *The Coming of Messiah in Glory and Majesty,* trans. with a preliminary discourse by Edward Irving (1827).

[50] A.-F. Vaucher, *Une celebre oubliee: Le P. Manuel de Lacunza y Diaz (1731-1801)* (Collonges-sous-SalEve,

[51] 'Reflections upon the Prophetic Inquiry and the Views advanced in it' (1829); Darby, *Collected Writings* (n.d.), ii. 7. In one of his tiresome polemics accusing Darby of deceitfulness, MacPherson draws attention at tedious length to the similarities in Darby's language to that of Lacunza and Irving; Dave MacPherson, *The Rapture Plot* (Simpsonville, SC, 1995), 90-99. The significance of the fact that many of the phrases cited are also biblical seems to be lost on him.

[52] Darby, *Collected Writings* (n.d.), ii. 20.

credentials were being questioned by many evangelicals. It is therefore all the more remarkable that Darby, a man who so rarely cited other writers with approval, felt free to commend them. However, these are exceptions and his writings give very little indication of what he was reading or what books he may have possessed in this early period.[53]

A further point needs to be made about Darby's experience in 1827-28. Some of his later accounts of it are immediately followed with other realizations, which came to him soon after and, which indeed were logical consequences arising from his experience. We may nevertheless identify three original elements that Darby stresses as the essence of his experience of deliverance.[54] First was the total faith that he was now able to place in the authority of the Scriptures. A second emphasis was the assurance that he (together with all Christians as opposed to Christendom) was risen and spiritually united with Christ in heaven. The third element, which he consistently related to his reading of Isaiah 32, was the converse of the second. As the Christian hope was a heavenly one, the earthly promises of the prophets must relate to the restoration of the Jews. Darby recognised in retrospect, 'I was not able to put these things in their respective places or arrange them in order',[55] and in the following account, his reference to forty years suggests that he may at this stage have been thinking in terms of some intervening events before Christ's return:

---

[53] According to Frank Newman, Darby explained that his reading of 2 Timothy 4:13 'saved me from selling my little library'; Newman, *Phases of Faith* (1860), 19. That library should not be confused with the substantial collection of his later years, the more important items of which were sold by auction after his death; *Catalogue of the Library of the Late J.N. Darby, Esq.* (1889). That the catalogue gives little indication of Darby's earlier reading is apparent for several reasons. It is not a comprehensive list – unnamed books are included in some lots. It includes nothing by Scott, Tillotson or Prideaux (with whose works we know Darby was familiar) and scarcely one of the volumes of which Darby published reviews or refutations. For example there are no works by Edward Irving, S. R. Maitland or William Burgh, with all of whom he entered into published controversy; Darby, *Collected Writings* (n.d.), ii. 6-10, 32-42, xxxiii. 1-12. Most of the books listed were published after 1830 or before 1800.

[54] All three elements are to be found in the following accounts – the year of writing is shown in brackets: [Darby], *Letters of J.N.D* (n.d.), [185?] iii. 298-9; [Darby], *Letters of J.N.D* (n.d.), [1863] i. 344; Darby, *Collected Writings* (n.d.), [c. 1865] i. 38, 36; [Darby], *Letters of J.N.D* (n.d.), [1878] ii. 433.

[55] [Darby], *Letters of J.N.D* (n.d.), [185?] iii. 299.

Isaiah xxxii. it was that taught me about the new dispensation. I saw there would be a David reign, and did not know whether the church might not be removed before forty years' time. At that time I was ill with my knee. It gave me peace to see what the church was. I saw that I, poor, wretched, and sinful J.N.D., knowing too much yet not enough about myself, was left behind, and let go, but I was united to Christ in heaven.[56]

In fact for some years after his experience of deliverance there was something decidedly ambivalent about some of the positions adopted by Darby. Eschatologically, his two pamphlets in 1829 and 1830 indicate that he was sympathetic but by no means irretrievably committed to a futurist premillennialism.[57] Ecclesiastically he was by no means fully detached from the establishment. Mter his time of convalescence he does not appear to have returned to Calary but for a year or two worked in a variety of parishes as a freelance missioner. A threatening letter from 'Captain Rock' (a variant on the more notorious 'Captain Moonlight') telling Darby to keep his 'Bible business' out of Corosin (2 February 1829) suggests that he was working with the somewhat maverick Protestant landlord Edward Synge in County Clare.[58] It would have been during this time that he

---

[56] *Bible Treasury* xii. 353. I am grateful to Mr Andrew Poots for this reference, which is not in the *Collected Writings*. Darby's realisation in 1827-28 that earthly Jewish promises should not be appropriated by the Christian church is circumstantially corroborated in Frank Newman's letter to B. W. Newton (17 April 1828), written after Darby's deliverance experience, where he makes a similar distinction between the promises made to Israel and those made to the Church: 'But where it is merely a prediction under the form of a promise...we are not justified in saying that "Israel" means anything other than the nation of the [sic] Israel'; transcribed in Wyatt MS ii. 120 and recopied in Fry MS 63 (JRULM, CBA 7049).

[57] Darby, *Collected Writings* (n.d.), ii. 1-42. In these pamphlets he asks almost as many questions as he answers and some important prophetic topics are almost ignored. For example there is scarcely a single reference to Antichrist. In contrast his critique, in the *Christian Herald,* of William Burgh's *Lectures on the Second Advent* and *The Apocalypse Unfulfilled* (1832) is rather less tentative. He basically approves of Burgh's interpretation with regard to the Jewish prophecies but takes issue with his analysis of Revelation and the nature of the Gentile apostasy. He decidedly rejects Burgh's idea of a future personal antichrist, insisting that 'The time and principles of Antichrist I believe to be daily developing themselves'; Darby, *Collected Writings* (n.d.), xxxiii. 2.

[58] Captain Rock to J. N. Darby, 2 Feb 1829 (JRULM, CBA 5540 [188]); Flan Enright, 'Edward Synge, The Dysert Proselytiser', *The Other Clare* vi (1982), 8. Edward's father, George Synge (1757-1837), was an uncle of John Synge

worked in Cloughjordan with Frederick Trench to whom we shall refer shortly. At some point between 1830 and 1834 Darby was invited to be an assistant chaplain at the Magdalen Asylum in Leeson Street, Dublin. The suggestion was presumably made by the principal chaplain, Joseph Henderson Singer, who as a leading evangelical Fellow of Trinity College would have been anxious to keep Darby from secession and therefore may have hoped to provide him with a position where there would be few restraints on him. [59] In fact, Darby's decision to leave Ireland in 1830 may have been prompted by the uncertainty of his position. [60]

Much has been written of the impact of his visit to Oxford in 1830, but Darby also recalled that earlier in the year he had visited Cambridge where he had been given a less sympathetic hearing. [61] His experience there has been ignored by most Brethren historians but it effectively indicates how ill at ease Darby was beginning to find himself with some aspects of traditional evangelicalism. Frederick FitzWilliam Trench, a friend in whose parish of Cloughjordan Darby had assisted with mission work, had been converted as a student at Peterhouse, Cambridge, sometime between 1818 and 1822. [62] In 1830 Trench took Darby to meet Charles

---

of Glanmore Castle. Darby's association with Synge is confirmed in Newton's recollections; Fry MS 239 (JRULM, CBA 704).

[59] Bellett, whose chronology is unreliable, says that in 1834 Darby decided against the appointment and began to worship regularly with the Brethren in Aungier Street. From internal evidence in Bellett's account, 1832 is a more probable date; see J. G. B[ellett] *et al., Interesting Reminiscences of the Early History of "Brethren"* (n.d.), 8. The Diocesan Records confirm that there was a hiatus in the assistant chaplaincy between 1828 and 1836; see J.B. Leslie and W. J. R. Wallace (eds), *Clergy of Dublin and Glendalough: Biographical Succession Lists* (Belfast, 2001), 135. For Darby's association with Singer in 1831, see Stunt, *From Awakening to Secession* (2000), 258 n.65.

[6] For his ecclesiastical undecidedness in London and Oxford (1830-31), Plymouth (1830-31) and Limerick (1832), see Stunt, *From Awakening to Secession* (2000), 253, 258, 291-2, 276-7. Hitherto it has been assumed that Darby's first visit to Plymouth was in December 1830. However as early as 20 October 1830 the *Falmouth Packet and Cornish Herald* reported that 'the Rev. J. N. Darby' had recently addressed the annual meeting of the Plymouth auxiliary of the London Society for Promoting Christianity among the Jews.

[61] [Darby], *Letters of J.N.D* (n.d.), iii. 301, to Tholuck, 1855.

[62] Frederick FitzWilliam Trench (1799-1869), the perpetual curate of Cloughjordan (1823-54), was a cousin of Richard Chenevix Trench, later Archbishop of Dublin. He must not be confused with another cousin, Frederick FitzJohn Trench, who was the father of John Alfred Trench (a

Simeon, who had been the instrument of his conversion. We must bear in mind that Darby wrote his account of the episode more than thirty years after the event, in the context of an ongoing controversy with Trench. Whatever the exact details of the interview may have been, it is clear that the enthusiastic Darby felt that he had been rebuffed by the doyen of the evangelical movement whose eschatology was decidedly postmillennialist.[63] It is only conjecture, but the experience may have contributed- perhaps more than he realised- to the hardening of Darby's premillennialism.

There are two accounts of Darby's activities in 1830, which indicate that even before he went to Cambridge and Oxford, the undecided Irish separatist had visited Paris. One of these was published in the *Schaff-Herzog Encyclopedia* and was written by Edward Elihu Whitfield, who as an Oxford undergraduate had corresponded with Darby but who later seems to have moved to a less exclusive Brethren position.[64] The other account is the brief statement, by a more recent Brethren writer, Theodore William Carron, that Darby 'visited the Continent for the first time in 1830 when he supported the labours of F. P. Monod in France'.[65] We should note that two of Darby's former neighbours in Ireland were also visiting Paris in the spring of 1830. Robert Daly, with whom Darby was beginning to be ecclesiastically estranged, was there from 21 March to 4 April, while among the letters of Lady Powerscourt (later associated with the Plymouth Brethren), one dated 6 April and two others from May and June were written in Paris.[66] We cannot

---

personal friend of Darby) and of George Frederick Trench who is included in H. Pickering (ed.), *Chief Men among the Brethren* (1931), 133. For details of Fitzwilliam Trench see J. A. Venn (ed.), *Alumni Cantabrigienses* (Cambridge, 1922-54), ii. 6. 226; J. B. Leslie (ed.) 'Biographical Succession Lists', Representative Church Body Library, Dublin; and the sympathetic reminiscences in R. S. Brooke, *Recollections of the Irish Church* (1877), 46-9.
[63] Darby, *Collected Writings* (n.d.), x. [1863] 133-4.
[64] In S. M. Jackson *et al.* (eds), The *New Schaff-Herzog Encyclopedia of Religious Knowledge* (New York, 1908-12), iii. 357, Whitfield is described as a 'Retired Public Schoolmaster, London'. He was a graduate of Oriel College, Oxford; C. L. Shadwell (ed.), *Registrum Orielense* (1902), ii. 558. Darby's letter of 1870 was written to Whitfield; [Darby], *Letters of J.N.D* (n.d.), iii. 410-12. Still later Whitfield contributed an article on Darby to the Open Brethren publication H. Pickering (ed.), *Chief Men among the Brethren* (1931), 11-15.
[65] T. W. Carron, The *Christian Testimony Through the Ages* (Worthing, 1956) 346. I am indebted to Mr Andrew Poots of Belfast for this reference.
[66] Mrs H. Madden, *Memoir of the late Right Rev. Robert Daly, Lord Bishop of Cashel* (1875), 168-75; R. Daly (ed.), *Letters and Papers of the late Theodosia*

say whether these friends were in touch with Darby, but it is quite possible.

For Daly's visit to Paris, his journal is informative. Besides deploring the apparent godlessness of the Parisians, he visits the Louvre and the second-hand bookshops. He also attends services in the English Church and the Oratoire as well as a Protestant mission house in the Faubourg de Mt. Parnasse, meeting a variety of English residents and French-speaking Protestants like Fran<;ois Olivier ('Mr Oliviet') and Frederic Monod ('Mr M.').[67]

In addition to these fairly predictable responses to the life of the French capital Daly recorded what he was told about the 'descendants of the Jansenists' in Paris 'who knew the truth, and, though they held many Roman Catholic errors, rejoiced in hearing the doctrines of grace'. He also learnt of another group of former Roman Catholics (with Jansenist origins), *'La Petite Eglise'*, who, in protest against the desecration of the Church by the French revolutionaries and the concordat signed between the Pope and Napoleon, had broken away from the Pope and from the French clergy.[68] It is surely not unreasonable to suppose that if these developments interested a long-standing Protestant like Daly, they would have been of even greater interest to Darby whose formative period had been dominated by Catholic thinking. The ideals of Jansenism could only arouse his sympathetic approval and for reasons, which will shortly become apparent, we must glance briefly at some aspects of the movement.

The Jansenists had been meticulously devout in their practices and had shunned the worldliness of the Roman Catholic Church.[69] With the suppression of the Jesuits in 1773 they seemed to have lost their *raison d'etre* but the rampant atheism of the French Revolution gave them a late burst of energy. They were appalled at the desecration of the churches and the Erastianism of the new *regime* as much as by the concessions made by the Church in the face of such interference. Witnessing at close quarters the cataclysmic

---

A. *Viscountess Powerscourt,* 5th ed. (1845), 84, 108, 111. Lady Powerscourt may well have been the unnamed lady to whom Daly spoke disapprovingly on 23 March (169) 'about her conduct at Brussels' where Lady Powerscourt had been earlier in the month (107).

[67] For further details see Stunt, *From Awakening to Secession* (2000), 163.

[68] Madden, *Memoir of...Robert Daly* (1875), 172, 173-4.

[69] For Jansenism in the eighteenth century, see the magisterial work by J. McManners, *Church and Society in 18th Century France* (Oxford, 1998), ii. chapters 39 and 48. For later Jansenist developments and the origins of *La Petite Eglise* in Lyon, see J.-P. Chantin, *Les Amis de l'CEuvre de la Verite: Jansenisme, miracles et fin du monde au XIXe siecle* (Lyon, 1998).

events of the 1790s, they believed, perhaps with more cause than anyone, that they were living in the last times. They had long been pre-occupied with the question of the return of the Jews to Palestine and more than ever they turned to the study of prophecy.[70]

One of the foremost among them was the Dominican Bernard Lambert (1738-1813), who had formerly been the *protege* of Malvin de Montazet, the Jansenist-sympathising Archbishop of Lyon. From 1776 Lambert, an energetic writer and controversialist, was a member of the Dominican community in the Rue du Bac, in Paris.[71] He vigorously protested on behalf of the Dominicans (ominously known as Jacobins in France until the revolutionary party took over their name as well as their convent), fearlessly denounced the 'blasphemies and calumnies of the church's enemies' and rebuked the Church for its readiness to compromise. In 1793 he published a pamphlet explaining that the apostasy of the church suggested that the return of the Jews was imminent and increasingly from that point he appears to have been pre-occupied with the implications of living in the last times.[72] It is possible that he knew of Lacunza's work, which was circulating in MS after 1790, but some time before *La Venida del Mesias en gloria y magestad* was in print Lambert published his own *Expositions des predictions et des promesses faites à l'Eglise pour les derniers temps de la gentilité* in 1806.[73]

---

[70] For the Jansenist fascination with the return of the Jews, see the earlier chapters of D. Vidal, *La Morte-Raison: Isaac la juive, convulsionnaire janseniste de Lyon 1791-1841* (Grenoble, 1994).

[71] For Lambert see the articles by M. J. Picot in M. Michaud (ed.), *Biographie Universelle: Ancienne et Moderne* (Paris, 1843), xxiii. 51-2; and by M. D. Chenu in A. Vacant *et al.* (eds), *Dictionnaire de Theologie catholique* (Paris, 1925), viii. 2470. More precise details are in B. Plongeron, *Les Reguliers de Paris devant le serment constitutionnel: Sens et consequences d'une option 1789-1801* (Paris, 1964), 140-46, 360-1. For a brief taste of Lambert's low view of the Enlightenment see the quotations in J. E. Bradley and D. K. Van Kley (eds), *Religion and Politics in Enlightenment Europe* (Notre Dame, IN, 2001), 3. Lambert's outlook must be differentiated from that of the Jansenist reformers discussed by W. R. Ward in 'Late Jansenism and the Habsburgs', *idem,* 154-86.

[72] *Avertissement aux fideles, sur les signes qui annoncent que tout se dispose pour le retour d'Israel et l'execution des menaces faites aux gentils apostats* (Paris, 1793). My attention has been kindly drawn by Mr Will Irvine to the interest shown in the Parisian Jansenists by the Irish revolutionary millenarian Thomas Russell in 1802; see J. Quinn, *Soul on Fire: A Life of Thomas Russell 1767-1803* (Dublin, 2002), 230.

[73] Lambert's book was published in two volumes in Paris (1806). I have only belatedly discovered that there is a copy in the Bibliotheque Nationale de France, Paris, but that it is not listed under 'Lambert, Bernard' because the

A younger Jansenist writer, the Parisian lawyer and judge Pierre-Jean Agier (1748-1823) also became fascinated by eschatological studies in the last decade of his life, publishing an analysis of Lacunza's *Venida* in 1818[74] as well as his own work on *Les propheties concernant Jesus-Christ et lEglise* (1819) and a commentary on *Revelation* (1823). Agier's version of Lacunza's work was used by Lewis Way who was living in Paris in the 1820s and it was probably he who introduced the work to Irving in 1825.[75] The great authority on Lacunza, Alfred-Felix Vaucher, closely studied Lambert's *Expositions des predictions* as well as his supplementary rebuttal of his critics, and carefully identified the similarities and the differences between the work of Lacunza and Lambert. Both interpretations of the prophetic scriptures are literalist and premillennial but, in one important respect at least, Lambert's must be distinguished from that of Lacunza. While the Jesuit sees Christ's return as one simple event ('tout court') at the beginning of the millennium, Lambert expects the event to be in two stages and forsees an intermediate coming ('un avenement intermediaire') when Christ first gathers his saints.[76] On the other hand Vaucher argues that although Agier also wrote of an intermediate coming in his earlier commentary on the *Psalms* (1809), he appears to have abandoned the idea after studying Lacunza's work.[77]

The justification for what may appear to be an unwarranted digression into Jansenist eschatology is quite simple. Bearing in

---

author is given as 'Le P[ere] Lambert'. I have therefore been constrained to use the summary of Lambert's prophetic views in E. B. Elliott, *Horae Apocalypticae or a Commentary on the Apocalypse, Critical and Historical,* 4th edition (1851), 507-513 (5th edition, 530-36), and in Vaucher, *Une celebrite oubliee* (1941), 87 *et passim.*

[74] [P-J. Agier], *Vues sur le second avenement de J.-C., ou Analyse de l'ouvrage de Lacunza sur cette importante matiere* (Paris, 1818).

[75] Vaucher, *Une celebrite oubliee* (1941), 37, 139 n. 66. For Agier see the article by Fallot in Michaud (ed.), *Biographie Universelle* (1843), i. 222-224; other references in Vaucher, *Une celebrite oubliee* (1941), 145 n. 189.

[76] Vaucher, *Une celebrite oubliee* (1941), 87, 88, 177 n. 460. The same distinction is made by Elliott: Lacunza's account of Christ's premillennial advent is 'not a second intermediate advent, before the third and last to final judgment, so as Lambert'; Elliott, *Horae Apocalypticae,* 4th edition (1851), iv. 515 n. 1.

[77] Vaucher, *Une celebrite oubliee* (1941), 178 n. 466. In the liberal Roman Catholic *Chronique Religieuse* ii (1819), 184ff, the reviewer of Abbe Giudici's *Lettres Italiennes sur l'avenement intermediaire et le regne de Jesus-Christ* (Lugano, 1816-17) noted that Giudici was following Lambert when he envisaged three comings as opposed to Lacunza who expected only two (188).

mind Darby's earlier Catholic orientation, we may be pretty sure that when he was in Paris (if not before) he became acquainted with the works of Lambert and Agier. It is doubtful whether he had yet made up his mind about a two stage second coming (as found in his later distinction between Christ's napoucrta and the later l:mcpcivEta), but almost certainly he was familiar with the idea before he went to Cambridge and Oxford and therefore before he went to Row in Scotland later in 1830.

Much has been made, in the contemporary eschatological controversy, of Darby's visit to Row and his having heard a prophecy ofMargaret Macdonald.[78] It is true that one of her rather incoherent prophecies was circulating in manuscript in the early 1830s and was later published by her widower Robert Norton in 1840.[79] Irving was impressed by the urgency (rather than the teaching) of the prophecy and it may have played a part in the development of the distinctive Irvingite premillennialism that characterised the writings of the *Morning Watch*. There is however no reason to claim that this was the source of Darby's idea of the pretribulation rapture, as he had already encountered the idea in Lambert's work. The textual scholar Samuel Prideaux Tregelles recalled in 1857 that 'Lambert and Agier were the writers Mr. J. N. Darby studied earnestly before he left the Church of England. I remember his speaking much about them in 1835.'[80] For Darby's debt to Lambert there is a further piece of circumstantial evidence which is at least partially corroborative. The French Protestant pastor of Cambrai, Achille Maulvault, wrote an article on Lambert for the *Encyclopedie des Sciences Religieuses* in the late 1870s in which he refers to the Dominican's *Exposition des predictions*. The article concludes with a curiously unexpected observation: 'Ce livre, [se. *£'exposition]* chose etrange, tres en honneur chez les chretiens darbystes, parait avoir ete la source, avec

---

[78] For Darby's own account of his visit to Row and his reasons for not being impressed, see Darby, *Collected Writings* (n.d.), vi. 284-85.

[79] See M. Oliphant, The *Life of Edward !ruing*, 2nd edition (1862), ii. 139; R. Norton, *Memoirs of James and George Macdonald of Port Glasgow* (1840).

[80] S. P. Tregelles to B. W. Newton, 29 January 1857, JRULM, CBA 7181 (7). Tregelles was first associated with the Brethren at Plymouth in 1835. Darby's earlier mention of Lambert and Agier may have prompted Tregelles in September 1850 to visit the Jansenist Archbishop of Utrecht who lent him copies of Lambert's and Agier's works. See S. P. Tregelles, The *Jansenists: Their Rise, Persecution by the Jesuits, and Existing Remnant: A Chapter in Church History* (1851), 96-97. Tregelles's Dutch visit is ignored by Ruth Clark, *Strangers and Sojourners at Port Royal: Being an account of the connections between the British Isles and the Jansenists of France and Holland* (Cambridge, 1932).

le livre de Lacunza, ou M. Darby et les theologiens de son ecole semblent avoir puise leurs doctrines particulie'\res.'[81]

As Lambert's work was never translated into English, it was perhaps only in France that Darby found it appropriate to recommend his work to his listeners. This in turn may have contributed, in the 1830s and 1840s, to an eschatological perspective among Darby's French followers that was rather different from that of the English speaking brethren. There was a curiously 'millenarian' episode at the end of 1844 when some of the Brethren, near Tence on the border of the Haute-Loire and the Ardeche, were persuaded by the Brethren evangelist Dentan and his wife that Christ would return on the last day of the year. This and the ensuing excesses were clearly a source of concern to Darby who wrote to warn some French sisters that 'we have no need of a dream with respect to matters clearly revealed by God.'[82] I am unaware of any comparable incident among English-speaking Brethren.

Before summarizing our conclusions we have to bear in mind that

---

[81] 'This book [se. *L'expositionL* strange to relate, is held in great honour among the Darbyite Christians. It appears to have been the source, together with Lacunza's book, from which Monsieur Darby and the theologians of his school seem to have drawn their distinctive teachings.' See the article on Lambert by A. Maulvault in F. Lichtenberger (ed.), *Encyclopedie des Sciences Religieuses* (Paris 1880), vii. 693. That Lambert was a source for the idea of 'the secret rapture of the saints' was recalled in Thomas Croskery's hostile account of the Brethren. The fact that he refers to Pere Lambert as 'Pierre [sic] Lambert, a Jesuit [sic] Father' suggests an oral tradition rather than his being familiar with Lambert's writings; T. Croskery *Plymouth Brethrenism: A Refutation of its Principles and Doctrines* (London, Belfast, 1879), viii. Croskery, a Presbyterian minister from Londonderry (1830-86), was probably the author of the article 'Plymouth Brethrenism' in the *British Quarterly Review* (Oct 1873), 409, where the same inaccurate attribution is made. His earlier *Catechism on the Doctrines of the Plymouth Brethren* had reached its 6th edition in 1868; on that basis he had been invited to contribute an article on 'The Plymouth Brethren' for the *Princeton Quarterly* i (1872), 48. It is perhaps worth noting that although Neatby made no mention of Lambert, the earliest historian of the Brethren drew parallels with Jansenism on at least three occasions; W. B. Neatby, *A History of the Plymouth Brethren,* 2nd edition (London, 1902), 173, 216, 267.

[82] [Darby], *Letters of J.N.D* (n.d.), i. 76. For the background to these events see three important sources for religious developments in the region all written or edited by Christian Maillebouis, *La dissidence religieuse à Saint-Voy, canton de Tence- "Les Momiers" 1820-1845* (Le Chambon sur Lignon, 1990); *Vie et pensees d'un Darbyste: A. Dentan, 1805-1873* (Le Chambon sur Lignon, 1991); *La Chronique "Deschomets" de Mazelgirard, pres de Tence, en Velay* (Le Chambon sur Lignon, 1992).

we are navigating between a Scylla and Charybdis of controversy, with a *prima facie* obligation to reject the agenda of both sides. The principal aim of R. A Huebner and some other dispensationalist admirers of Darby seems to be to show that Darby's later eschatology and ecclesiology were already established in his mind and can be found in his earliest writings in the late 1820s.[83] At the other end of the polemical spectrum, Dave MacPherson, with the vigorous approval of various opponents of dispensationalism (and of the Scofield Bible), is intent upon discrediting Darby and his hermeneutic. With this object, he proclaims that Darby was a plagiarist who borrowed without acknowledgement from Lacunza, Irving and more particularly Margaret Macdonald (who in turn is accused of occultism).[84] Both positions effectively demonstrate the danger of over-simplification and the temptation to forget that historical truth is 'never pure and rarely simple'.

In conclusion therefore we must emphasize that Darby was a very complex person whose understanding of scripture and theology was continually evolving. Indeed his reluctance to cite his authorities may have arisen from an awareness that his mind was far from made up. It is worth noting that in 1844 he made no attempt to hide the fact that he had conversed on the subject of ministries and gifts with Irving 'at least fourteen years ago' though he insisted that this was 'before the system, to which he [Irving] gave his name, was manifested'.[85] However, years before he met Irving Darby was drawn to eschatological enquiry. Pretribulationist eschatology was undoubtedly a significant element in Irvingite teaching, but this does not necessarily mean that Darby adopted it from them.[86] There was an eclecticism in his early writings that fastened with approval on some points while rejecting others with some virulence. On the other

[83] See R. A. Huebner, *Precious Truths Revived and Defended through J.N. Darby* (Morganville, NJ, 1991), i. v, where he claims that although Darby's 'recovery of truth...in reality was accomplished by 1835, its foundation was understood in Dec. 1826-Jan. 1827'.

[84] The fullest exposition of this line is Dave MacPherson, *The Rapture Plot* (Simpsonville, SC, 1995). I have commented on some of the implications of this book in 'The Tribulation of Controversy: A Review Article', *BAHNR* 2:2 (2003), 91-98.

[85] 'On the presence and action of the Holy Ghost in the Church'; Darby, *Collected Writings* (n.d.), iii. 264. I am most grateful to Dr Tim Grass for helping me find this reference.

[86] For an excellent discussion of Irvingite pretribulationism and also some very apposite examples of Darby's ongoing undecidedness; see M. Patterson and A. Walker, '"Our Unspeakable Comfort": Irving, Albury and the Origins ofthe PretribulationRapture', *FH*31 (1999), 66-81.

hand, his earlier years of high-church observance following the rejection of his family's rationalist optimism at his conversion and prior to his experience of deliverance in 1827-28 contributed significantly to his spiritual development. It is clearly from these years that we should date his strong opposition to Erastianism and his growing premillennial expectations. The fact that premillennialism was beginning to be more acceptable in evangelical circles may have made it easier for these expectations to be carried over into his own variety of evangelicalism after 1827.

These continuing emphases from the earlier period may help us to appreciate his readiness to learn from Lacunza, and his enthusiasm for the work of Lambert and Agier. By the same token, although the experience of 1827-8 was liberating for his soul and strengthened his faith in Scripture, there evidently remained uncertainties in both his ecclesiology and eschatology for some years. We have not dealt with such questions as Darby's belief in 'the ruin of the church' and his systematic dispensationalist hermeneutic as he did not fully formulate them until after 1834 when he finally broke with the establishment. The ambiguities of his personal position between 1827 and 1833 must have contributed to his reluctance for quite a time finally to commit himself on eschatological and related issues.

CHAPTER 4

# 'The Ecstasy of Perfected Love':
# The Eschatological Mysticism of J. N. Darby

Gary L. Nebeker

John Nelson Darby (1800-1882) is often regarded as the originator of
the theological system known as dispensationalism. From the best
historical evidence, he also appears to be the principal architect of
dispensationalism's doctrine of the pretribulational rapture. While
these may be his more enduring legacies, a feature often overlooked
in Darby's thought is his synthesis of pre-existing bridal mysticism
with an emerging futurist premillennial theology. This synthesis
would become a distinguishing trait of the piety of British and
American evangelicalism in the nineteenth and early twentieth
centuries. I have termed this synthesis 'eschatological mysticism'.
Darby's eschatological mysticism can be described as a desire for the
rapture that holds forth perfected love between the believer and
Jesus as the blissful zenith of hope. This expectation is a spiritual
yearning couched in the endearing language of nuptial mysticism. It
is the believer's 'sighing' for a perfect love relationship with Christ in
heaven. The rapture serves as the entryway into the consummation
of love between Christ and His Church in the heavenlies. By
referring to this synthesis as 'eschatological mysticism', it is crucial
to clarify that Darby disavowed 'mysticism' as a mediated supra-
rational personal consciousness of God that one experiences in the
Christian life. Still, his hope of 'heavenly glory' was mystical in an
anticipatory sense when he spoke of the believer's union with Christ
in heaven at a point yet future. Darby's ample use of bridal imagery
places him in a long tradition of nuptial mystics, including Origen,
Gregory of Nyssa, Pseudo-Dionysius the Aeropagite, Bernard of
Clairvaux, Johannes Tauler, Thomas à Kempis, Richard Rolle,
Julian of Norwich, and Waiter Hilton. Therefore, the rubric 'eschatological mysticism' is apropos when describing Darby's hope of

heaven. This essay will examine the bridal flourishes in Darby's writings. The antecedents of Darby's nuptial mysticism will be explored, as will the theological antecedents of heavenly glory as a state of perfected love.

Some come away with the impression that Darby's pretribulational rapture theory was nothing more than an acute form of escapism. However, without appropriate elucidation, this assessment is incomplete. Was Darby's rapture hope an escape? Yes, it was a flight from the turmoil of the world and from the ravages of sin. But more than simply these, it was a deliverance into the embrace of Christ's satisfying love. Once we realize that the impetus underlying Darby's hope was his vision of a perfected relationship with Christ in heaven, then we are in a better position to understand the importance of the rapture in his framework of thinking. The rapture, blessed as that event would be, was but a corridor to the greater bliss of an infinity of *agape.* Darby believed that mystical union with Christ in glory was the culmination of eschatological expectancy.

> The proper hope of the saint is not Christ's appearing – it is not even glory as displayed to the world, not to be at the right hand or the left in the kingdom, glorious and undeserved as it may be, – but to be with Christ Himself. That is not the appearing. It is another kind of hope, a hope of another nature altogether. It is being with Himself for ever, and in the Father's house.[1]

While Darby would regard the pretribulational rapture of the Church as an important impetus of hope, the essence of hope was not the rapture *per se,* but what the rapture would effect, namely, a lasting relationship of joyful and intimate communion with Christ in heaven. For this reason, Darby could write, 'The hope of the Church is not alone salvation, that is, to escape the wrath of God, but to have the glory of the Son Himself.'[2] Hope was the anticipation of the ecstasy of heavenly glory, the indescribable eternal joy that consisted of being glorified, the expectancy of being loved by Jesus and by God the Father forever.

## A Caveat Concerning Psychobiography

Political, ecclesiastical, and theological factors notwithstanding, personal temperament, emotional conflicts, and psychopathologies

---

[1] John Nelson Darby, *The Collected Writings of J. N. Darby,* ed. William Kelly (Sunbury, PA, 1971), x. 260.
[2] Darby, *Collected Writings* (1971), ii. 283.

may also serve as the impulses behind one's eschatological expectations. Religionists of different persuasions have conceded that hope, as an inherent and universal yearning of mortals, is awakened whenever the disparities, incertitudes, and tumult of life confront the soul. This applies to our consideration of the mystical hope of John Nelson Darby. Some observers of Darby have noted that his life reflected a certain psychological complexity.[3] One might suspect that the traumas of life and other psychological factors lent expression to the otherworldliness of his hope. Unfortunately, the available evidence of Darby's childhood amounts to a few sentences in the biographies. Likewise, available archival materials do not yield enough information to gain a complete picture of Darby's earliest days.

As fascinating as the idea of a 'psychobiography' of Darby would be, and as fitting as the connection is between religious hope and psychology,[4] LaCapra prudently cautions, 'There is always the possibility that a psychobiography will tell us more about its author than about the author being studied.'[5] We are thus wont to project our contemporary obsessions, anxieties, and insecurities into our interpretations of history.[6] Coad arrives at the nub of the matter: 'The problem, of course, is to get sufficiently close to the ambience and influences of his [Darby's] early childhood to be able to draw any valid speculations — and even then, speculations are what they

---

[3] Upon Darby's passing, Neatby remarked, 'Not often have men been called to mark the passing of a stranger or more complex personality'; William Blair Neatby, *A History of the Brethren Movement,* second ed. (London, 1902), 308. Ernest Sandeen described Darby as, 'a man with magnetic, electric personal qualities combined with a tyrant's will to lead and intolerance of criticism. Perhaps he should be described as a petty tyrant, for he was most tyrannical of petty things'; Ernest Sandeen, *The Roots of Fundamentalism: British and American Millenarianism, 1800-1930* (Chicago, 1970), 31. Krapohl offers this reflection, 'History must judge whether Darby's good intentions have been drowned by a plethora of questionable acts'; Robert Henry Krapohl, 'A Search for Purity: The Controversial Life of John Nelson Darby' (unpublished Ph.D. thesis, Baylor University, 1988), 458.
[4] On the relationship between psychology and religious hope, see W. W. Meissner, 'Notes on the Psychology of Hope', *JRHealth* 12 (1973), 7-29.
[5] Dominick LaCapra, 'Rethinking Intellectual History and Reading Texts', in Dominick LaCapra and Steven L. Kaplan (eds), *Modern European Intellectual History: Reappraisals and New Perspectives* (Ithaca, NY, 1985), 61.
[6] J. F. C. Harrison, *The Second Coming: Popular Millenarianism, 1780-1850* (New Brunswick, NJ, 1979), 220.

remain.[7] To be sure, psychology is itself subject to its own prejudices and assumptions about what it considers normal behaviour. Hence, a psycho-biographical explanation of Darby could take any number of trajectories depending upon the *gestalt* that one chooses to explore.

For these reasons, then, this essay will attempt to understand Darby's otherworldly hope principally from the primary and secondary sources. While psychological factors may well have lent expression to Darby's vision of heavenly glory, this should not be unduly pressed to the exclusion of a complex of other considerations. Regarding the efforts to unscramble the factors that gave rise to British millenarianism, Sandeen sums up the matter well:

> It has not been possible to determine which of these forces – the psychological state of the believer, the biblical prophecies of judgement and destruction, or the historical situation- was primary and which secondary, or to determine whether there were causal links between them. But the presence and mutually supportive role of all three factors both in the millenarian movement as a whole and in the individuals associated with it is clear.[8]

In short, a complicated nexus existed between the psychological, theological, and historical factors that shaped the eschatological belief systems of British and Irish prophetic advocates in the early nineteenth century. While attempts to unravel these factors may be next to impossible, what can be conceded is that these factors were present in the milieu and linked together in some intricate way.

## Bridal Mysticism in Darby's Writings

Among the many themes that appear throughout Darby's writings, hope of heavenly glory is one that receives pre-eminence. His expectation of the eternal state consisted of the believer's transformation into Christlikeness when Christ returns for his Church at the rapture, and the believer's consequent eternal enjoyment of perfected love in the heavenly domain. That this idea is a normative paradigm in his writings is evidenced by the all-pervasive references to hope of glory in his scholarly essays as well as in his devotional material, hymns, and personal correspondences.

Darby's understanding of heavenly glory was directly connected to his understanding of the believer's heavenly position in Christ. Heavenly glory comprehended both the 'now' and the 'not yet'. Of this tension, Darby wrote, 'The great result of this salvation will be

---

[7] F. Roy Coad, Letter, Shropshire, England, 5 March 1995.
[8] Sandeen, *Roots of Fundamentalism* (1970), 14.

our being with Christ in the glory by and by: but even now, by faith, we can see ourselves 'in Christ Jesus'...there.'[9] The significance of union with Christ for eschatological hope was specifically stated in Darby's tract, 'The Church- What is It?':

> The 'hope' of the Church, as such, is identified with, and founded on, the relationship in which it is placed as united to the Lord Jesus Christ in heaven. It is true she is here as a pilgrim on earth, but, at the same time, she is the bride on earth. United to her Head in heaven, seated in heaven in Him, she waits to be there. The one proper hope of the church has no more to do with the world than Christ has, who is in heaven. She will see things set right in the kingdom, but this is not her hope: her hope, as her actual association, is with the Lord Jesus Christ in heaven, where she knows Him. Where did Paul know Christ? In the heavenly glory. And Paul knew the church to be one with Christ there.[10]

As regards future glory, this would consist of the Bridegroom's transformation of the Church into moral perfection when the Bridegroom returns for His Church at the rapture.[11] This would thus effect a relationship of the most intimate nature, that is, perfected beings (the Church) apprehending Perfection (God the Father and God the Son) in an infinity of perfected love.

Darby employed Paul's metaphor of the Church as the Bride of Christ to portray the intimate communion that would exist between the believer and Christ in heavenly glory. Although he believed that the pretribulational rapture of the Church would serve as a vital impetus for Christian hope, the core of New Testament hope was the longing for eternal communion and lasting intimacy with Christ. This is seen in an important clarification made in an 1840 lecture given in Geneva: 'The hope of the Church is not alone salvation, that is, to escape the wrath of God, but to have the glory of the Son Himself.'[12] By this, Darby meant that the perfection of eternal joy consisted of being glorified, being loved by Jesus, and by God the Father.[Y] Or, as he explained, "help meet for him' (Gen. 2:18) in His glory, full of thoughts of her beloved, and enjoying His love, she will

---

[9] Darby, *Collected Writings* (1971), xii. 244; see also Darby, *Collected Writings* (1971), xii. 186-97, 239, 350; John Nelson Darby, *Synopsis of the Books of the Bible* (Oak Park, IL, 1970), i. 28; John Nelson Darby, *Letters of J. N. Darby* (Sunbury, PA, 1971), i. 40, ii. 33.

[10] Darby, *Collected Writings* (1971), xii. 381.

[11] A central passage in this connection was 1 Corinthians 15:47-48. See the essay, 'As is the Heavenly', Darby, *Collected Writings* (1971), xvi. 348-59.

[12] Darby, *Collected Writings* (1971), ii. 283.

[13] Darby, *Collected Writings* (1971), ii. 283.

be the worthy and happy instrument of His blessings; whilst, in her condition, she will be the living demonstration of their success.'[14] Hence, dwelling in the heavenlies in a divine mode of being (i.e., in a resurrected body), as blissful as that would be, was 'an inferior thing, compared to the enjoyment of Christ Himself.[15]

In countless essays and tracts where Darby described the hope of the Church, conjugal language was used to refer the Bride's longing for Christ. Darby not only reiterated the bridal metaphor of Ephesians 5:25-32, but he took the metaphor further by expanding its implications for the Church in eternity. Darby did not regard the references to the Bride of Christ in the Book of Revelation (18:23; 19:7; 21:2, 9, 17) as having a bearing on Christ's present intimate relationship with the Church. Darby insisted that the idea of Christ's present relationship and identification with the Church were uniquely Pauline.[16] Paul's depiction of Christ as the bridegroom is preparatory, whereas John's depictions in Revelation speak of the marital consummation of Christ and His Bride in heaven.[17] Darby also conflated the Pauline metaphor with his particular spiritual reading of the Song of Solomon. Darby's comments on the love dynamic that exists between the Beloved and the Shulamite corresponds to the nuptial language he used elsewhere to describe the nature of Christian hope:

> The assembly – loved, redeemed, and belonging to Him – having by the Spirit understood His perfections, having known Him in the work of His love, does not yet possess Him as she knows Him. She sighs for the day when she will see Him as He is. Meanwhile, He manifests Himself to her, awakens her affections, and seeks to possess her love, by testifying all His delight in her. She learns also that which is in herself – that slothfulness of heart which loses opportunities of communion with Him. But this teaches her to judge all that in herself which weakens the effect on her heart of the perfections of the Beloved. Thus she is morally prepared, and has capacity for the full enjoyment of communion with Him; when she shall see Him as He is, she will be like Him. It is not the effort to obtain Him; but we seek to apprehend that for which we have been apprehended by Christ. We have an object that we do not yet fully possess, which can alone satisfy all our desires-an object whose affection we need to realise in our hearts- an end which He in grace pursues, by the testimony of His perfect love towards us, thereby cultivating our love to Him, comforting us even by the sense of our weakness, and by the revelation of His own perfection, and thus

---

14 Darby, *Collected Writings* (1971), ii. 289.
15 Darby, *Collected Writings* (1971), xxxiv. 387.
16 Darby, *Letters* (1971), iii. 55-56.
17 Darby, *Letters* (1971), iii. 56.

shewing us all that in our own hearts prevents our enjoying it. He delivers us from it, in that we discover it in the presence of His love.[18]

Although Darby believed that the Song of Solomon was originally addressed and applied to the remnant of Israel, the book also contained an important spiritual application for the Church: 'Christ can give His approval to those he loves. The saint, Jew or heavenly, enjoys His love, [and] can describe His excellencies with delight.'[19] Regarding the bridal metaphor in Ephesians 5:23-32, Darby wrote, 'This passage teaches us that there is, in the union of Christ and the Church all the intimacy that exists between a husband and a wife beloved.'[2] Concerning the Bride's earthly pilgrimage, Darby maintained that 'she sighs after her country, but still more after the Bridegroom who will come to receive her to Himself, that, where He is, there she may be with Him.'[21] The hope, then, of the Bride is a yearning for intimate communion with Christ: 'United to her Head in heaven, seated in heaven in Him, she waits to be there...She will see things set right in the kingdom, but this is not her hope: her hope, as her actual association, is with the Lord Jesus Christ in heaven, where she knows him.'[22]

For Darby, then, the culmination of hope was Christocentric and 'mystical'. That is to say, hope was 'mystical' in the sense that it comprehended a yearning for ultimate spiritual communion with Christ that was to be realized through the medium of perfect love. The bridal imagery that is employed in Darby's writings might be best described as a form of 'nuptial mysticism'.[23] Turner, one of Darby's earliest biographers, dubbed him as 'the mystic engrossed in the heavenlies'.[24] Such a designation, however, is not entirely appropriate in light of Darby's own disdain of 'mysticism'. In his essay, 'On Mysticism,' Darby reviewed the biography of the Russian mystic Julie de Kriidener (1764-1824). He concluded that mysticism

---

[18] Darby, *Synopsis* (1970), ii. 272-73.

[19] Darby, *Collected Writings* (1971), xxx. 161

[20] Darby, *Collected Writings* (1971), iii. 360.

[21] Darby, *Collected Writings* (1971), iii. 382; see also xiii. 12-13.

[22] Darby, *Collected Writings* (1971), xii. 381.

[23] Bouyer describes 'nuptial mysticism' as 'the discovery of the divine *agape* coming to us, awakening in us an *eras* which exceeds and transcends altogether the *eras ouranios* of the loftiest Platonism'; Louis Bouyer, *The Christian Mystery: From Pagan Myth to Christian Mysticism*, trans. Illtyd Trethowan (Edinburgh, 1990), 241. See also, Pierre Adnes, 'Marriage mystique', in M. Viller *et al.* (eds), *Dictionnaire de spiritualite, ascetique, et mystique, doctrine et histoire* (Paris, 1937-1995), vol. 9 col. 388-408.

[24] W. G. Turner, *John Nelson Darby* (1901; rpr. London, 1951), 61.

in general was far too introspective and far too focused upon one's desire for God, rather than God Himself.[25] Darby believed that enjoyment of God first consisted of a spiritually-induced knowledge of one's union with Christ: 'What God has done, what He is, has given me peace; and I have divine leisure (because nothing is uncertain in my portion) to contemplate that which is perfect in the object of my affections, without being occupied with myself.'[26]

'Mysticism', as the term is generally used, refers to a mediated supra-rational personal consciousness of God, a consciousness that is experienced in Christian life.[27] Darby was averse to any such consciousness of God this side of heaven. At the same time, his hope of heavenly glory was mystical in an anticipatory sense when he spoke of the believer's union with God in heaven at a point yet future. In this sense it can be argued that there was a decided mystical influence in Darby's understanding of union with God.

The work of Darby that provided the most vivid depiction of the essence of heavenly glory is 'The Hope of the Christian'. This piece warrants an extended overview because of its elaborate exposition of mystical communion. When compared to other works that betray a more scholarly approach to the topic of Christian hope, 'The Hope of the Christian' is a decidedly devotional piece. Unfortunately, what is woefully true of his other writings applies to this essay as well; his grammar and style is cumbersome, and his rambling thought is not always lucid.

In written correspondence to an unnamed Christian who inquired on the nature of Christian hope, Darby responded with two principal points:

> The first important point which this result [response] brings powerfully home to the heart and conscience is, that the source of this hope, and the only means of rightly estimating it, the only sure ground on which the heart can rest in appropriating it, is that all that I hope for is the fruit of the grace of Jesus, that in which His own heart finds its delight, in giving to us, because it is that of which He knows in Himself the blessedness, and because His love is perfect toward us. His interest in us is as perfect as Himself. This is essentially characteristic of perfect love.[28]

Darby's thought here is ambiguous and he does not develop this

---

25 Darby, *Collected Writings* (1971), xxxii. 218-26.
26 Darby, *Collected Writings* (1971), xxxii. 221.
27 See, for example, Bernard McGinn, *The Foundations of Mysticism: A History of Western Christian Mysticism* (Chicago, 1991), i. xi-xx.
28 Darby, *Collected Writings* (1971), xvi. 224.

point in the body of his essay. One might hazard that the gist ofthis first point is that hope consisted of the expectancy of perfected love. His second point is provided below:

> where there is perfect love on the one hand, and capacity of enjoyment through possession of the same nature on the other, love will seek to introduce its object into the common enjoyment of that which it possesses, and finds its blessing and happiness in. This is true of a friend, a parent, and every genuine human attachment; though, of course, in these cases, imperfection is attached to the affection itself, and to its power of accomplishing its wish to make happy. But the perfection of Christ's love does not, since it is love to us, make our introduction into the enjoyment of His blessedness a thing not to be hoped for because it is too excellent, but just lays the sure ground for this hope. It is his own delight to make us happy, a part of the perfection of His nature, His own satisfaction.[29]

Though equally obscure, his thought seems to be that through love Christ seeks to bless the Church with His own perfection. In brief, the relational language of 'love' employed in these two opening points again reflects Darby's mystical piety of hope.

In this correspondence as in his many other works, the essential theme of the believer's union with Christ emerges. In this regard, Darby conceived a close connection between 'hope' and 'union with Christ': 'Our possession of the life of Christ, His being our life, so that it can be said of it, in its nature and fruits, 'which thing is true in him and in you,' is the basis of our hope, and that which makes us, in connection with His work on the cross, capable of enjoying it.'[30] Elsewhere he describes this concept as 'the glorious truth of the exalted Man'.[31] That is to say, because of Israel's rejection of Christ, Christ has become 'wholly a heavenly person'.[32] As regards His role in the present 'heavenly economy', it is 'no longer the Messiah of the Jews, but a Christ exalted, glorified'.[33] Consequently, God is presently choosing 'a people for the enjoyment of heavenly glory with Jesus Himself.[34] While the Church is now positionally seated in heavenly glory and reveals that glory only partially through hope she awaits for the culmination of her glory at the rapture.[35]

---

[29] Darby, *Collected Writings* (1971), xvi. 224.
[30] Darby, *Collected Writings* (1971), xvi. 225.
[31] Darby, *Collected Writings* (1971), x. 268.
[32] Darby, *Collected Writings* (1971), ii. 376.
[33] Darby, *Collected Writings* (1971), ii. 376.
[34] Darby, *Collected Writings* (1971), ii. 376.
[35] Darby, *Collected Writings* (1971), ii. 288-89.

In the remainder of 'The Hope of the Christian', Darby appealed to 1 John 1:1-2, 5:11-12 to demonstrate that the Holy Spirit 'connects us with Christ in life, position, and, consequently, hope'.[36] This is essentially a reiteration of 'the glorious truth of the Exalted man'. Then, after citing 1 John 3:2-3, a central text in the essay, Darby remarked:

> born of God, we have the nature (morally) and position of that true, blessed and eternal Son made man, that in His glory we may be with Him and be like Him. We are children of God, unknown by the world consequently as He was. We shall be perfectly like Him in glory, seeing Him as He now is above in heavenly glory, and hence can bear no lower standard now. Having this hope in Christ, reaching to, and founded on Himself, we seek to be as like Him now as possible in the inner man, and in our ways we purify ourselves as He is pure. What a picture of the moral position of the Christian is here, through his living connection with Christ![37]

Darby devoted considerable space to 1 John 3:2-3, and his discussion of the eternal exchange of nuptial love between Christ and the believer fairly teems with such descriptive adjectives as 'perfect', 'satisfying', 'sweet', 'happy', and 'blessed' and similar abstract nouns as 'delight', 'joy', 'enjoyment', 'perfection', and 'excellence'. In short, Darby speaks of hope as hope of relationship, specifically, perfection (the Church) enjoying and apprehending Perfection (Christ).

Darby also maintained that the nuptial love and communion between Christ and His Church in heavenly glory issue from the love of God the Father. In a rather laboured discussion that conflates ideas from 1 John 3, John 14, and John 17, Darby argued that the Father's love for Christ was demonstrated by His removal of Christ from the world. Christ's desire was that the Father's love would be in the Church and that the Church would be where He was, that is, in heaven in the Father's presence. In the meantime, the Church was to remain in the world; yet the Church will eventually be removed and placed within her heavenly domain. Darby made this summary:

> What a hope is this, and blessed be God, founded on a present blessing, only as yet in an earthen vessel, and known in present imperfection! And if we are with Christ, it is in the Father's house, where He is in the Father's love. He is not alone, He is gone to prepare a place for us; nor will He be content to send and fetch us. He will come and receive us to Himself, that where He is we may be also. This same chapter (John xiv) shews that it is our present knowledge of the Father, as

---

36 Darby, *Collected Writings* (1971), xvi. 225.
37 Darby, *Collected Writings* (1971), xvi. 226.

revealed in the Son that is the means of knowing what this joy is, and coming to the enjoyment of it. We shall be there with the Lord, ever with Him: no interruption, no decay of joy, but rather ever increasing delight, as there always is when the object is worthy of the heart, and here it is infinite: and this in the relation of the Father's affection for the Son. We are with Him in that place, with Himself, and with Him in the joy, infinite joy, which He has in the Father's love, a love resting on Him as Son, but in His excellency as such, loved before the world was, and now the accomplisher of redemption.[38]

While Darby attempted to use this argument as an inducement for hope, for the contemporary reader, his explanation gives the appearance of a strained attempt to maintain the modal distinction between heavenly and earthly peoples.

Mter completing his lengthy exposition of 1 John 3:2-3, other Scripture texts are offered to reveal the believer's heavenly identification and association with Christ and the quality of that glorious blessedness (John 17:22; Pss. 16; 17; Luke 9; Rev. 2:17; Ps. 145). From John 17:22, 'The glory which thou gavest me I have given them; that they may be one, even as we are one,' Darby surmises, 'If Christ is in us now the hope of glory, He will be in us then the display of glory.'[39] The glory of Christ is now the believer's portion in part, but the culmination of glory is the object of the believer's hope. Darby's Christological reading of Psalm 16:11 ('In thy presence is fulness of joy; at thy right hand there are pleasures for evermore') instils Christian hope by demonstrating that in God's presence in heaven, the fullness of joy abides forevermore. Psalm 17:15 ('I will behold thy face in righteousness: I shall be satisfied, when I awake, with thy likeness') is also read through a Christological lens and finds its ultimate referent in heavenly glory where the believer will see Christ face-to-face. Luke 9:28-36, the narrative of Christ's transfiguration on the Mount, is a picture of the believer's intimacy with Christ, that is, of entering heavenly glory. Finally, the promise of a 'white stone...[with] a new name written' (Rev. 2:17) speaks of the believer's 'joy and communion and personal knowledge of the Lord, which was for him alone who had it, between his soul and Christ'.[40]

Near the conclusion of this correspondence, Darby reiterated that the object of Christian hope is none other than Christ himself:

---

[38] Darby, *Collected Writings* (1971), xvi. 229.
[39] Darby, *Collected Writings* (1971), xvi. 229.
[40] Darby, *Collected Writings* (1971), xvi. 228-32.

how bright and blessed is the hope that is before us, founded on the
acceptance of Christ himselfl to see Him – be like Him – with Him in
His own relationship with the Father – to converse with Him with
divine intelligence – be before God with Him – enjoy the unmingled,
unclouded blessedness of His presence – with and like Him – yet to
receive it all from Him-to owe it all to Him.[41]

Darby closed his letter with this benediction:'May hope be as living
in the saints as the object of it is worthy of all their hearts. May they
abound in hope, by the power of the Holy Ghost.'[42]

As regards the nature of Christian hope, there are few works in
Darby's literary corpus that surpass the level of Christological
relational intimacy that comes across in this correspondence. While
the association between hope and pretribulationalism is more
arrestingly seen in other works by Darby, 'The Hope of the Christian'
describes hope in the language of nuptial love.[43] Hope of heavenly
glory is the expectancy of perfected love, in particular, that Christ
will bless the Church with His own perfection. Hope of heavenly
glory is the longing of an eternity of *agape,* an unending exchange of
joyful love between the Bridegroom and his Bride. Thus, the
ultimate object of hope is the enjoyment of the heavenly glory of
Christ himself.

## The Theological Antecedents ofDarby's Nuptial Mysticism

Although Darby is sometimes thought of as a theological iconoclast,
his hope of heavenly glory found precedent in earlier Church writers.
Whether knowingly or unknowingly, Darby utilized the pre-existing
construct of bridal mysticism. Jaroslav Pelikan has described nuptial
mysticism as 'a complex and subtle synthesis between Neo-Platonic
and biblical elements'.[44] Sparked initially by the allegorised
interpretations of the Canticles by Origen in the second century[45]
and coming to an elaborate exposition in the Middle Ages in the

---

[41] Darby, *Collected Writings* (1971), xvi. 231.

[42] Darby, *Collected Writings* (1971), xvi. 233.

[43] Darby's earliest argument for the linkage between hope and
pretribulationalism is the essay, 'Is the Coming of Christ for His Saints the
Proper Hope of the Church?'; Darby, *Collected Writings* (1971), x. 257-69.
This piece was written in the mid-1840s as a response to the historic
premillennialism of Benjamin Wills Newton.

[44] Jaroslav Pelikan, *Jesus Through the Centuries: His Place in the History of
Culture* (New Haven, 1985), 124.

[45] SeeR. P. Lawson, 'Introduction', *Origen: The Song of Songs, Commentary
and Homilies* (Westminster, MD, 1957), 6.

writings of Bernard of Clairvaux,[46] nuptial mysticism, in its varied expression, would assume an important role in the history of Christian spirituality Y With respect to the operative dynamic oflove that exists between the Trinity and the glorified Christian in heaven, an underlying assumption of nuptial mysticism is that the unity of creation must be restored, completed, and transcended in both its collective and personal union with the Incarnate God-Son. To become united in love with the Son, humankind becomes the object of the wooings of the Holy Spirit. Thus, as nuptial union comes to its ultimate expression in the eternal state in the realm of heaven, an inseparable link is seen between nuptial mysticism (intimate union with the Son) and the mysticism of essence (the return to the Father of all that emanated from Him).[48]

Mter Origen, nuptial mysticism saw progressive development in the spirituality of the Christian church. Largely through the writings of Gregory of Nyssa and Pseudo-Dionysius the Aeropagite in the fourth century, and ultimately those of Bernard of Clairvaux in the twelfth century, Johannes Tauler in the fourteenth century, and Thomas à Kempis in the fifteenth century, nuptial mysticism became a prominent motif in Christian spirituality. During the later Middle Ages, the nuptial theme was also present in the writings of such English mystics as Richard Rolle, Julian of Norwich, and Waiter Hilton.[49] Consequently, nuptial mysticism existed in certain forms of English spirituality before it was given added impetus in later generations by writers in the Reformed tradition.[50] In the Reformation era, Martin Luther disavowed the ideas of mystical ascent in Dionysius and others, but adopted the bridal mystical motif to describe the believer's union with Christ.[51] Similarly, Calvin held scorn for medieval mysticism, but implemented the nuptial motif to depict the believer's union with Christ that begins with the believer's justification.[52] Calvin also stated that marriage of Christ to the

---

[46] Bernard of Clairvaux, *On the Song of Songs*, trans. Kilian Walsh (Spencer, MA, 1971), volume 1.

[47] Pelikan, *Jesus Through the Centuries* (1985), 124.

[48] Bouyer, *Christian Mystery* (1990), 292-93.

[49] David Knowles, *The English Mystical Tradition* (New York, 1961), 1-38.

[50] Gordon S. Wakefield, 'Anglican Spirituality', in Luis Dupre and Don E. Saliers (eds), *Christian Spirituality: Post-Reformation and Modern* (New York, 1989), 257.

[51] David W. Lotz, 'Continental Pietism', in Cheslyn Jones *et al.* (eds), *The Study of Spirituality* (New York, 1986), 450.

[52] For an enumeration of primary texts in Calvin, see Dennis E. Tamburello, *Union with Christ: John Calvin and the Mysticism of St. Bernard* (Louisville, KY, 1994).

Church would have its consummation in the eternal state.[53] Beginning in the seventeenth century, nuptial mysticism found a place in the writings of the puritans.[54] Unlike certain Catholic mystical ideas of absorption and 'inner light', puritan authors generally spoke of a Christocentric mediated *communion* with justification as a point of departure as opposed to an unmediated theocentric *union* with sanctification as an end in view.[55] In the sixteenth century, the nuptial motif was prevalent in Continental Pietism that owed its debt to the spirituality of Luther and the Christ-centred forms of bridal mysticism of the Middle Ages.[56]

In Darby's era, the late eighteenth and early nineteenth centuries, the broader sweep of spirituality within British Protestantism was coloured by Continental Pietism of the seventeenth century.[57] For conservatives of Darby's period, the nuptial themes of continental Pietism and Puritanism continued to play a leading role in spirituality.[58] Interestingly, Theodosia Viscountess Powerscourt, a close associate of Darby, described Christian hope in the language of nuptial mysticism.[59] A contemporary of Lady Powerscourt observed that 'she seemed as if she lived in heaven, and barely touched the earth'.[60]

Did the European Romantic revival of the late eighteenth and

---

[53] Gordon S. Wakefield, *Puritan Devotion: Its Place in the Development of Christian Piety* (London, 1957), 108.

[54] Geoffrey F. Nuttall, 'Puritan and Quaker Mysticism', *Theology* 78 (1975), 518-31; Gordon S. Wakefield, 'Mysticism and Its Puritan Types', *LQHR* 35 (1978), 34-45; Dewey Wallace, The *Spirituality of the Later English Puritans: An Anthology* (Macon, GA, 1987), 241, 243; and Lean J. Podles, The *Church Impotent: The Feminization of Christianity* (Dallas, 1999), 116-17.

[55] Wakefield, *Puritan Devotion* (1957), 101-108.

[56] Lotz, 'Continental Pietism' (1986), 450.

[57] See, for example, John S. Andrews, 'German Influence on English Religious Life in the Victorian Era', *EQ* 44 (1972), 218-33; Dale W. Brown, *Understanding Pietism* (Grand Rapids, 1978), 15-19; George Brown, Jr., 'Pietism and the Reformed Tradition', *RR* 23 (1970), 143-52; and F. Ernest Stoeffler, The *Rise of Evangelical Pietism*, Studies in the History of Religions, vol. 9 (Leiden, 1970), 15-16.

[58] Wakefield, 'Anglican Spirituality' (1989), 274.

[59] Robert Daly (ed.), *Letters and Papers of the Late Theodosia A. Viscountess Powerscourt* (London, 1838), 10, 20, 39-40, 164, 203, 246, and 276. Regarding the letters of Lady Powerscourt, R. B. McDowell states that they were, 'one of the most poignant literary survivals of the [Evangelical] movement in Ireland'; R. B. McDowell, *Public Opinion and Government Policy in Ireland, 1801-1846* (1952; rpr. New York, 1975), 27.

[60] Quoted by Mrs. Hamilton Madden, *Personal Recollections of the Right Rev. Robert Daly, D.D.* (London, 1872), 23.

early nineteenth centuries lend greater expression to Darby's nuptial piety? Is there a definite link between medieval mysticism and nineteenth-century Romantic emphases upon spirituality and the afterlife? Was not the aesthetic and spiritual allure of perfected love in eternity compatible with the Romantic spirit? Indeed, some of the distinguishing features of Romanticism correspond to emphases in Darby's thought (i.e., otherworldliness, a craving for infinite values, a disillusioned view of society, contempt for tradition, preoccupation with the inner life, practical spirituality, and an awareness of the duality of man's constitution).[61] Arguably, there is something uncanny, even Romantic, about a gentleman trained in law who abandoned his legal profession and wealth to become a globe-trotting spokesman of a complicated prophetic system of belief. Be all this as it may, the difficulty of making Darby the product of Romantic influences is finding tangible evidence that reveals a direct link between him and his contemporaries. This is not to dismiss the probability that specific Romanticist inducements were tied to Darby's life and thought and that he was conversant with the literature of his Romantic contemporaries. At the same time, the evidence in this connection is more suggestive than it is substantive. There is as much dissimilarity between Darby and Romanticism as there is similarity.[62] The likelihood is strong that Darby's brand of nuptial mysticism was more a carry-over of Continental Piety than a product of Romanticism.[63]

Much like puritan authors and unlike Catholic mystical writers, Darby did not believe that ecstatic mystical transport was to be

---

[61] For discussion of Romanticism in early nineteenth-century British millennialism, see David W. Bebbington, *Evangelicalism in Modern Britain: A History from the 1730s to the 1980s* (London, 1989), 80-81; David W. Bebbington, 'Evangelical Christianity and Romanticism', *Crux* 26 (1990), 9-15; and for Romanticism in general, G. S. R. Kitson Clark, 'The Romantic Element: 1830 to 1850', in J. H. Plumb (ed.), *Studies in Social History: A Tribute to G. M. Trevelyan* (London, 1955); Arthur O. Lovejoy, 'The Meaning of Romanticism for the Historian of Ideas', *JHI* 2 (1941), 257-78; M. H. Abrams, 'English Romanticism: The Spirit of the Age', in Northrop Frye (ed.), *Romanticism Reconsidered: Selected Papers from the English Institute* (New York, 1963), 26-72; Tom Dunne, 'Haunted by History: Irish Romantic Writing 1800-50', in Roy Porter and Mikulas Teich (eds), *Romanticism in National Context* (Cambridge, 1988), 68-91.

[62] The plausibility of Romantic influences in Darby's view of the afterlife is explored in Gary L. Nebeker, 'The Hope of Heavenly Glory in John Nelson Darby (1800-1882)' (unpublished Ph.D. thesis, Dallas Theological Seminary, 1997), 87-95.

[63] See Andrews, 'German Influence on English Religious Life' (1972), 208-29.

experienced by the Christian in the present life. As noted above, Darby's nuptial mysticism found its application in an anticipatory sense, at the rapture when Christians were conformed into the likeness of Christ's heavenly glory and experienced the consequent blessing of perfected love. As he understood the term, Darby disavowed the introspective excesses of 'mysticism', but nuptial mysticism was, in fact, the language he used to speak of the believer's yearning for intimacy with Christ in heavenly glory. With the imminent prospect of Christ's return for His Church, hope could be thought of not only as a longing for 'the glory of Christ himself, but also a longing for deliverance from the corrupted world very soon to be judged. The nearness of the rapture, by virtue of its pretribulational sequence, lent urgency to one's yearnings for ultimate union with Christ. However, in the final analysis, more than hope of deliverance from coming wrath, it was hope of perfected love in heavenly glory that was emphasized in Darby's writings. One facet, then, of Darby's eschatological vision was to view himself and the Church as the objects of Christ's perfected love. This perfected love would find its culmination in heaven.

What remains unclear in the broad sweep of Darby's writings is his how carefully he distinguished between the corporate and individual aspects of nuptial mysticism. Did Darby apply the bridal metaphor to the individual soul simply because that soul was a member of the Church? The general impression given is that Darby blurred this distinction. Certainly, the Church collective was the Bride of Christ, but in some sense the individual union with Christ in heaven served as the Christian's sustaining vision for the here and now.

### Heavenly Glory as a State of Perfected Love

In the same way that Darby drew upon pre-existing concepts of nuptial mysticism, he also espoused an Augustinian view of heaven as a state of perfected love.[64] In his conclusion to *The City of God* (22.29), Augustine spoke of heaven as a place of everlasting rest, vision of God, love of God, and praise of God.[65] Of the beatific vision

---

[64] Representative texts for Augustine's concept of perfected love in heaven are found chiefly in *On the Psalms,* 36.1.12; 66.10; 83.8, 20-22; 86.8-9; 87.13; 117.22; 122.4; 124.3-4; 136.16; 144.2, 11; 149-10. This concept is considered at length in John Burnaby, *Amor Dei: A Study of the Religion of St. Augustine* (London, 1938).

[65] Augustine, The *City of God,* in *Basic Writings of Saint Augustine,* ed. Whitney J. Oates (Grand Rapids, 1980), 2:656-60.

in heaven, Augustine wrote, 'Your whole strength there is to love what you see, and your greatest happiness to have what you love.'[66] The Augustinian insights into heaven as a state of perfected love were eloquently elaborated on in the works of Bernard of Clairvaux, Bonaventure and Duns Scotus. Bernard described heaven as a community of love originating in and being fulfilled in the love of God- Father, Son, and Holy Spirit.[67] Despite the different emphases within Christian tradition concerning the nature of heaven,[68] the essential Augustinian idea of heaven as a place of perfected love, praise, rest, and vision remained intact over the centuries.[69] Darby's perspective of heaven as a state of perfected love with the Triune God reiterated the essential elements seen in Augustine and Bernard. In one sense, Darby regarded heaven as both a state and a place. Heaven was a place distinct from the earth, which the redeemed of Israel and believing Gentiles were to inhabit.[70] At the same time, heaven was also a state where the joy of perfected love in God's presence would be experienced everlastingly.

How did Darby's vision of heavenly glory compare with those of his contemporaries? Thomas Scott (1747-1821), a popular Anglican Bible commentator and preacher who wielded some measure of influence upon Darby's thought,[71] regarded heaven as nothing other than the enjoyment of Christ himself.[72] Thomas Erskine (1788-1870),

---

[66] Augustine, *The Literal Meaning of* Genesis, trans. John Hammond Taylor, Ancient Christian Writers 41 (New York, 1982), 12, 26. For discussion of Augustine's understanding of love in the eternal state, see D. J. Leahy, *St. Augustine on Eternal Life* (London, 1939), 54.

[67] Bernard of Clairvaux, *On Loving God,* ed. Halcyon C. Backhouse (London, 1985).

[68] For a discussion of the beatific vision as it has been discussed in Protestant and Catholic scholastic tradition, see G. C. Berkouwer, *The Return of Christ* (Grand Rapids, 1972), 372-79.

[69] Peter Toon, *Heaven and Hell: A Biblical and Theological Overview* (Nashville, TN, 1986), 149-56; David W. Lotz, 'Heaven and Hell in the Christian Tradition', *RL* 48 (1979), 87.

[70] Darby believed that the Church in heaven obtains a superior glory to that of Israel upon the earth; see Darby, *Collected Writings* (1971), i. 243-44; xi. 348.

[71] Whether Scott had influenced Darby in the articulation of Christian hope remains to be seen. Of Scott's importance in clarifying issues of personal assurance of salvation, Darby wrote, 'I think Scott's essays gave a strong determination to my thoughts at one time, while my mind was working upon it [personal assurance of salvation]' (Note on 2 Tim. 1:12, JRULM, CBA, 5540 [529]).

[72] Thomas Scott, *Essays on the Most Important Subjects in Religion,* 9th ed. (London, 1822), 124-25.

a Scottish Episcopalian, concluded in his 1828 work *The Unconditional Freeness of the Gospel* that heaven was 'the joy of God ...[and we] cannot enter the joy of God without entering into the character of God...[heaven] is the name for a character conformed to the will of God.'[73] A typological understanding of heaven as the eternal Sabbath was the common interpretation among Evangelicals and Tractarians within the Anglican Church during the early nineteenth century. At the same time, it was believed that holiness in this life was a token of eternal blessedness. Participation in the Eucharist feast provided the worshipper with a foretaste of heaven. The hymnody of these traditions presented heaven in a transcendent spiritual light as opposed to a projection of earthly desires.[74] Later in the nineteenth century, however, a diversity of views on the nature of heaven would emerge. Heaven became a topic of populist fascination as well as academic debate.[75]

Darby's vision of heavenly glory shared more than a passing affinity with that of at least one contemporary. Though the two men stood at opposite ends of the ecclesiastical spectrum,[76] Darby's vision of heavenly glory corresponded closely to that of the Anglo-Catholic divine, Edward B. Pusey (1800-1882), who in the heyday of the Oxford Movement wrote:

God is all-glorious; and glory 'is the very name of our future being...'
Glory shall fill the Elect above the brightness of the sun, shall make

---

[73] Thomas Erskine, *The Unconditional Freeness of the Gospel: In Two Essays* (Edinburgh, 1828), 24, 9.

[74] Geoffrey Rowell, 'Heaven and Hell (3) In Victorian Times', *ER* 19 (1992), 14-23; and Michael Wheeler, *Death and the Future Life in Victorian Literature and Theology* (Cambridge, 1990), 120.

[75] Although their portrayal of the beliefs of conservative Protestant Evangelicals in Britain in the Victorian period is at times less than careful, the work of McDannell and Lang sheds important light on the emerging diversity of beliefs about heaven in the mid-nineteenth century; Colleen McDannell and Bernard Lang, *Heaven: A History* (New Haven, 1988). See also Wheeler, *Death and Life* (1990), 119-74.

[76] Turner compared Darby and Pusey with these words: 'In the year 1800 two of the most remarkable men of the nineteenth century were born. This century ... is admitted by all who are conversant with the so-called religious world of the period, to have been powerfully influenced by the personalities of Edward Bouverie Pusey and John Nelson Darby, both of whom made indelible marks upon the face of Christendom. Both became clergymen of the Established Church, and lived lives of unworldly piety; labouring, although in a wholly different way, to realise a great ideal (the visible unity of the Church of God). It is noteworthy that both ended their labours within a few months of each other'; Turner, *Darby* (1951), 9-10.

them transparent with light, all-bright, all-pure, and that, with the
imparted light of God...And loving with the love of God himself, shall
love God as God loveth himself...uplifted, filled, overflowing, receiving,
giving back so as again to receive, the unutterable love of God, and by
His love changed into His own unchangeableness...How can we ever
cease to love, when we love unceasing Love with His own Love...? In all
shall we see nothing but God; all shall be as mirrors, flashing back and
forth the rays of the Glory and Beauty and Love of God.[77]

The yearning for ultimate union with God is the focus of Pusey's
1845 sermon on 1 John 3:2. It is at this point where commonality
between Darby and Pusey is most clearly seen; hope is the longing
for perfected love with each member of the triune Godhead. Where
Darby and Pusey appear to be at variance is on the extent of such
heavenly union. Darby did not specify the extent of this union.
Pusey, on the other hand, followed a more Platonic idea of absorption
into the Godhead, and the notion of varying degrees of ascent into
love. Citing Bernard of Clairvaux, Pusey regarded ultimate union
with Christ to be a form of deification, a familiar theological theme
seen in the early Church Fathers:

> So to be affected is to be deified. As a little drop of water, poured into
> much wine, seems wholly to cease from itself, while it assumes both
> the taste and colour of the wine...so must then, in the saints, all
> human affection, in a certain ineffable manner, melt away from itself
> and be wholly transfused into the Divine Will.[78]

Pusey's idea of transfusion into the Divine Will is reflective of the
language of the Eastern Fathers that he incorporated into his
theology.[79] Darby, on the other hand, adopted a more Augustinian
emphasis upon perfected love as the defining characteristic of
heavenly glory. But despite this point of difference, Darby's view of
heaven differed little from those of his contemporaries in the

---

[77] Edward B. Pusey, *A Course of Sermons on Solemn Subjects Chiefly
Bearing on Repentance and Amendment of Life, Preached in St. Saviour's
Church, Leeds, During the Week After Its Consecration on the Feast of S.
Simon and S. Jude, 1845* (Oxford, 1845), 269-77.
[78] Cited by Pusey, in *A Course of Sermons* (1845), 276. When Pusey speaks of
being 'deified', he echoes a long-standing theological tradition dating back to
the fathers of the early Church. The idea does not refer to an ontological
removal of the Creator-creature distinction, but of the culmination of a life-
long process of sanctification that could only be attained at death with
glorified perfection in the presence of God.
[79] Geoffrey Rowell, *The Vision Glorious: Themes and Personalities of the
Catholic Revival in Anglicanism* (New York, 1983), 79-90.

Anglican communion.

The similarity between Pusey's and Darby's understanding of heavenly glory leads us to consider an observation that has been made in at least one sociological study of millennial phenomena. This is what might be termed as the aesthetic attraction that heavenly imagery provides for those living in tumultuous social contexts, or even in states of lasting emotional deprivation. Existing millennial traditions and corresponding views of heaven (Christian or otherwise), may lie in a period of dormancy until such a time when local conditions necessitate a vision of the afterlife that gives meaning and purpose to the present. Thrupp has suggested that theories of aesthetic attraction must make a distinction between contexts in which millennial imagery coexists with traditional views of the millennium and those contexts that vary with current views of the millennium.[80] This observation is applicable to Darby in the following sense. Darby incorporated an existing interpretation of heavenly glory, nuptial mysticism, into his futurist eschatology. Previous Christian eschatological traditions regarded the intimate communion of the believer with God as inevitable at death. But Darby's incorporation of nuptial imagery into his brand of futurist premillennialism, especially with its emphasis upon a pretribulational rapture, made this blissful communion all the more imminent. Although Darby's social context was particularly unstable, marked by unrest and rapid change, it is difficult to prove that he purposely used nuptial imagery in his newly formulated theological synthesis as a means of coping with existing societal distresses. Instead, Darby believed that the language he employed to describe heavenly glory was the language of Scripture, and as such, it served as an incentive for perseverance in the perilous times in which he lived. In short, the vision of perfected love with God the Father and with Christ in heaven – a reality that could be at any moment experienced by means of the rapture – was the attraction that sustained Darby during an unprecedented period of social upheaval.

Was aesthetic attraction for perfected love in the afterlife a means of compensating for the pain and disillusionment that E. B. Pusey underwent during his life? While Pusey was optimistic about the reform of England's many social woes, his personal life was marked by ongoing depression. Browbeaten by a domineering father

---

[80] Sylvia L. Thrupp, 'Millennial Dreams in Action: A Report on the Conference Discussion', in Sylvia L. Thrupp (ed.), *Millennial Dreams in Action: Studies in Revolutionary Religious Movements* (New York, 1970), 15-17, 26-27.

throughout childhood and early adulthood, Pusey eventually suffered an emotional collapse in his early twenties, and the larger part of his life after this was characterized by a 'sombre, ungenial, and unjoyous gravity'.[81] His gloom and austerities escalated with the death of his wife in 1839. A recent biographer suggests that throughout his lifetime Pusey sought relief from his sorrows in overwork.[82] Because of personal and life experience similarities between Darby and Pusey, one wonders if their aesthetic mystical attraction for heaven was prompted in large part by the deep personal pain that both had suffered in the earthly realm. Could it be that a vision of perfected love in eternity sustained two leading exponents of theological conservatism within the Anglican communion in the early nineteenth century? While in the end this may be true, such a postulation remains only that- a postulation.

Darby's understanding of heaven differed little from the views of his Anglican contemporaries. Furthermore, Darby maintained continuity with the long-standing Augustinian tradition of heaven as the place where perfected love is shared between the Triune God and the believer. Where Darby differed from his contemporaries and antecedent traditions was in his modal distinction between heaven and earth as the final destinations of heavenly and earthly peoples, and in his argument for the pretribulational timing of the return of Christ for His Church.

Darby's futurist hermeneutic did not markedly affect his anticipation of heavenly glory. At the same time, his understanding of hope stands in stark contrast to the hopes of his post- and premillennial contemporaries. In one sense, Darby's hope of heavenly glory was his reactionary corrective to the earthly fixation upon the millennium that characterized many of his millennia! contemporaries.[83] When we speak of Darby's hope, we must do so without labelling it as 'millennia!'. It is accurate to say that Darby was a premillennialist without a millennia bject of hope for himself or for the Church. Darby believed that Christ would return with His Church before the one thousand year reign of Revelation 20. Nevertheless, it was likewise his conviction that the Church would neither be dwelling upon the earth during the millennium, nor dwelling upon the earth in the eternal state following the

---

81 David Forrester, *Young Doctor Pusey: A Study in Development* (London, 1989), 6.
82 Forrester, *Young Doctor Pusey* (1989), xvi, 11.
83 For a fuller development of this differentiation, see Gary L. Nebeker, 'John Nelson Darby and Trinity College Dublin: A Study in Eschatological Contrasts', *FH* 34 (2002), 87-108.

millennium. His modal distinction between the people of heaven and the people of earth would not allow for this.[84] Instead, as has been seen, his hope was for what he understood to be the greater and more glorious domain of heaven. An earthly millennial hope was reserved for national Israel and Gentiles who would come to faith during the Tribulation. Much importance has been placed upon Darby's theory of the pretribulational rapture of the Church and how such a position engenders the nature of Christian hope. Nevertheless, for Darby the rapture was not what the Church was to long for in the ultimate sense. Darby's hope was in keeping with the traditional hope of amillennial interpreters since Augustine, namely, the desired expectancy to share in the perfected love of the Triune God in the heavenly domain. Discontinuity with the Augustinian tradition of heaven is seen in his newly devised modal distinction between the peoples of heaven and the peoples of earth and their allotted destinations in the eternal state. Moreover, Darby's *timing* of the rapture was a departure from the existing tradition of the time frame when the Church would participate in the beatific vision of heavenly glory at the end of history, that is, after the ultimate victory of Christ over the forces of evil, the general resurrection, the Great White Throne Judgement, the transformation of the created order, and the beginning of the eternal state. The pretribulational rapture made the anticipated glorious exchange of perfected love all the more imminent, not something distant, to be experienced at the end of time.

## Conclusion

Exported to America in the late nineteenth century, Darby's eschatological mysticism found a welcome audience. His nuptial eschatology was echoed in the writings of North American dispensational contemporary, William E. Blackstone, whose 1878 work *Jesus is Coming* remained a best seller well into the early twentieth century. Of the union between Christ and His Bride at the rapture, Blackstone wrote:

> Can there be anything more precious than the thought of Jesus coming to take unto Himself His Bride? It is full of tenderness and love...The ecstasy of that meeting is above the power of description by tongue or pen...THEN shall the Church experience the rest of love – the fullness

---

[84] See, for example, Darby, *Synopsis* (1970), v. 343, and Darby, *Collected Writings* (1971), ii. 344-83.

of communion – the rapture of her Lord's embrace, and be satisfied in the sweetness of His love.[85]

Handley C. G. Moule (1841-1920), Bishop of Durham, was a popular premillennialist speaker at the Niagara Bible Conferences in America in the late nineteenth and early twentieth centuries. His variety of eschatological mysticism is reflected in his thoughts on the Second Coming:

> He for whom we look is indeed the Bridegroom, the Beloved, hastening down 'the mountains of separation' to the Bride...At some time, probably at no distant time, is to dawn and beam upon us this personal arrival of the 'Altogether Lovely' turning midnight into morning, winter into the heavenly summer, age into immortal youth, into a life of holy happiness and happy holiness for ever...Finally, we to whom the Lord Christ is what Ignatius called Him, with reverent boldness, *ho emos eras,* 'my Passion,' the Beloved of the inmost heart.[86]

Hope of mystical union with Christ at the rapture became a distinguishing feature of piety within the dispensational tradition in America in the late nineteenth and twentieth centuries. However, eschatological mysticism would eventually wane. As proponents of the rapture theory became more doctrinaire in their defence of that viewpoint, the nuptial mystical element of eschatological expectancy faded. When a new era of dispensational 'scholasticism' emerged in the middle of the twentieth century, Darby's mystical and relational yearning for perfected love was eclipsed by pretribulational apologetics. To use Buber's language, dispensationalists became more focused upon an 'it' (the rapture) than on a 'Thou' (Christ).[87] Another factor for the demise of eschatological mysticism merits consideration. As later generations of dispensational scholars attempted to become more consistently 'literal' in their interpretation of the Bible, the spiritualised overtones in Darby's ideas held less appeal. This would include his 'spiritual' application of the Song of Solomon to the Church.[88]

---

[85] William E. Blackstone, *Jesus is Coming* (Grand Rapids, 1932), 205.

[86] H. G. C. Moule, *The Hope of the Near Approach of the Lord's Return and Its Influence Upon Life* (London, 1919), 19-22.

[87] Gary L. Nebeker, 'The Theme of Hope in Dispensationalism', *BS* 158 (2001), 15-17.

[88] For a catalogue of spiritual, allegorical, symbolic, and typological word associations in Darby's writings, see Floyd Saunders Elmore, 'A Critical Examination of the Doctrine of the Two Peoples of God in John Nelson Darby' (unpublished Th.D. thesis, Dallas Theological Seminary, 1990), 319-321.

Darby's eschatological mysticism, the synthesis of a pretribulational deliverance with bridal mysticism, thrived in a case specific period in history, from the early nineteenth to the mid-twentieth century. Due to Darby's proximity and influence, the expressions of eschatological mysticism may have been more pronounced within Brethren circles. If it can be proven that Romanticism added colour and contour to Darby's nuptial mysticism, this might serve as an additional explanation for why nuptial language is seldom used in contemporary eschatological expectations of Evangelical Christians. Yet, evidence thus far is wanting in this connection. As regards other reasons for the obsolescence of eschatological mysticism, dubious is Podles's explanation that,

> Bridal language used to describe a Christian's relationship with God has homosexual overtones to many men, unless they engage in mental gymnastics and try to think of themselves as women...Since normal men reject both homosexuality and femininity as incompatible with the masculinity for which they are always striving, bridal mysticism and the metaphors and attitudes to which it gave rise have placed a major obstacle to men's participation in the Church.[89]

While spiritualised romantic longings for Jesus may border on homoeroticism for some, Podles's appraisal works from un-stated assumptions concerning what constitutes healthy masculinity.

To be sure, nuptial mysticism served an important role in different streams of Christian thought, literature, and piety throughout the centuries. Yet, bridal mysticism in general and Darby's brand of it in particular are not immune to criticism. A fundamental problem is the legitimacy of applying the content of The Song of Solomon to Christ's love for the Church. Turner's suggestion of 'pagan neo-Platonism' as the operative influence behind Origen's interpretation of the Song of Songs implies guilt by association.[90] By revisiting Aquinas' principle of analogy, perhaps the matter can be stated in another way. The metaphysical underpinnings of Origen's spiritual exegesis of the Song led to a univocal, rather than an analogical, understanding of God. Knowledge of God is not similar to one's knowledge of the things in the world. While God is immanent, He transcends the analogies He provides of Himself in Scripture. Added to this is the truism that knowledge of God is mediated by one's experiences in the world. Because God is an independent being, His being markedly differs from that of His creation. Therefore,

---

[89] Podles, *The Church Impotent* (1999), 119.

[90] Denys Turner, *Eras and Allegory: Medieval Exegesis of the Song of Songs* (Kalamazoo, MI, 1995), 32.

words and entities within the created order cannot be applied with exactitude to God.[91] The bridegroom imagery used of God 'affirms that there is a likeness or correspondence between God and that being [a human bridegroom], which allows the latter to act as a signpost to God'.[92] The flaw of the nuptial mystic tradition is that it pressed analogous language too far.[93]

While the bridal language of Scripture is analogical and not univocal in character, the bridal language of Scripture is not equivocal language. That is to say, God has disclosed some aspects of His being to His creatures. The experience of marriage does provide a hint of the depth of commitment God holds for His people. Nonetheless, our fragmented and finite perspective places limitations on our grasp of the perfect love of God. To provide some controls on the limitations of analogical language, Ian Ramsey has suggested that biblical analogies must be understood collectively. Scripture provides a range of analogies of God (e.g. king, warrior, shepherd, judge, and father) that serve to qualify the analogies in their entirety. When viewed in their totality, these analogies provide a fuller and more consistent portrayal of God.[94] Whether prompted by conscious or unconscious personal need, there is a human tendency to emphasize certain biblical analogies of God to the neglect of others.

Origen's exegesis of the Canticles marked a departure from the traditional understanding of the Church collective as Christ's bride to an individualized understanding in which the Christian's soul was His Bride.[95] Nine centuries later Bernard of Clairvaux would write,

although none of us will dare arrogate for his own soul the title the bride of the Lord, nevertheless we are members of the Church which rightly boasts of this title and of the reality that it signifies, and hence may justifiably assume a share in this honour. For what all of us

---

[91] See William C. Placher, *The Domestication of Transcendence: How Modern Thinking About God Went Wrong* (Louisville, KY, 1996), 27-31.

[92] Alister E. McGrath, *Christian Theology* (1994; second edition, Oxford, 1997), 162.

[93] Although at points overstating the contemporary consequences of bridal mysticism, Podles enumerates specific historical aberrations of the bridal motif during the Middle Ages. See Podles, *The Church Impotent* (1999), 103-108.

[94] Ian T. Ramsey, *Christian Discourse: Some Logical Explorations* (London, 1965).

[95] Nelson Pike, *Mystic Union: An Essay in the Phenomenology of Mysticism* (Ithaca, NY, 1992), 68.

simultaneously possess in full and perfect manner, that each single one of us undoubtedly possesses by participation.[96]

Pelikan has observed that mystical individualism became a way of describing one's private relationship to Jesus, and Jesus' relation to Christians, to the exclusion of fellow Christians and other people in general. Tersely stated, nuptial mysticism subtly promoted a self-focused individualism.[97]

As applied to Darby, his unconscious mystic individualism overshadowed the corporate dimension of hope as depicted in the Epistle to the Ephesians. There is a corporate dimension of hope that is a legitimate expression of biblical hope (Eph. 4:4). The 'one hope' of which the author spoke is not individual and private. More properly, it is the harmonious communal expectancy of a unified and restored cosmos where all things are brought to harmony as a result of Christ. Stated in another way, biblical hope is not only a desired outcome for 'me', but also a desired outcome for 'us'. In one sense, Darby did adopt a corporate dimension of hope. Nevertheless, for him the corporate nature of hope was a mystical yearning for individualized heavenly ecstasy that one shared with fellow Christians in the here-and-now, and not so much the communal joy of perfected horizontal relationship with fellow believers in the eternal state.

As a theological construct, Darby's pretribulational rapture theory is less than two hundred years old. Despite the theological novelty of this doctrine, the rapture hope appears to be holding its own in the twenty-first century. At the same time, Darby's eschatological mysticism, a unique fusion of the rapture hope with bridal mysticism and an Augustinian vision of heaven, has become *passe.* Evidently, nuptial mysticism – *sans* eschatology – still holds a powerful allure for many believers.[98] Nevertheless, contemporary expressions of nuptial piety are apparently not compatible with the modern scholastic rigor that comes with determining the chronological sequence of the rapture. While the rapture is a cherished doctrine in contemporary evangelicalism, the current rapture hope has become silently, yet visibly estranged from the nuptial mystical hope of John Nelson Darby.

---

[96] Bernard of Clairvaux, *On the Song of Songs* (1971), i. 27.
[97] Pelikan, *Jesus Through the Centuries* (1985), 131-32.
[98] The currently popular devotional piece, The *Sacred Romance,* is a telling case in point. Void of any references to the rapture hope, this work is an interesting mixture of nuptial mysticism, neo-Romanticism, and psychology; Brent Curtis and John Eldredge, The *Sacred Romance: Drawing Closer to the Heart of God* (Nashville, TN, 1997).

# CHAPTER 5

# Edward Irving: Eschatology, Ecclesiology and Spiritual Gifts

Tim Grass

The name of Edward Irving (1792-1834) has traditionally been 'associated, in the popular memory, with "unknown tongues," unfulfilled predictions, and unintelligible polemics'.[1] Although there has been a renaissance of interest in Irving during recent decades, a reading of much modern writing about him might give the impression that his main concerns were eschatology, as 'prophet of the millennium',[2] Christology, the aspect of his thought which is taken most seriously by contemporary academics, or spiritual gifts, as 'forerunner of the charismatic movement'.[3] However, to take any one of these aspects of Irving's theology and study it in isolation from the whole risks failing to understand what lay uppermost on his

---

[1] W. Wilks, *Edward !ruing: An Ecclesiastical and Literary Biography* (London, 1854), 265. This is a revised version of a paper originally given at the Study Group for Christianity and History Conference, Birmingham, 22 April 1995, and published in *Christianity and History Newsletter* 15 (1995), 15-32.

[2] Sheridan Gilley, 'Edward Irving: Prophet of the Millennium', in J. Garnett and C. Matthew (eds.), *Revival and Religion since 1700: Essays for John Walsh* (London, 1993). The most cogent defence of this reading of Irving has been offered by Mark Patterson, 'Designing the Last Days: Edward Irving, The Albury Circle, and the Theology of *The Morning Watch*' (unpublished Ph.D. thesis, King's College, London, 2001), who asserts that 'Irving was a theologian of the millennium, and it is from this perspective, alone, that the real Irving, the whole Irving, may be understood' (150).

[3] See Arnold Dallimore, *The Life of Edward !ruing: Forerunner of the Charismatic Movement* (Edinburgh, 1984), and, from a charismatic viewpoint, C. Gordon Strachan, *The Pentecostal Theology of Edward !ruing* (London, 1973).

heart. I believe that the 'centre' of Irving's thought lay not so much in any aspect of his theology as in his sense of divine vocation. Irving saw himself primarily as a pastor, and I would submit that his thinking and writing should be viewed in this light. This being so, his ecclesiology should be given more prominence than it has usually received.

This paper offers an account of three significant aspects of Irving's thought, with some reflections on the relations between them: eschatology, ecclesiology, and his understanding of the nature and restoration of the charismata. In so doing, I am following in the footsteps of the nineteenth-century Anglican Edward Miller, who saw Irvingism as a result of the meeting of three religious currents:

> first, the tendency to look for a new outpouring of the Holy Spirit upon the minds of chosen individuals, apart from the traditionary indwelling of the Holy Ghost in the Catholic Church; secondly, the yearning for a more perfectly realized continuance of the Incarnation by means of complete Church machinery and worship; and thirdly, a tendency to expect immediately the Second Coming of our Lord Jesus Christ.[4]

Underlying Irving's thinking in these closely-related areas was his pastoral concern, which was manifest in a love for his flock and a burden to raise the standards of spiritual life and evangelistic effectiveness of the Church of Scotland. What happened when his concerns were rejected, and the impact of such rejection on his theology and practice, will become evident in what follows.

## Eschatology[5]

On 9 September 1822, Irving wrote in a letter to his friend Jane Welsh: 'I meditate a work upon the alienation of clever men from

---

[4] E. Miller, *The History and Doctrines of Irvingism* (London, 1878), ii. 202. Miller was a high Anglican seeking to stem the loss of Anglican clergy to the Catholic Apostolic Church.

[5] Irving's main eschatological works were *Preliminary Discourse to the work of Ben Ezra* (1827), *Babylon and Infidelity Foredoomed of God: A Discourse on the Prophecies of Daniel and the Apocalypse which relate to these Latter Times, and until the Second Advent* (1828), which began life as a sermon to the Continental Society in 1825; *The Last Days: A Discourse on the Evil Character of these our Times: Proving them to be the 'Perilous Times' of the 'Last Days'* (1828), the substance of his 1828 lectures on Revelation, which is referred to here in its second edition; *Sermons, Lectures and Occasional Discourses* (1829), vol. 3, 'On Subjects National and Prophetical'; *Lectures on the Book of Revelation* (1829), which was later reissued in two volumes as *Prophetical Works.*

their Maker.' His meditations bore fruit in a lengthy work published the following year, *For the Oracles of God, Four Orations: For Judgment to Come, an Argument, in Nine Parts.* This was intended as an example of two new methods of teaching – the oration and the argument, directed at particular social groups whom he wished to reach with the gospel.[6] Influenced by Romantic currents of thought, his aim was to appeal to the heart as well as the mind. He sent a copy of the work to Coleridge, who wrote in it, 'Let this young man know that the world is not to be converted, but judged.'[7] The 'Sage of Highgate' appears to have led Irving to exchange the popular evangelical hope of seeing the world's conversion and a gradual progress into the millennia!age for a pessimism which foresaw only a steady decline until all the institutions of society should be overthrown and destroyed, a decline in which the Church would share unless it were afforded supernatural assistance.[8] Through this relationship, Irving also gained a reverence for the ideal, a contempt for expediency, and a strengthened belief in the importance of ecclesiastical order as expressive of spiritual reality.[9] Friendship with Coleridge was to cool as Irving became absorbed by the study of prophecy.

For all his strength of conviction when facing opposition, there was an impressionable streak in Irving's character: at several points, his convictions took a new turn as a result of the influence of others. It had happened when he met Coleridge; now it was to happen again through an eager prophetic student by the name of James Hatley Frere. In 1815 Frere had published *A Combined View of the Prophecies of Daniel, Esdras, and St John, Shewing that All the Prophetic Writings are Formed upon One Plan,* in which he portrayed the Second Coming as imminent, although not literal. He sought a man of influence whom he could convince of the truth of his scheme of interpretation. Lighting upon Irving, he concluded that he had found the man he was looking for, and applied himself to convincing him of the validity of his eschatological scheme- a task made easier by the pessimism Irving had learned from Coleridge.[10]

---

[6] Wilks, *Edward !ruing* (1854), 64.

[7] [W. W. Andrews], *Edward !ruing: A Review* (Edinburgh, 1864), 51.

[8] A. L. Drummond, *Edward !ruing and his Circle* (London, [1937]), 67; M. O. W. Oliphant, The *Life of Edward !ruing, Minister of the National Scotch Church, London,* fifth edition (London, [1870]), 92-3.

[9] D. W. Bebbington, *Evangelicalism in Modern Britain: A History from the 1730s to the 1980s* (London, 1989), 80.

[10] Carlyle described Frere as 'the Honourable Something or other, great in Scripture Prophecy, in which he had started some sublime new idea, well

Although a year passed before Irving was finally convinced by Frere's arguments, the extent of Frere's influence can be gauged from the fact that Irving dedicated to him a work, based on a sermon to the Continental Society in 1825, entitled *Babylon and Infidelity Foredoomed of* God. [11] In this work, Irving followed the historicist principle of interpretation that in prophecy a day is equivalent to a year in history. He based his calculations of the date of the Second Advent on the Edict of Justinian issued in 533 as the beginning of the Papacy as an object of prophecy; 1260 years (the 1260 days or forty-two months of Daniel and Revelation) continued until 1793, a date seen by many prophetic interpreters as significant because of the beheading of Louis XVI in France, an act which symbolised the rise of infidel democracy and the overthrow of papal power. Since 1793 the first six vials of Revelation had been outpoured, and the seventh would last for forty-five years until 1868 and the second coming. Immediately before this, Armageddon would usher in a period of success for the Gospel; following the second coming would be the millennium. Like Frere, Irving did not yet view the second coming literally: 'I express no decided opinion concerning the personal or corporeal appearance and reign of Christ, to consummate wrath, and commence blessedness.' [12] In all this, Britain was destined to play a unique role, and would be spared the judgments to fall upon the nations of the former Roman Empire, provided that the nation and its established churches remained faithful:

> when the rulers of this nation shall permit, to the worshippers of the Beast, the same honours, immunities, and trusts, which they permit to the worshippers of the true God, that day will be blackest in the history of our fate. That day our national charter is forfeited in heaven, and we are sealed no longer. [13]

From this we can see why Irving was so opposed to Catholic emancipation, and why, thereafter, he began to view the condition of the established churches in more negative terms.

Coleridge disapproved of Irving's admiration for Frere, [14] and arranged a meeting with Irving to study Revelation, 'if so I might

---

worth prosecuting, as Irving had assured me'; Thomas Carlyle, *Reminiscences* (London, 1932), 279.

[11] Iain H. Murray, *The Puritan Hope: Revival and the Interpretation of Prophecy* (Edinburgh, 1971), 189.

[12] Irving, *Babylon and Infidelity Foredoomed* (1828), 377.

[13] Irving, *Babylon and Infidelity Foredoomed* (1828), 546.

[14] E. L. Griggs (ed.), *Collected Letters of Samuel Taylor Coleridge* (Oxford, 1971), vi. 557.

withdraw him from what I cannot regard as other than a Delusion, of a very serious nature, were it only for it's [sic] consequences on his character, and therewith on his Utility'.[15] The attempt failed; but while Irving's friendship with Coleridge was cooling, that with Henry Drummond (whom Irving had first met as a result of preaching a sermon on behalf of the Continental Society, which Drummond had founded[16]) was growing warmer.

Drummond was to play a crucial role in Irving's later career, not least as host of the Albury Conferences. These originated with a proposal by the Rev. Lewis Way (secretary of the London Society for the Promotion of Christianity among the Jews) for a conference to study scripture prophecy concerning the prospects of the Church in what was seen as a time of crisis.[17] Occasional meetings took place in London during June 1826, and Drummond invited all whom he knew to be interested in the subject, of whatever denomination, to confer at his mansion, Albury Park in Surrey.[18] For four years they did so each Advent, with a final conference in July 1830; the matters discussed in the first four conferences are fully detailed in the form of three volumes of *Dialogues on Prophecy,* edited by Drummond. Irving gave an enthusiastic account of the 1826 conference in his *Preliminary Discourse to the Work of Ben Ezra,* stressing the harmony of understanding which prevailed among the participants. The syllabus indicates that the conference covered a large amount of ground:

> First, The doctrine of holy scripture concerning the times of the Gentiles. Secondly, The duties of Christian ministers and people, growing out thereof towards the gentile churches. Thirdly, The doctrine concerning the present and future condition of the Jews. Fourthly, The duties growing out of the same towards the Jews. Fifthly, The system of the prophetic visions and numbers of Daniel and the Apocalypse.

---

[15] Letter to Edward Coleridge, 8 March 1826; in Griggs (ed.), *Collected Letters of Samuel Taylor Coleridge* (1971), vi. 570.

[16] H. C. Whitley, *Blinded Eagle: The Life of Edward !ruing* (London, 1955), 45.

[17] Irving, *Preliminary Discourse* (1827), 197; L. E. Froom, *The Prophetic Faith of our Fathers* (Washington, DC, [1946]), iii. 449; E. A. Rossteuscher, 'The Rebuilding of the Church of Christ upon the Original Foundations', original German edition (1850) trans. L. A. Hewett (1871); MS in British Library, shelf mark 764n13,22.

[18] Irving, *Preliminary Discourse* (1827), 197; Miller, *History and Doctrines of Irvingism* (1878), i. 37. Way had argued since 1822 for a personal return of Christ and had influenced Drummond on this point; see Bebbington, *Evangelicalism in Modern Britain* (1989), 83.

Sixthly, The scripture doctrine concerning the future advent of the Lord. And lastly, The duties to the church and the world arising out of the same.[19]

The participants reasoned that **if** the Second Coming is associated with the restoration of the Jews to their land, then the Millennium must follow rather than precede it, a conclusion fraught with important consequences for ecclesiology and missionary strategy.[20]

Irving's own premillennialism had crystallised through reading early in 1826 a work by a South American Jesuit, Manuel Lacunza, who wrote under the pseudonym of Ben Ezra.[21] Finding that it reflected his own views, Irving translated it into English as *The Coming of Messiah in Glory and Majesty,* adding a *Preliminary Discourse* outlining the development of his convictions.[22] Evidently he was still following an historicist approach, as he made clear his rejection of Lacunza's futurist interpretation of the Apocalypse.[23] However, his thinking had moved on since *Babylon and Infidelity Foredoomed,* his main contentions being that the Gentile Church was ripe for judgment, a conclusion derived from study of the signs of the times and the prophetic numbers; that Christ would prepare another ark of testimony, and would probably use faithful Gentiles to bring about revival among the Jews: this outpouring of the 'latter rain' (Pentecost being the 'former rain') would lead to opposition, antichristianity against the Gentiles and infidelity against the Jews; and that judgment would conclude in the personal appearance of Christ, followed by the millennium.[24]

The pessimism which had characterised Irving's thought for some years was reinforced by awareness of the parallels to be drawn between the Jewish and Christian dispensations: both were marked by apostasy and consequent rejection. Furthermore, an early

---

[19] Irving, *Preliminary Discourse (1827),* 198.

[20] Bebbington, *Evangelicalism in Modern Britain* (1989), 83.

[21] Drummond had been instrumental in introducing Irving to this work; see Grayson Carter, *Anglican Evangelicals: Protestant Secessions from the via media, c. 1800-c. 1850* (Oxford, 2001), 174.

[22] Murray, *The Puritan Hope* (1971), 189-90; Irving, *Preliminary Discourse* (1827), 197.

[23] Irving, *Preliminary Discourse* (1827), 30.

[24] Irving, *Preliminary Discourse* (1827), xlix, 5-7, 199. The idea of a 'spiritual coming' recurred in Baxter's prophecies of 1832, though now as a precursor of a literal Second Advent; R. Baxter, *Narrative of Facts, Characterizing the Supernatural Manifestations, in Mr. !ruing's Congregation, and Other Individuals, in England and Scotland, and Formerly in the Writer Himself* (London, 1833), 78.

formulation of the concept of the rapture of believers makes its appearance.[25] All the same, he had not yet given up all hope for the institutional church: in spite of the anticipation of the apostasy of Christendom, he believed that revival could come to the church through prophetic study.[26]

Irving's premillennial eschatology received further development at subsequent Albury Conferences, and we shall see later the implications of these ideas for Irving's ecclesiology. Mter the 1829 conference, a summary of conclusions so far reached was circulated:

1. That the present Christian Dispensation is not to pass insensibly into the millennia!state by gradual increase of the preaching of the Gospel; but that it is to be terminated by judgments, ending in the destruction of this visible Church and polity, in the same manner as the Jewish dispensation has been terminated.

2. That during the time that these judgments are falling upon Christendom, the Jews will be restored to their own land.

3. That the judgments will fall principally, if not exclusively, upon Christendom, and will begin with that part of the Church of God which has been most highly favoured, and is therefore most deeply responsible.

4. That the termination of these judgments is to be succeeded by that period of universal blessedness to all mankind, and even to the beasts, which is commonly called the Millennium.

5. That the second Advent of Messiah precedes or takes place at the commencement of the Millennium.

6. That a great period of 1260 years commenced in the reign of Justinian, and terminated at the French Revolution; and that the vials of the Apocalypse began then to be poured out; that our blessed Lord will shortly appear, and therefore it is the duty of all, who so believe, to press these conclusions on the attention of all men.[27]

Given that by all accounts Irving played a leading role in discussions, we may well view these as representing his own convictions. Irving's eschatology was now fully developed in its essentials, and we turn to consider how it impacted on his ecclesiology.

---

[25] Patterson, 'Designing the Last Days' (2001), 56, 141.
[26] Patterson, 'Designing the Last Days' (2001), 57.
[27] [H. Drummond (ed.)], *Dialogues on Prophecy*, vol. i (London, 1828), ii-iii.

## Ecclesiology[28]

Irving's early convictions may well have derived from his occasional Sabbath attendance at the Burgher Seceders' meetinghouse in Ecclefechan, a few miles from his home in Annan. Here he would have imbibed the seventeenth-century Scottish ideal of a baptised nation in covenant with God.[29] Echoes of this are evident in his strong belief (until his theology came under sustained attack) in a national establishment, and his theology of baptism (which receives comment below). While still a student in Edinburgh, however, he began to read Richard Hooker,[30] whose *Laws of Ecclesiastical Polity* strengthened his convictions concerning establishment, and concerning the divine authority of a minister.[31] Another work which

---

[28] Irving's main ecclesiological and pneumatological works were *For Missionaries after the Apostolical School* (1825); 'Homilies on the Sacraments' (1827), in G. Carlyle (ed.), *Collected Writings* (London, 1864-5), ii. 247-642; *Discourse and Charges at the Ordination of the Reverend H. B. MacLean, Scotch Church, London Wall, 15th March* (1827); *An Apology for the Ancient Fullness and Purity of the Doctrine of the Kirk of Scotland* (1828); *The Church and State Responsible to Christ, and to One Another: A Series of Discourses on Daniel's Vision of the Four Beasts* (1829); 'On the Doctrine, and Manifestation and Character of the Apostasy in the Christian Church' (1829), *Morning Watch* (hereafter abbreviated as MW) 1 (1829), 100-115; 'Signs of the Times and the Characteristics of the Church', *MW* 1 (1829), 641-666, *MW* 2 (1830), 142-162; 'The Church, with her Endowment of Holiness and Power', *MW* 2 (1830), 630-668, originally part of his *Lectures on the Apocalypse* and republished in *CW* (1864-5), v. 449-506; 'On the Gifts of the Holy Ghost, commonly called supernatural', *MW* 2 (1830), 850-869; 3 (1831), 473-96; 4 (1831), 84-101, republished in *CW* (1864-5), v. 509-61; *The Confessions of Faith and the Books of Discipline of the Church of Scotland, of date Anterior to the Westminster Confession* (1831); *The Day of Pentecost, or the Baptism with the Holy Ghost* (1831); 'Facts connected with the Recent Manifestations of Spiritual Gifts', *Fraser's Magazine*, January 1832, 754-61; March 1832, 198-205; April 1832, 316-320 (also published separately); 'A Judgment, as to what course the ministers and the People of the Church of Scotland should take in Consequence of the Decisions of the Last General Assembly' (1832), *MW* 5.84-115 (also published separately).
[29] Bebbington, *Evangelicalism in Modern Britain* (1989), 95; see also Irving, *The Last Days* (1828), xxxviii. This notion was central to Catholic Apostolic apologetic, and was prominent in the 'Testimonies' issued at intervals to religious and political leaders throughout Christendom.
[30] Oliphant, *The Life of Edward !ruing* (1870), 19; Whitley, *Blinded Eagle* (1955), 10.
[31] P. E. Shaw, *The Catholic Apostolic Church* (Morningside Heights, NY, 1946), 12. When a new building was opened for him in Regent Square in 1827, Irving reputedly had it named 'The National Scotch Church' because

he read with enthusiasm was the *Convocation Book* of the seventeenth-century Bishop Overall, which put forward the belief that political power was derived from above and was responsible for upholding true religion.[32]

Crucial to Irving's ecclesiology was the sense of a reaction against the pragmatically-orientated religious world, and the desire for something higher. The difficulties which he experienced in obtaining an opening for ministry would have reinforced his low opinion of the contemporary church; another factor influencing his views may have been his experience of the inadequacy of the parish system, while serving as assistant to Chalmers in Glasgow. The result was that Irving became something of an ecclesiastical loner (though not an isolationist). In a letter of April 1822, about the time of his removal to London, he wrote:

> There is a sea of troubles, for my notions of a clergyman's office are not common, nor likely to be in everything approved. There is a restlessness in my mind after a state of life less customary, more enterprising, more heroical, if I might apply the word to a sacred use, certainly more apostolical. My notions of pulpit eloquence differ from many of my worthy brethren. In truth I am an adventurer on ground untried.[33]

His introduction to Coleridge led him to venture further onto such ground, with the result that, as Bebbington has commented, 'The substance of [Irving's] exalted ecclesiology was Coleridgean.'[34] This is evident in his work *For Missionaries after the Apostolical School:* man being body as well as spirit, spiritual realities must have an outward form whereby to influence him, just as God's attributes have the outward forms of the heavens, the Law and the Gospel. In particular, 'the visible Church is the sensible form of the heavenly communion.'[35] Pleading for a move away from pragmatism to an attempt to implement what he believed was the 'Missionary Charter' given by Christ in Matthew 10, he expressed his conviction that the offices of Ephesians 4:11 – apostle, prophet, evangelist, pastor and teacher – should always be present in the Church: 'These five offices

---

he could not bear to be regarded as a dissenter; D. Brown, 'Personal Reminiscences of Edward Irving', *The Expositor,* 3rd series, 6 (1887), 218.

[32] Oliphant, *The Life of Edward !ruing* (1870), 121, 139-40.

[33] Irving to A. Robertson; quoted in J. Hair, *Regent Square, Eighty Years of a London Congregation* (London, 1898), 34.

[34] Bebbington, *Evangelicalism in Modern Britain* (1989), 80.

[35] Irving, *For Missionaries after the Apostolical School* (1825), 85.

arise out of the everlasting necessities of the Church.'[36] In this way the Church's form would give expression to the nature of the spiritual reality which it had been constituted to make manifest. Since there were still heathen for apostles to win, backsliders for prophets to admonish, opponents of the truth for doctors to confute, it was impossible to make do with evangelists and pastors as the religious world sought to do.[37]

Such sentiments had startled the evangelical congregation who had first heard them preached at the London Missionary Society's Annual Meeting of 1824, and provoked an outraged reaction when they appeared in print, especially as the work was dedicated to Coleridge with the words: 'you have been more profitable to my faith in orthodox doctrine, to my spiritual understanding of the Word of God, and to my right conception of the Christian Church, than any or all of the men with whom I have entertained friendship and conversation.'[38] Being the kind of man he was, and holding the views that he did, Irving's conviction of the rightness of his views was probably strengthened by such opposition. Although his attitude towards the empirical church did change fairly significantly after this, the substance of his ecclesiology remained the same, and would receive institutional expression with the emergence of what was to become the Catholic Apostolic Church.

Building on this foundation, Irving set out his understanding of the meaning and function of the Church in his *Homilies on Baptism,* based on sermons preached in 1827.[39] According to these, the Church owed its visible existence to the sacrament of baptism, the seal of a covenant which both implied obligations and conferred regenerating grace.[40] From this rite were to be deduced the divine government of the Church as Christ's body and the practice of church discipline by a body responsible to Christ.[41] Although baptism conferred obligations as part of a community in covenant with God,[42] there were elect and reprobate within the Church; indeed, at the end the Church would be almost entirely reprobate.[43]

The exalted nature of Irving's theoretical ecclesiology meant that

[36] Irving, *For Missionaries after the Apostolical School* (1825), xxi.

[37] Irving, *For Missionaries after the Apostolical School* (1825), xxi-xxii.

[38] Irving, *For Missionaries after the Apostolical School* (1825), vii-viii.

[39] Whitley, *Blinded Eagle* (1955), 65.

[40] *CW* (1864-5), ii. 385.

[41] *CW* (1864-5), ii. 386.

[42] Elsewhere he described baptism as 'constituting a people in covenant, and responsible for the privileges of the covenant'; Irving, *Last Days* (1828), xxxviii.

[43] *CW* (1864-5), ii. 404.

he viewed contemporary ecclesial reality in all the darker terms because of the contrast which it presented, just as the early Brethren were beginning to do and as the Tractarians would do a few years later. This was reinforced by the development in his eschatology, which paved the way for a significant shift of emphasis, from the Church as an established entity in a nation in covenant with God, to the Church as a remnant of the faithful, called to separate from apostate religion in the face of imminent judgement. In particular, the eschatological scheme of the Albury Conferences had an impact on Irving's ecclesiology in the areas of unity and apostasy.[44] In a vindication of the Protestant Reformers written in 1829, 'On the Doctrine and Manifestation and Character of the Apostasy in the Christian Church', he set out the scriptural expectation of such an apostasy, concluding that God had planned that the Church should include both wheat and tares; that the wicked would be more numerous and more powerful in the Church, and would increase towards the end; and that persecution was to be expected from the wicked within the Church rather than from unbelievers outside it– a point which was to be reflected in his own experience as the storm over his Christological writings gathered strength.[45] Since the institutional church was expected to decline in this way, it is not surprising to find Irving asserting that 'a church, in the apostolic and true sense, means any two or three met together in the name of the Lord.'[46]

The balance which had existed since 1823 between Irving's attachment to the Establishment principle and his conviction that the professing church was in terminal decline now shifted in favour of the latter, after the passing of the Roman Catholic Emancipation Act in 1829 (which he described as 'the late great act of national apostasy'[47]) and the condemnation by the Church of Scotland's

---

[44] [Drummond] (ed.), *Dialogues on Prophecy* (1828), ii. 4-5; iii. iii.

[45] [Drummond] (ed.), *Dialogues on Prophecy* (1828), i. 115.

[46] Irving, 'Facts connected with the Recent Manifestation of Spiritual Gifts', *Fraser's Magazine* (March 1832), 202.

[47] Irving, *Church and State* (1829), xiv. Writing to Thomas Chalmers after the 1828 Albury Conference, he described the participants as 'more convinced than ever of the judgments which are about to be brought upon Christendom, and upon us most especially, if we should go into any league or confederacy with, or toleration of, the papal abomination'; Oliphant, *The Life of Edward !ruing* (1870), 255. The high Toryism and premillennial pessimism of Drummond would have led him to interpret the crises of the 1820s over political reform in eschatological, and even apocalyptic, terms; Carter, *Anglican Euangelicals* (2001), 158. Such an interpretation would

General Assembly of Irving's friends Campbell, Scott and Maclean
and of his own writings in 1831.[48] This was evident in his response 'A
Judgment, as to what course the ministers and the People of the
Church of Scotland should take in consequence of the Decisions of
the Last General Assembly'. Irving had never felt any great affection
for the General Assembly, and stood their condemnation on its head
by viewing *them* as the ones who were teaching error, primarily by
their denial that Christ took fallen human flesh; the faithful should
separate from them in obedience to 2 John 10.[49] If there was no
sound ministry within reach, those so awakened should follow the
example of the Waldenses, Albigenses and the early Scottish
Reformers, and 'meet together, and worship amongst themselves,
crying to the Lord to raise them up Apostles, Evangelists, Prophets,
Pastors and Teachers, and Elders and Deacons, and the other office-
bearers in his house'.[50] He acknowledged that he had formerly
opposed such separation as schismatic, but he could not justify
knowingly remaining under false teaching;[51] in any case (and this is
another significant development), the Church is primarily local, not
denominational: 'the view which God takes of a church is a body of
Christians gathered under the ministry and government of their
pastor, with his council of elders and deacons; not a confederation of
churches gathered under a Confession of Faith.'[52] All the same, we

---

have been shared by Irving, whose Toryism was fully as high as
Drummond's.

[48] He still believed in the necessity of the establishment of the Church, but
he located it in the future rather than the present. In a sermon preached
later in 1832, he asserted that the Church was destined to reign on earth; it
was 'a nursery for kings', in which God's people were to be trained for future
government. Believers could only be fitted for this coming kingdom by
receiving the Holy Ghost; Irving, 'Exposition and Sermon on 8th August
1832', 2-4, in *Sermons by Edward Irving and Nicholas Armstrong* (London,
1831-33).

[49] Irving, *A Judgment* (1832), 21-2. Interestingly, this shift to what might be
called a 'remnant' ecclesiology was by no means associated with Calvinist
views concerning election: Irving had come to a belief in universal
atonement several years earlier, under the influence of Campbell and Scott;
J. P. Newell, 'A. J. Scott and his Circle' (unpublished Ph.D. thesis, New
College, Edinburgh, 1981), 50.

[50] Irving, *A Judgment* (1832), 23. He considered that this is what took place
at the start of the Reformation (27).

[51] For example, 'I hold it to be an act of schism, to go forth and separate from
any church which is not of the Apostasy'; Irving, *Church and State* (1829),
568.

[52] Irving, *Church and State* (1829), 24; see also Irving, *Confessions of Faith*
(1831), cii-ciii, where he derives his emphasis on the local nature of the

must not forget that Irving was advocating secession from the establishment because of its errors, rather than because he was opposed to establishment *per se;* he urged Scott not to cut himself off from the Church of Scotland before it had pronounced its verdict on his views.[53]

By now, he had ample reason for his belief that Christendom was in an irreversible decline: 'I hold it as a simple axiom, that every change in the civil and ecclesiastical state of Christendom, is a change for the worse, however much it may pretend to the contrary.'[54] As for the Church of Scotland, he considered its General Assembly to be 'the most wicked of all God's enemies upon the face of the earth' and with it he could have 'no relationship but that of open and avowed enmity'.[55] The nation in covenant with God has become the apostate nation, the visible church has been cast off as apostate, and believers are forced to separate from it; only with the advent of the millennium will the true church regain its rightful place at the centre of human society.

## Spiritual Gifts

Carlyle was of the opinion that Irving's interest in spiritual gifts was produced by the same cause as his interest in eschatology: he 'is forgotten by the intellectual classes, but still flourishes among the fanatical classes, whose ornament and beacon he is'.[56] Many have followed Carlyle, but this interpretation does not do justice to Irving or to his ideas. On the other hand, Strachan has somewhat overstated the case in saying that the gifts reappeared in response to the sustained and systematic exposition of Scripture.[57] The story is

---

Church from Revelation 2-3; and *CW* (1864-5), v. 372-3. Emphasis on the Church's local aspect coheres well with Irving's developing 'remnant' ecclesiology. It could also account for Irving's difficulties in submitting to the charismatic ministries as they began to appear at Newman Street: he had no real framework within which to place ministries intended for the Universal Church.

[53] Newell, 'A. J. Scott and his Circle' (1981), 119, following *Daily News,* 26 May 1862.

[54] Irving, 'An Interpretation of the fourteenth Chapter of the Apocalypse', *MW* 6 (1832), 282.

[55] Irving to the Presbytery, 13 October 1832 (New College, Edinburgh, Chalmers MSS, Box 9.3.19).

[56] Carlyle to Jane Welsh Carlyle, 15 August 1831, quoted in J. A. Froude, *Thomas Carlyle: A History of the First Forty Years of his Life 1795-1835* (new ed., London, 1896), ii. 121.

[57] Strachan, *The Pentecostal Theology of Edward !ruing* (1973), 14-15.

rather more complex than either of these explanations might imply. Looking back, Irving believed that he had accepted the responsibility of the Church for the gift of the Holy Ghost, as well as the intended permanence of spiritual gifts and offices, since the opening of his new church in 1827; although the gifts disappeared as God's judgment on an unbelieving and apostate Church, they would be restored after the Second Coming. The first articulation of a belief that the gifts should still be in operation in the Church came that year in a sermon later published in his *Homilies on Baptism*, in which he contended that real spiritual grace was conferred on the elect through this ordinance. Baptism not only conferred remission of sins, but the gift of the Holy Ghost, manifest in the gift of inward sanctification but also in that of outward power. Irving needed a better explanation than the mere fact that the latter had been withdrawn to convince him that it was no longer to be expected, especially since he saw no division in Scripture between the ordinary and extraordinary gifts of the Spirit.[58] In spite of this, Irving later admitted that he had not encouraged his flock actively to seek the restoration of spiritual gifts; although his assistant A. J. Scott used to tell him that he should be seeking their restoration himself, he took little notice.[59] Scott, who has often been regarded as the theological *eminence grise* behind the reappearance of the gifts, had by 1828 influenced McLeod Campbell to believe that spiritual gifts were intended to be available in all ages of the Church; the latter encouraged his congregation at Row (or Rhu), near Helensburgh in the west of Scotland, to pray for the outpouring of the Spirit.[60] Scott was attracted to spiritual gifts as signs of the life which he felt ought to be more evident as the moving power of the Church, and while in Greenock during 1829-30 he preached from 1 Corinthians 12 on the subject of spiritual gifts. A minority of those who had been influenced by Campbell's preaching were moved to begin home meetings to seek the outpouring of the Spirit, among whom was Mary Campbell (no relation), whom Scott sought to convince of the

---

[58] Irving, 'Facts connected with the Recent Manifestation of Spiritual Gifts' (1832), 754-5; *idem, CW* (1864-5), ii. 276-7; see also Strachan, *Pentecostal Theology*, eh. 5. Irving drew his high view of the Church and its sacraments from the Scots Confession (1560).

[59] Irving, 'Facts connected with the Recent Manifestation of Spiritual Gifts' (1832), 755-6.

[60] Newell, 'A. J. Scott and his Circle' (1981), 37, following Campbell to Thomas Chalmers, 28 April 1830 (New College MSS, CHA 4.134.21), and D. Campbell, *Memorials of John McLeod Campbell* (London, 1877), i. 48.

distinction between regeneration and baptism with the Holy Ghost.[61]

Irving's Christology weighed heavily in favour of the idea that spiritual gifts were to be restored to the Church.[62] For some years, he had taught that 'all the works of Christ were done by the man anointed with the Holy Ghost, and not by the God mixing himself up with the man.' The implication was obvious, as Mary Campbell grasped: 'if Jesus as a man in my nature thus spake and thus performed mighty works by the Holy Ghost, which he even promiseth to me, then ought I in the same nature, by the same Spirit, to do likewise "the works which he did, and greater works than these."'[63] On 30 March 1830, she was the first to speak in unknown tongues.[64]

News of the gifts and the accompanying healings reached Irving in London at a critical point in his life: his son Samuel was seriously ill, and died on 6 July.[65] Irving wanted to believe that the gifts of which he heard, and whose reappearance appears to have come as a surprise to him, were real. Writing to Henry Drummond the following day, he expressed the conviction that if there had been one in London gifted with the power to work miracles, his son need not have died, and suggested that those who had remained at Albury after he left the Conference consider 1 Corinthians 12-14.[66] They studied Scott's recently-published work on 1 Corinthians 14, *Neglected Truths*,[67] concluding that it was the duty of believers generally to pray for the restoration of supernatural gifts, and their

---

[61] Irving, 'Facts connected with the Recent Manifestation of Spiritual Gifts' (1832), 755; Newell, 'A. J. Scott and his Circle' (1981), 67, 71.

[62] Strachan, The *Pentecostal Theology of Edward !ruing* (1973), 59. Campbell was already known for his advocacy of the doctrine of assurance of salvation; in contrast to the prevailing view in the Church of Scotland, he regarded it as the norm for Christians to experience the love of God shed abroad in their hearts by the Holy Ghost. This, for Campbell, was rooted in his understanding of the gospel, which stressed the universality of the love of God. This stress on the Spirit's work in the individual as something which could be felt would doubtless have strengthened the desire for the restoration of the supernatural spiritual gifts, as these also represented divine supernatural breaking upon human consciousness.

[63] Irving, 'Facts connected with the Recent Manifestation of Spiritual Gifts' (1832), 757.

[64] Strachan, The *Pentecostal Theology of Edward !ruing* (1973), 66.

[65] Oliphant, The *Life of Edward !ruing* (1870), 298.

[66] Northumberland Collection, C9/5. Thanks are due to His Grace the Duke of Northumberland for permission to quote from the letters in this collection.

[67] Newell, 'A. J. Scott and his Circle' (1981), 99; following C. W. Boase, *Supplementary Narrative to the Elijah Ministry* (Edinburgh, 1868), 750.

own responsibility to investigate the events taking place.[68]

It was not long before Irving began to reflect in print on the significance of the 'Gareloch Pentecost'. In the *Morning Watch* for September 1830, he published an article entitled 'The Church, with her Endowment of Holiness and Power', which showed how Christ exercised his rightful kingship over the world by means of the power of the promised Holy Spirit active in and through the Church.[69] Although they had been estranged for some years by this point, one can still hear echoes of Coleridge in Irving's words:

> The body is the organ by which the spirit within a man doth manifest itself to the world; and the body of Christ, which is the Church, is the organ by which He, acting from the invisible seat of the Father by the invisible Spirit, must manifest Himself unto the world. There is no other medium of communication between Christ abiding with the Father and the world but the Church in the flesh; and herein the Church in the body hath a manifest importance, and, I would say, preeminence of usefulness, over the Church disembodied, in that she is the organ of communication between the invisible Christ and the visible world.[70]

The gift of the Spirit to the Church consisted of inward holiness (the fruit of Christ's work in the flesh) and outward power (the first fruits of Christ's work at his coming again);[71] the supernatural powers mentioned in Mark 16:15-20 were the first fruits of Christ's rule over creation.[72] They confirmed the truth of the message preached, providing men with tangible evidence of the reality and power of God which would prove far more effective than the accepted evangelical means of outreach:

> The word preached is, that Christ hath redeemed men from the power of death; and in sign thereof we do in His name heal all manner of diseases, and upon occasion raise the dead, (as is recorded both of Peter and Paul;) and the conclusion is, that the name of Christ is indeed able to effect those things preached. The sign is part and parcel of the thing preached, and by being so confirms it. It is not an appeal to blind power, but it is an appeal to Jesus to confirm the truth preached, by giving a sign of His possessing this power which we assign to Him, and a first-fruits of that action which we preach Him about to perform.

---

[68] H. Drummond, *Narrative of the Circumstances which led to the Setting Up of the Church of Christ at Albury* (Albury: Privately published, 1834), 13.
[69] *CW* (1864-5), v. 451.
[70] *CW* (1864-5), v. 454.
[71] *CW* (1864-5), v. 453, 503.
[72] *CW* (1864-5), v. 460-5.

It is not by the transmission of this through eighteen centuries of tradition, that the unlearned world are to be convinced- a process by which, I will venture to say, that none but a few antiquaries were ever convinced; but it is by the abiding of them in, and the putting of them forth by, the Church, wherever and so long as she is established, until Christ come, that the world is to be taught that Jesus of Nazareth is the world's gracious Healer, and wise Teacher, and merciful Redeemer, and righteous Governor. It is not by putting a book into every man's hand, of the genuineness and authenticity of which it takes no mean store of learning to be convinced, but it is by a continuous Church holding forth the word of the gospel of life to the nations, and attesting the truth of what they declare concerning Jesus, by calling His name over all distressed nature, and giving it redemption and joy.[73]

Such signs had been lost through the Church's unfaithfulness, self-sufficiency and lack of mercy. Because believers were not using that into which they were baptised, the world had been deprived of a testimony and the purpose of God frustrated.[74] However, supernatural gifts had been intended to last until Christ's return, and though decayed they had not ceased.[75] Indeed, their renewal was inevitable, since the Church could not die: it must be revived, which meant that it would act according to the law of its constitution as the Church, i.e. in power as well as holiness, and thus manifest the work of Christ.[76] At this point, therefore, Irving provided an exposition of the purpose and theological significance of the various gifts.

In the *Morning Watch* for December 1830 Irving began a sequel to the previous article, 'On the Gifts of the Holy Ghost, commonly called supernatural'.[77] In the first section he expounded Psalm 68 and Ephesians 4, demonstrating that the gifts were given that Christ might construct a habitation in which God could dwell: 'Christ's work with the Spirit is to prepare for God such a living temple, such a speaking, acting body, as shall declare His presence to every beholder.'[78] This habitation, the Church, was built up as each gifted member was placed in position.[79] Irving now made a clear

---

[73] *CW* (1864-5), v. 476. The concluding sentences would have challenged the prevailing evangelistic methodology, which majored on the circulation of Scripture by Bible societies and the formation of para-church agencies for evangelistic purposes.

[74] CW(1864-5), v. 477.

[75] *CW* (1864-5), v. 499.

[76] *CW* (1864-5), v. 502.

[77] Strachan, *The Pentecostal Theology of Edward !ruing* (1973), eh. 9, provides a full exposition of this.

[78] *CW* (1864-5), v. 510, 516.

[79] CW(1864-5), v. 512, 517.

connection between Christ's union with us in our flesh, and our
union with him in his glorified state as the supernaturally
empowered giver of the Spirit.[8] Conversely, he connected the
Church's denial of the miraculous gifts with its denial that Christ
had assumed our human flesh.[81] The second section of 'The Gifts of
the Holy Ghost' appeared in June 1831.[82] It began by expounding
Isaiah 8:18 and then considered Isaiah 28 and 1 Corinthians 14,
again defending the necessity and permanence of the gifts, and in
particular the gift of tongues. The third section appeared in
September; continuing his exposition of 1 Corinthians 14, Irving
concluded that

> the true reason why the gift of tongues hath ceased to be in the Church
> is, the exaltation of natural methods of teaching above, or into
> copartnery with, the teaching of the Holy Ghost, the meanness of our
> idea, and the weakness of our faith, concerning the oneness of Christ
> glorified, with His Church on earth; the unworthiness of our doctrine
> concerning the person and office of the Holy Ghost, to knit up the
> believer into complete oneness with Christ, every thread and filament
> of our mortal humanity with His humanity, immortal and glorious; to
> bring down into the Church a complete Christ, and keep Him there,
> ever filling her bosom, and working in her members; the shortcoming
> of our knowledge, in respect to the gifts themselves; our having ceased
> to lament their absence, and to pray for their return; our want of
> fasting, and humiliation, and crying unto the Lord; our contentment to
> be without them; our base and false theories to account for their
> absence, without taking guilt to ourselves. Any one of these causes
> were sufficient, all of them are far more than sufficient, to account for
> their long absence from the bosom of the Church. These are the true
> reasons; and the commonly given reason, that they were designed only
> for a short time, is utterly false and most pernicious.[83]

Christology thus combined with Romantic idealism and
supernaturalism to produce a heady mixture. But what were the
effects to be in practice? One of those who had visited Scotland to
witness the charismata was J. B. Cardale, a young London lawyer
who attended the evangelical ministry of the Rev. Baptist W. Noel at
St. John's, Bedford Row. On his return in October, Cardale and
others testified to large meetings of what they had seen and heard,

---

[80] Strachan, *The Pentecostal Theology of Edward !ruing* (1973), 91.
[81] Strachan, *The Pentecostal Theology of Edward !ruing* (1973), 93.
[82] See Strachan, *The Pentecostal Theology of Edward !ruing* (1973), chapter
11, for an exposition.
[83] *CW* (1864-5), v. 560.

and groups began to meet in homes to pray for the gifts.[84] The first answer to their prayers came at Cardale's house on 5 April 1831, when his wife spoke 'in the power' (the phrase often used in describing manifestations of the gifts of tongues, interpretation and prophecy), 'The Lord will speak to His people! The Lord hastens His coming! He comes, He comes.' [85]

Irving seems to have proceeded more cautiously in relation to the gifts than is often believed. He had only been convinced that they were genuine after attending one of Cardale's prayer meetings in October 1830, and events in his church (presumably the investigation of his Christology by the Presbytery of London) kept him preoccupied until May 1831.[86] That month he instituted prayer meetings daily at 6:30 a.m. for the General Assembly of the Church of Scotland. His increasing isolation as a result of the condemnation of his doctrines by the General Assembly provided all the more impetus to seek supernatural tokens of divine approval upon his doctrines, which the manifestations would provide:

> We met together about two weeks before the meeting of the General Assembly, in order to pray that the General Assembly might be guided in judgment by the Lord, the Head of the Church; and we added thereto prayers for the present low state of the Church. We cried unto the Lord for apostles, prophets, evangelists, pastors, and teachers, anointed with the Holy Ghost, the gift of Jesus, because we saw it written in God's Word that these are the appointed ordinances for the edifying of the body of Jesus. We continued in prayer every morning, morning by morning, at half-past six o'clock; and the Lord was not long in answering our prayers.[87]

All the same, Irving was as yet unwilling to allow the gifts to be exercised in the Sunday services. At this stage, he sought to test both the manifestations and the gifted persons, and to allow opportunity for the congregation to examine the gifts for themselves in the

---

[84] Rossteuscher, 'The Rebuilding of the Church of Christ upon the Original Foundations' (1850), 231.

[85] Rossteuscher, 'The Rebuilding of the Church of Christ upon the Original Foundations' (1850), 237-8. Note the eschatological tone of the utterance, which was characteristic.

[86] Rossteuscher, 'The Rebuilding of the Church of Christ upon the Original Foundations' (1850), 232.

[87] Oliphant, *The Life of Edward !ruing* (1870), 318; see also W. Harding, *Trial of !ruing before the London Presbytery,* third edition (London, [1832]), 23.

context of the prayer meetings.[88]

Such caution, however, was overtaken by the events of Sunday 16 October 1831. During the morning service, a Miss Hall felt compelled to speak in tongues and prophesy and was constrained to leave the sanctuary, in accordance with the Trustees' stipulation that no utterances were to be permitted in the main building. Irving, it seems, had considered that it would be disorderly for the gifts to be manifested during a Sunday service, but he proceeded to interpret her hasty departure as symbolising the congregation's unwillingness to hear God's voice.[89] She could be heard speaking in the vestry, and pandemonium broke out. That afternoon, Miss Cardale warned Irving 'in the power' against resisting the Spirit and urged him and his Session to 'go outside the camp' to bear the reproach which would follow the manifestations. At the evening service he therefore reversed the Trustees' ruling.[90] Uproar the following Sunday led to Irving again banning charismatic manifestations during the services.[91] However, since the police were unwilling to provide protection unless allowed to arrest any speakers except the preacher, Irving changed his mind yet again, deciding to trust God rather than man, and lifted the ban from 20 November, making space for the gifts to be exercised in worship.[92]

Irving's actions led to long and anxious consultations with the Kirk Session.[93] Now prepared to lay everything on the line because of his belief that the manifestations were God-given, he offered a robust and principled defence of them. He considered the issue a doctrinal

---

[88] Rossteuscher, 'The Rebuilding of the Church of Christ upon the Original Foundations' (1850), 242-5.

[89] J. O. Tudor to Robert Baxter, 26 October 1831, in possession of Iain H. Murray, Edinburgh.

[90] For the events of the day, see R. Baxter, *Irvingism, in its Rise, Progress, and Present State* (London, 1836), 16-17; C. G. Flegg, *Gathered Under Apostles: A Study of the Catholic Apostolic Church* (Oxford, 1992), 51-2; E. Trimen, 'The Rise and Progress of the Work of the Lord' (transcript of lectures delivered in 1904, held in the Library of the British Orthodox Church, London), 21.

[91] Flegg, *Gathered Under Apostles* (1992), 52. In so doing, he may have been influenced by his recollections of a disastrous visit to Kirkcaldy in 1828, when at least thirty-five people died after a gallery packed with people who had come to hear him preach gave way and panic ensued; Oliphant, *The Life of Edward Irving* (1870), 235.

[92] Rossteuscher, 'The Rebuilding of the Church of Christ upon the Original Foundations' (1850), 249, 251.

[93] For details of this, see 'Regent Square Church: Trustee's Minute Book 1825-1848', United Reformed Church Historical Society Library, London.

one: these were gifts of God, to be received and submitted to, and he set out in a letter to the Trustees how he intended to regulate public manifestations, justifying his conduct in terms of the Church of Scotland's First and Second Books of Discipline.[94] The majority of the Trustees, however, did not accept his fundamental premise that God rather than a human being was speaking, and were unhappy at the disruption caused by the manifestations. For them, the question was one of discipline rather than doctrine, and thus it was to be settled not by Scripture but by the regulations obtaining in the Church of Scotland: the Trust Deed stipulated that worship was to be conducted by those authorised by the Church of Scotland. They offered Irving the compromise of allowing the gifts at the prayer meetings only, which he refused.[95] With evident reluctance to act thus against one whom they loved, they appealed to the Presbytery of London, who agreed to receive their complaint.[96] The trial began on 26 April; explaining the history of the manifestations in his church and how he had dealt with them, Irving again stated as his basic premise the belief that 'it is not persons but the Holy Ghost that speaketh in the church.'[97] Through the manifestations God was showing his Church what it should be:

> how shall the Lord show to us what he would have his church to be but by restoring to us the gift which was originally in his church? What can reconstitute his church but that which constituted it at first?[98]

Allowing the relevance of Irving's insistence that the court determine whether or not it was God who spoke through the manifestations, the Moderator nevertheless concluded that they were an unscriptural delusion, and contrary to the standards of the Church of Scotland.[99] Judgment was given that Irving should be removed as pastor, and when members of his congregation arrived for prayer on 4 May, they found themselves locked out of the building.[100] Mter a

---

[94] The letter appears in Oliphant, *The Life of Edward !ruing* (1870), 335-6.
[95] Davenport, *Albury Apostles* (1973), 62; Rossteuscher, 'The Rebuilding of the Church of Christ upon the Original Foundations' (1850), 265, 278.
[96] C. G. Strachan, 'Edward Irving and Regent Square: A Presbyterian Pentecost', *JPHSE* 14 (1968-72), 186. The Presbytery was appointed in the Trust Deed to arbitrate in disputes between the minister and the Trustees.
[97] Harding, *Trial of !ruing before the London Presbytery* (1832), 41.
[98] Harding, *Trial of !ruing before the London Presbytery* (1832), 50.
[99] Harding, *Trial of !ruing before the London Presbytery* (1832), 71-2, 82. Contrast Irving's belief that the permanence of the gifts was upheld by the standards of the Church of Scotland; Irving, *Confessions of Faith* (1831), xc.
[100] Harding, *Trial of !ruing before the London Presbytery* (1832), 87.

brief sojourn in the Socialist lecture hall off Gray's Inn Road, they settled in a converted picture gallery in Newman Street.

A major blow to Irving was the defection of one of the prophets, Robert Baxter, on the morning his trial began. An evangelical Anglican from Doncaster, Baxter had been occasionally associated with the group of 'Gifted persons' in Irving's church for about six months in 1831-32. His prophecies shaped the theology of the new movement, and foretold the rejection of existing orders of ministry and their replacement by new ones given by God, the 'spiritual ministry' (especially the reappearance of Apostles) endowed with supernatural gifts;[101] the condemnation of existing churches as apostate;[102] and a period of 1260 days to terminate on 14 July 1835, a date which he interpreted as referring to the rapture or translation of believers before the Second Coming, but which Catholic Apostolics afterwards referred to the 'Separation of the Apostles'.[103] Baxter's first two prophecies would have come as no surprise to Irving, given the conclusions of the Albury conferences quoted above. Baxter's defection was seized upon by the religious world, and served to isolate Irving still further. Ironically, this was the last thing Baxter wanted, since he believed that ostracism would only harden Irving's followers in their errors.[104]

Irving's stormy relationship with his spiritual mother now came to a head with his trial for heresy at Annan on 13 March 1833. When the sentence of condemnation was pronounced, Irving's friend David Dow (Church of Scotland minister at Irongray, near Dumfries) prophesied against the assembled body before being silenced; Irving rose to follow him out with the words, 'As many as will obey the Holy Ghost, let them depart!'- words which symbolised his ecclesiology as it had now developed.[105]

Irving's position as a minister became still more unclear: Drummond's ordination at Christmas 1832 as 'Angel' ('bishop' in the Ignatian sense) of the congregation in Albury led to consideration by

---

[101] Baxter, *Irvingism, in its Rise, Progress, and Present State* (1836), 20, 22; Davenport, *Albury Apostles* (1973), 60.

[102] Shaw, *The Catholic Apostolic Church* (1946), 41.

[103] Baxter, *Irvingism, in its Rise, Progress, and Present State* (1836), 19-20, 23; Shaw, *The Catholic Apostolic Church* (1946), 41.

[104] Baxter, *Irvingism, in its Rise, Progress, and Present State* (1836), 40. Hall also confessed to having faked prophecies, though her confession does not appear to have made the impact that Baxter's did (her written confession is in the hands of Iain H. Murray, Edinburgh).

[105] *Trial of Mr. Edward !ruing, late minister of the National Scotch Church, Regent Square, London; before the Presbytery of Annan, on 13th March, 1833* (Dumfries, 1833), 26.

the Prophets of Irving's situation. On 5 April 1833 Taplin announced that God 'purposed giving the mystery of the candlestick in the Holy Place', in other words, that a new pattern for church order was about to be revealed.[106] Shortly after this, Irving was temporarily inhibited from exercising his ministerial functions, which he saw as the Spirit's ratification of the sentence pronounced upon him by the Church of Scotland: 'I discerned, that He had indeed acknowledged the act of the fleshly church, taking away the fleshly thing.'[107] He was then ordained as Angel, prophecy indicating that as man had taken away fleshly ordinances God would give spiritual ones.[108]

Although his teaching had prepared the way for the manifestation of spiritual gifts in his congregation, Irving (with his high Reformed view of the pastoral ministry) did not always find it easy to accept the results.[109] He found it no easier living with Apostles (whose calling may have caught him off-balance just as Miss Hall's prophecy had done)[110] than he did with Prophets: 'I receive my instructions through the Apostle, but when he has delivered them to me, he must be the 1st to observe them, and I shall take care that he does so.'[111] Furthermore, it seems likely that his view of apostolic ministry, which had focused on their calling to break fresh ground with the Gospel, was at odds with the concept developing among those who were actually being called as apostles, which was much more concerned with ruling the church. Irving's death in December 1834 was seen as chastisement for his rebellion against the apostleship.[112] However, we would be wrong to accept Mrs Oliphant's picture of Irving as the good man brought down by the leaders of the new

---

[106] H. B. Copinger, 'Annals: The Lord's Work in the Nineteenth and Twentieth Centuries' (transcribed and edited by S. Newman-Norton, transcript, n.d., in British Orthodox Church Library, London), 33.

[107] Irving to D. Dow, April 1833, quoted in H. Drummond, *Narrative of the Circumstances* (1834), 34.

[108] F. V. Woodhouse, *Narrative of Events Affecting the Position and Prospects of the Whole Christian Church*, second edition (London, 1885), 20. It is possible to see these 'spiritual' ordinances as an anticipation of the millennia era.

[109] For evidence of this, see T. G. Grass, "The Taming of the Prophets': Bringing Prophecy under control in the Catholic Apostolic Church', *JEPTA* 16 (1996), 58-70.

[110] Rossteuscher, 'The Rebuilding of the Church of Christ upon the Original Foundations' (1850), 395.

[111] Rossteuscher, 'The Rebuilding of the Church of Christ upon the Original Foundations' (1850), 487.

[112] Woodhouse to Drummond, 14 December 1834 (Northumberland Collection, C9/50).

church, since he chose to submit to those called to office by the gifted persons, and Baxter was not far from the truth in stating that 'all the changes which took place in Mr. Irving's views and church arrangements, were in subservience and strict obedience to these utterances.'[113]

Neither should we accept the view that he recanted his belief in the manifestations. Catholic Apostolic sources imply that he died accepting the divine origin of the work:

> A few hours before his death, he sent for Mr. Woodhouse saying that he wished to confess his sins in resisting the bringing out of the Apostleship, and his jealousy of those who were his children, lest they should lead the flock astray. Having received absolution, he almost immediately passed away.[114]


### How did Irving Relate these Aspects of Theology?

The chief outlet for the views of the Albury circle was the quarterly *The Morning Watch.* It published many articles by Irving, and, as Mrs. Oliphant wrote,

> the chief thing which appears to me remarkable in these early numbers of the *Morning Watch,* is the manner in which Irving pervades the whole publication. Amid eight or ten independent writers his name occurs, not so much an authority, as an all-influencing, unquestionable presence, naturally and simply suggesting itself to all as somehow the centre of the entire matter.U[5]

According to Patterson, 'The Second Coming of Christ was made the lens through which every event and doctrine was interpreted and applied.'[116] While this judgment has a considerable measure of truth, we need to understand how things worked out over time. Although the journal began with an emphasis on eschatology and Christology, there does seem to have been a shift to consideration of ecclesiological issues (perhaps as a result of considering the place of the Church and the Jews in prophecy). When the miraculous gifts reappeared the journal devoted much of its space to examining them

---

[113] Baxter, *Irvingism, in its Rise, Progress, and Present State* (1836), 10.
[114] Copinger, 'Annals: The Lord's Work in the Nineteenth and Twentieth Centuries' (n.d.), 50. Woodhouse, who had been called as an apostle, had been sent to Glasgow to minister to Irving.
[115] Oliphant, The *Life of Edward !ruing* (1870), 258.
[116] Patterson, 'Designing the Last Days' (2001), 99.

and responding to evangelical opposition, which was viewed in terms of eschatological apostasy. It seems that the journal's changing emphases mirror what was going on in Irving's thinking and his ministry; but it is also clear that the writers saw eschatology, ecclesiology and pneumatology as intimately related.

The interplay between Irving's eschatological convictions and the charismatic manifestations is of particular interest. Preaching fostered the expectation of the gifts, and the gifts testified to the content of the preaching. According to Irving, the gifts would feature in the millennia! kingdom, and might even precede (and thus prepare for) its full manifestation.[117] Thus his developed eschatology clearly predisposed him to accept the idea of a revival at the end of the dispensation of the gifts which had marked its beginning, and to accept claims that this was taking place. But Irving's eschatologically-orientated preaching also fostered the expectation of such a restoration: 'it is the preaching of the Lord's coming which has re-awakened the Spirit in the church,' and since that doctrine was most strongly advocated at Regent Square, it was there that the gifts had been restored to confirm it.[118] Furthermore, Irving considered his proclamation of the doctrines of Christ's first coming in our flesh and his Second Coming in glory to be an essential prerequisite for the revival of the gifts, since apart from it there would have been nothing to which the Spirit could bear witness through the gifts.[119] The gifts thus testified to the validity of his theological views. In particular, they testified that restoration of the gifts was intended to prepare the Church for the imminent return of Christ.[120]

As part of this preparation, the manifestations testified to the belief that existing ordination was merely external and God would replace it with something better.[121] The gifted persons were the first

---

[117] Patterson, 'Designing the Last Days' (2001), 172, following *MW* 2 (1830), 302.

[118] Irving, 'Exposition on 18th December 1831', in *Sermons by Edward !ruing and Nicholas Armstrong* (1831-33), 43.

[119] Irving, 'Facts connected with the Recent Manifestation of Spiritual Gifts' (1832), 755. One of the main tests applied to the early 'gifted persons' was 1 John 4:1, which was interpreted as referring to Irving's Christology. For an example of this, see T. C. F. Stunt, 'Trying the Spirits: The Case of the Gloucestershire Clergyman', *JEH* 39 (1988), 95-105. Conversely, a decisive factor in Baxter's *uolte face* was his conclusion that Irving's Christology was in fact unorthodox; T. C. F. Stunt, *From Awakening to Secession: Radical Euangelicals in Switzerland and Britain 1815-35* (Edinburgh, 2000), 266.

[120] Baxter, *Iruingism, in its Rise, Progress, and Present State* (1836), 17.

[121] R. Norton, *Memoirs of James and George Macdonald, of Port-Glasgow* (London, 1840), 179.

fruits of a body separated from the apostate Church, which would testify to the Second Coming of Christ and be accredited by miracles.[122] The early church had failed to go on to perfection, but this time God's purpose would be fulfilled.[123] On the other hand, he also asserted that 'The work which God is setting his hand to, is not of reconstituting the primitive church, but redeeming his church out of the captivity of Babylon.'[124] We also see developed in the manifestations the idea of a restored Apostleship, seen as an eschatological sign. One who was at the early prayer meetings recalled, 'I remember hearing the cry in the Spirit, "Send us apostles – send us apostles." The room used to ring with it.'[125] However, the gifts were not the only factor in this expectation; another must be the idea (which Irving derived from Coleridge) of a certain outward form as necessary for the perfection of the Church. Since apostles were crucial to the working of the early Church, they must still be needed (as Irving himself had pointed out in *For Missionaries after the Apostolical School)*. More generally, since there was a real union between Christ and the church through the Spirit, the wonder was not that the gifts had reappeared, but that they should ever have ceased.[126] From this evidence, and from the events outlined above, we can see how the testimony of the manifestations both reinforced Irving's 'remnant' ecclesiology and gave shape to it.

Hugh McNeile, Drummond's rector at Albury, criticised the eschatologically-motivated idealism of Irving and Drummond:

> Filled with admiration of the predicted holiness and beauty of the *perfected* Church of Christ, at the second advent of her Lord, and looking at this truth alone, to the neglect of present duties arising out of other portions of holy Scripture [they] have become impatient of human infirmity, and determined to have a holy company even now. Forgetful of what manner of spirit they are themselves, they have hastily seceded from the militant and imperfect Church in which they

---

[122] 'Immediate events in the church unfolded from prophecy' (4 March 1832), in *Sermons by Edward Irving and Nicholas Armstrong* (1831-33), 9.
[123] Irving, 'An Interpretation of the fourteenth Chapter of the Apocalypse', *MW6* (1832), 266-7.
[124] Irving, 'An Interpretation of the fourteenth Chapter of the Apocalypse' (1832), 284.
[125] Quoted in R. Norton, *The Restoration of Apostles and Prophets in the Catholic Apostolic Church* (London, 1861), 25.
[126] Irving, 'Facts connected with the Recent Manifestations of Spiritual Gifts' (1832), 319.

were baptized, gone into diverse excesses of extravagant excitement, and denounced all who will not go with them.[127]

While there was a greater or lesser element of this in the attitude of most of the early leaders of what became the Catholic Apostolic Church (including Irving), such a verdict needs to be balanced by the recognition that Irving never considered that he or his congregation had arrived, in charismatic terms. Indeed, in 1833 he expressed the opinion that they had seen nothing yet: 'I am more and more convinced that the voice which we have in the church is not to be ranked in the order of the gifts, but as the voice in the wilderness preparing the steps of our King, and setting us therein'; gifts and ministries would come as a development of this.[128] He recognised, too, that however much his church went on to experience of the gifts, it would still only represent the first fruits of Christ's work as glorified King, which would not be completed until his return. This was the object of his hope as a theologian and as a pastor, and it was in this hope that he sought to shepherd his flock.

---

[127] Hugh McNeile, *Letters to a Friend* (1834), quoted by Carter, *Anglican Evangelicals* (2001), 187.
[128] Irving to Drummond, 27 March 1833 (Northumberland Collection, C9/16).

# CHAPTER 6

# A Millennia! Maelstrom: Controversy in the Continental Society in the 1820s

Kenneth J. Stewart

An inquisitive visitor to London during May in the 1820s had open before him the prospect of surveying the annual general meetings of some of the most dynamic Christian agencies in the world – the London Missionary Society, the Religious Tract Society and the British and Foreign Bible Society.[1] Though to modern minds, accustomed to rapid global dissemination of information, the idea of trekking from one society's annual meeting to another is distinctly unappealing, the Georgian evangelical did not necessarily see it this way. There was then no superior way of monitoring the pulse of these great agencies than the one just named: progressing from the annual meetings of one pan-evangelical agency to another.[2]

The meetings of the London Missionary Society (founded 1795), the Religious Tract Society (founded 1799) and the British and Foreign Bible Society (founded 1804) were, in fact, scheduled in a staggered fashion. Ministers of the Gospel and laymen from the regions and the capital city were often present for a succession of these meetings.[2] There was often overlap among the Boards of

---

[1] The author is happy to acknowledge the assistance rendered to him by Drs. Don Lewis and Ian S. Rennie, Vancouver, Canada, Timothy C. F. Stunt, Newtown, CT, and Mr. David Stewart, Princeton, NJ, in their reading and commenting on a preliminary draft of this paper.

[2] This era of pan-evangelical cooperation is well described in Roger Martin, *Evangelicals United: Ecumenical Stirrings in Pre-Victorian Britain, 1795-1830* (London, 1983).

[3] One person who has left a record of his sequential attendance at various May meetings is Sampson Wilder, an American merchant at Paris who journeyed to London to be present in 1816 and 1820. He thereafter helped to found affiliate Bible, tract and mission societies in the French capital. See

Directors of the agencies – a practice which could only encourage collaboration and sharing of resources. Similarly, it was not unknown for the same distinguished foreign visitor to be featured in the meetings of more than one society. Each of these agencies represented the collaborative efforts of evangelicals in the National and Dissenting Churches, though the L.M.S., flanked by explicitly Baptist and Anglican mission societies, primarily existed to further the missionary aspirations of Independents, Calvinistic Methodists and Presbyterians.

But our concern is not with these first-generation co-operative agencies (though they form the backdrop of our investigation), but with an agency of the second generation, the Continental Society for the Diffusion of Religious Knowledge. It too held annual meetings each May in Georgian London. Yet it had been conceived of only in early 1817 and formally inaugurated at London in the following year. The Continental Society was, to a large degree, the continuator of concerns for Europe which had always been present in the minds of the directors of the three older societies just named.[4] These had already placed some agents, Christian publications and Bibles in Europe since their own foundations; but as Europe was never more than a subsidiary interest of these agencies with their global objectives, there was clearly room left for collaboration and fresh initiative.

The new society was the joint inspiration of two British evangelicals of immense wealth: one a banker and former M.P., Henry Drummond, and the other a Scottish laird-turned preacher, Robert Haldane. The paths of the two had crossed at Geneva in the

---

*Records from the Life of S.V.S. Wilder* (New York, 1865), 76, 145. See also the record of the attendance at the May meetings in Robert Philip, *The Life, Times, and Missionary Enterprises of John Campbell* (London, 1841), 313.

[4] This continuity of purpose was especially evident between the London Missionary Society and the Continental. Of the thirty-six persons memorialised by John Morison in *Fathers and Founders of the L.M.S.* (London, 1844), ten were numbered among the supporters of the Continental Society in the 1820s. Of that number, three had journeyed for the L.M.S. to France in 1802 to investigate missionary prospects. The need for Scriptures in French figured significantly in the origin of the British and Foreign Bible Society; see Roger Martin, 'The Bible Society and the French Connection', *JURCHS* 3:7 (1985), 278-290. See also K. J. Stewart, 'Restoring the Reformation: British Evangelicals and the *Reveil* at Geneva 1816-1849' (unpublished Ph.D. dissertation, University of Edinburgh, 1991), chap. 4. L.M.S. founder John Townsend spoke in the 1823 meeting of the Continental Society of the continuity of effort between the cooperating agencies; see *Proceedings of the Continental Society* (1823), 76-7.

spring of 1817 as the Scot, Haldane, was completing a series of expository lectures on Paul's letter to the Romans. These lectures had not only gathered a large proportion of the theological students of the university, but had led to the conversion of many and the establishing of others who were poorly grounded in the Christian faith. As Haldane prepared to leave the city for Montauban in the south of France, Drummond – himself a recent convert to the evangelical faith- arrived from Genoa, where he had learned of the stirrings at Geneva from Swiss businessmen. Drummond in effect inherited a situation which Haldane had helped to create.[5] There were now theological students at Geneva whose own path to ordination and placement in the canton of Geneva and beyond would be blocked on account of their identification with Haldane and his attacks on the clergy and theological faculty of the city. As well, an independent evangelical church was in process of formation. Something would need to be done to deploy these enthusiastic young evangelicals. And so the idea of a missionary society employing indigenous workers began to be conceived. The society, which would pursue the principle of employing European evangelists and colporteurs with British funds, began fledgling efforts there and then with two workers;[6] Drummond and Haldane were operating on a 'handshake' basis. More consultation followed at Paris in April of 1818 with the society formally inaugurated at London, on October 20 of that year.[7]

---

[5] Regarding Henry Drummond, see Donald M. Lewis (ed.), *Blackwell Dictionary of Evangelical Biography* (Oxford, 1995), s.v. The standard source on Haldane is that of his nephew; see Alexander Haldane, *The Lives of Robert and James Alexander Haldane* (London, 1852). An account of the Genevan activity of both is found in A. L. Drummond, 'Robert Haldane at Geneva, 1816-17', *RSCHS* 9 (1947), 69-82; A. L. Drummond, *The Kirk and the Continent* (Edinburgh, 1956); Deryck W. Lovegrove, 'The Voice of Reproach and Outrage: The Impact of Robert Haldane on French-Speaking Protestantism', in D. W. D. Shaw (ed.), *In Divers Manners* (St. Andrews, 1990); Stewart, 'Restoring the Reformation' (1991); Lewis (ed.), *Blackwell Dictionary of Evangelical Biography* (1995), s.v. 'Robert Haldane'; and T.C.F. Stunt, 'Geneva and British Evangelicals in the Early 19th Century', *JEH* 32:1 (1981), 35-46, and *From Awakening to Secession: Radical Evangelicals in Switzerland and Britain 1815-35* (Edinburgh, 2000), *passim*.

[6] *Report of the Continental Society* (1819), 8.

[7] The young American pastor, Matthias Bruen, then in London, was present at the inaugural London meeting. He was also an eyewitness of Haldane's Geneva ministry; Mary Lundie, *Memoir of Matthias Bruen* (New York, 1832), 108.

## The Continental Society: A Strong Beginning

An organization which was undergirded by so extensive a reconnoitering of the European scene as had just been carried out by Haldane and Drummond and which had at its call so extensive a network of potential workers in Switzerland and France was assuredly poised for a strong formal launch.[8] As it turned out, a considerable following was gathered for the inauguration of the society at London. Especially of note was the fact that the Continental Society was a truly interdenominational mission agency – uniting Anglicans, Presbyterians, Independents, Baptists, and Methodists in support of European mission. The posture was a deliberate one which found expression in a stated objective: 'To assist local native ministers in preaching the gospel and in distributing Bibles, Testaments and Religious publications over the Continent of Europe, but without the design of establishing any distinct sect or party'.[9] The society sought, furthermore, to safeguard this stance of non-sectarianism by pledging that Britain's denominational differences would not be exported to Europe. No Briton would ever be employed.

A survey of the early annual reports of the society makes plain that this agency was rapidly successful in meeting its objectives at home and abroad. It could soon count among its members and contributors such Anglicans as Charles Simeon, Zachary Macaulay, Josiah Pratt and Hugh McNeile, such Independents as David Bogue, Rowland Hill, George Burder, John Angell James, and John Pye Smith, Presbyterians such as Alexander Waugh, Robert Gordon, John Love, and Edward Irving, Scottish Baptists such as Robert and James A Haldane, and the Methodist leader Jabez Bunting.[10] At least eight past or current members of Parliament were connected with the society – the most famous being William Wilberforce.[11] Not only in support, but in extent of operations there was great reason to be encouraged. From the initial two agents employed in impromptu

---

[8] Haldane's work among theological students at Geneva was followed by similar work at Montauban, then home to France's only Reformed seminary; Haldane, *The Lives of Robert and James Alexander Haldane* (1852), chapter 19.

[9] *Report of the Continental Society* (1819), 3, 4.

[10] The names of these representative supporters are found listed either as committee members or as contributors in the *Report* (from 1822, *Proceedings) of the Continental Society* (London, 1819-1832).

[11] The others being Thomas Baring, Henry Drummond, R. H. Inglis, Thomas Lefroy, George Montagu, Spencer Perceval Jr., and Abel Smith. Again, these may be noted in the *Reports* or *Proceedings.*

fashion at Geneva in the spring of 1817 for ministries of itinerant preaching and Scripture distribution, the number had grown to four by the time the first published *Report* was issued for the 1819 annual meeting; fifteen were at work by 1822 and thirty-one by 1829. London Independents and Presbyterians gathered on a number of occasions beginning in 1821 to examine and ordain those agents for whom such certification was necessary to satisfy the European authorities.[12]

While the initial and major sphere of operation was Francophone Europe, by the 1821-22 period the Society was seeking to place an agent in Spain.[13] European committees were established in two cities to aid in the selection of local workers.[14] In 1823, the Society employed a German who had temporarily resided in Scotland as its agent in Hamburg and by 1825 claimed to employ five agents in German regions.[15] An agent first visited Austria in 1823 while another settled in Norway in 1828.[16] The committee of the Continental Society sent one of their own number, a Captain Cotton, to visit personally each European site in which their agents laboured in 1827.[17] This energetic interdenominational labour brought very welcome words of encouragement from a European Christian of stature, Professor August Tholuck of Halle, who addressed their annual meeting in 1825 and urged the rapid expansion of their work.[18]

Such exponential growth could only be sustained by the mounting

---

[12] Agents Henri Pyt and M. Falle were so ordained in July 1821 at Poultry Chapel, London; Felix Neff was similarly ordained in May 1823. See Emil Guers, *Vie de Pyt* (Toulouse, 1850), 130; and Ami Bost, *Life of Felix Neff* (London, 1855), 110, 111. Agent Carlos Von Bulow was ordained in the same church in the spring of 1827; *Proceedings* (1827), 51.

[13] *Report* (1821), 15. An agent visiting Spain in 1823 stayed long enough to distribute 500 Spanish New Testaments; *Proceedings* (1824), 6.

[14] *Proceedings* (1822), 36, would indicate only that the two cities with personnel committees were 'G_' and 'M_' (likely Geneva and Montauban). It was believed that the security of operations required this measure of anonymity.

[15] *Proceedings* (1824), 6, 49-52, and John Hunt Cooke, *Johann Gerhard Oncken* (London, 1908), 24. Oncken appeared in person to speak at the meeting of 1828; *Proceedings* (1828), 42. Oncken's work has most recently been investigated by Wayne Detzler, 'Johann Gerhard Oncken's Long Road to Toleration', *JETS* 36:2 (1993), 229-40.

[16] *Proceedings* (1827), 51; *Proceedings* (1828), 7. The agent was Carlos von Bulow. See also footnote 12, above.

[17] *Proceedings* (1827), 7.

[18] *Proceedings* (1825), 41.

of a much wider appeal to the Christian public. A promotional trip through Scotland in March 1821 led to the creation of auxiliary societies in Edinburgh and Glasgow, and supporting committees in Dundee, Perth, Stirling and Paisley.[19] By the following year, such auxiliary societies existed at Belfast and Dublin, in Ireland,[20] and by 1826 the society had auxiliaries in thirty English cities.[21] Such a support base made possible a rise in mission income from £200 in 1821 to £1625 by 1825, and £2733 by 1826.[22] These were very considerable sums for an organization only a decade old. Collaboration with the longer-established pan-evangelical agencies made the Continental Society's resources go farther. The printed *Proceedings* repeatedly pay tribute to the benevolence of the Bible and Tract societies in making Christian literature and Scriptures available for economical distribution through the agents of the younger society.[23] These resources were often channelled through the European auxiliary societies which the Bible and tract organizations had nurtured and encouraged at the end of the Napoleonic Wars.

## The 1820s: Four Waves of Controversy for the Continental Society

Why should not this upward trajectory of progress and expansion have continued indefinitely? The sober fact is that the decade of the

---

[19] *Report* (1821), 9, 10. The promotional tour was undertaken on behalf of the Society by its secretary, Isaac Saunders, and one regular member, the Rev. S. R. Drummond.

[20] *Proceedings* (1822), 5, 6. Robert Haldane and a French agent, Pierre Mejanel, had itinerated through Scotland and Ireland on behalf of the Continental Society in this period.

[21] *Proceedings* (1825), 1.

[22] The *Proceedings* of 1821 is the first report to list specific receipts and expenditures. Yet it can be stressed that the £200 contributed for 1820-21 exceeded the expenditures of the L.M.S. or R.T.S. for Francophone Europe for any year in this era. See 'L.M.S. handlist: Disbursements to France 1800-1837', L.M.S. Archive, University of London; William Jones, *Jubilee Memorial of the Religious Tract Society 1799-1849* (London, 1849), 284. For the purpose of overall comparison it may be noted that the total annual income in mid-decade for the R.T.S. was £12,568 and for the L.M.S. £38,860. See Jones, *Jubilee Memorial* (1849), Appendix 1; and Richard Lovett, *History of the L.M.S.* (London, 1899), ii. 753.

[23] See, for example, *Report* (1821), 19; *Proceedings* (1822), 38, 39; *Proceedings* (1824), 15; *Proceedings* (1829), 10. Oddly, the biographer of Haldane claims that the B.F.B.S. refused to supply Scriptures to prominent Continental Society agents; Haldane, *Lives of Robert and James Alexander Haldane* (1852), 507.

1820s was one in which the Continental Society passed through four controversies which aggregately worked to dissolve the bond of pan-evangelical goodwill. Of the four controversies, only one – the first – was a strictly internal matter.

## *1. Baptistic and Restorationist Practices*

As early as 1821, evidence emerged that some agents of the Society in Francophone Europe had engendered strife by advocating practices which the majority of the sponsoring membership in Britain could not endorse. The annual meeting at London requested to know, 'what are the sentiments of the agents in doctrine and discipline?' In reply it was explained that while the majority of the agents were connected to the Reformed Church of France, there were also two Baptists and two ex-Catholics. Two of these (presumably the Baptists) had in fact engaged in advocacy of adult baptism and had carried out this rite in two settings.[24] Plainly, such practices went contrary to the convictions of many Society members; an explanation was therefore demanded. The governors did their best to douse these flames of controversy by providing assurances that the agents of the Society were all in doctrinal accord with the Articles of the Church of England and the Shorter Catechism. Yet their efforts to assure the membership that all was well seem to have involved only a partial disclosure of a complex situation. These problems of doctrine and discipline would continue to plague the society as a direct outworking of the fact that so many of the agents had been recruited through earlier contacts with Henry Drummond and Robert Haldane.

These men, whom we have identified as the originators of the Society, were themselves of a decidedly 'restorationist' outlook. Haldane, the older of the two, had moved beyond his national Church (the Church of Scotland) in 1799 and passed successively through a sponsoring of connectional Independency to what may be called a Sandemanian Baptist position, all in advance of his journey to Europe. He had plainly imparted more than a simple 'ruin and redemption' exposition of Romans to his young Francophone disciples; restorationist practices such as the weekly Lord's Supper, the kiss of peace, multiple eldership (i.e. joint pastorates), and mutual admonition (spontaneous utterances delivered in a fellowship meeting) seemed to crop up regularly in the wake of his travels. Those influenced by him were seldom afterwards so warmly

---

[24] *Proceedings* (1821), 15-16.

inclined as before to ally themselves with national churches.[25] Drummond, for his part, while still likely a communicant of the Church of England at the time of the society's foundation,[26] was plainly moving in the direction of suspecting all national churches of apostasy. The troubles among the agents, then, in 'doctrine and discipline' were troubles which Haldane and Drummond would have done nothing to prevent and quite likely, something to promote. In 1821 the Society accepted the assurances given, and carried on.[27] Yet

---

[25] That all these practices occurred in the Genevan circle from which Haldane parted is clearly indicated by the record of participants and visitors; see *New Evangelical Magazine* 4 (1818), 96. David Bogue and James Bennett, *A History of Dissenters from the Revolution Under King William to the year 1808* (London, 1808), iv. 124-5, had attributed all these features to the pre-European ministry of Haldane. It is Stunt's view that these restorationist practices were already in place among persons attending a Moravian-pietist circle in Geneva, the Societe des Amis, which included numerous theological students subsequently influenced by Haldane; see T.C.F. Stunt, 'Diversity and Strivings for Unity in the Early Swiss Reveil', in R. N. Swanson (ed.), *Unity and Diversity in the Church* (Oxford, 1996), 351-362. The present writer acknowledges the prior existence of that circle, but believes the correspondence of the practices championed by Haldane c. 1808 in his homeland and those occurring at Geneva c. 1817 to be too great for the theory of local origin to explain them. The matter was certainly not clarified by the nineteenth century Haldane biographer, who emphatically denied that while his subject was in Geneva, he in any way 'advocated the questions which agitated and divided the Congregational Churches of Scotland'; Haldane, *Lives of Robert and James Alexander Haldane* (1852), 425, 229, 431.

[26] We infer Drummond's continuation in the Church of England primarily from his exercise of patronage in the appointing of Hugh McNeile to the living of Albury in 1823. Drummond considered himself a member of William Dodsworth's Chapel at Margaret Street when in London until 1831 when he began to attend Irving's chapel; see Stunt, *From Awakening to Secession* (2000), 167. However, Grayson Carter indicates that Drummond had some involvement with a member of another prominent London banking family, Thomas Baring, who was active in the Western Schism of 1815, a movement among certain evangelicals in the West Country leading to withdrawal from Anglicanism; see Lewis (ed.), *Blackwell Dictionary of Evangelical Biography* (1995), s.v. 'Henry Drummond'. Yet Carter admits that it is not certain that Baring (who would later be president of the Continental Society, 1818-1827) himself seceded. See Grayson Carter, *Anglican Evangelicals: Protestant Secessions from the via media, c. 1800-1850* (Oxford, 2001), 111, 160-72.

[27] Robert Haldane had been first the patron and latterly the scourge of early Independency in Scotland upon his own withdrawal from the Church of Scotland in 1799. But he upset an Independent movement (consisting of

the underlying issues pertaining to the doctrine and practice of the agents were never truly resolved.[28] The supporters of the young Society had never anticipated that persons with perspectives so different from their own on these questions would be their pioneer agents.

## *II. The Apocrypha Controversy*

There were also three issues not properly part of the Society's own internal affairs, which adversely affected the organization's ability to function. The involvement of prominent Society members as individuals in these controversies reverberated through the Continental Society as a whole. I will refer to the first and last of these here in a compressed way so as to develop most fully the second. Mention has already been made, above, of the cordial and fraternal working relationship enjoyed by the Continental Society with the older British and Foreign Bible Society. In its first half-decade of existence the former was more than happy to engage in Scripture distribution in Europe in league with the British and Foreign Bible Society and its European affiliates. The older society provided the Scriptures and the younger provided the colporteurs who distributed. In this half-decade, the Continental Society raised no objection to the distribution of the Bible most familiar to Francophones, the De Sacy New Testament and Martin Bible; the latter naturally contained the apocryphal or deutero-canonical

---

eighty-five congregations), which looked to him as financial patron, when, with his brother, he adopted a restorationist and Baptistic perspective in 1808. This was all remembered clearly in 1818, when a writer for the Nonconformist *Eclectic Review* reminded his readers of 'the chilling effects' of Haldane's earlier predilection for 'the Sandemanian hypothesis'; *Eclectic Review* 27 (1818), 13. This was a clear reference to the disruptiveness of 1808.

28 One of the earliest and most enduring agents of the Society, Henri Pyt, never overcame his restorationist and Baptistic principles, though for a time he struggled to overcome the latter. Churches formed under his labours in the 1820s often wished to be called 'neither Protestant or Catholic'. Yet in 1832, the Society accepted a proposal that he be made their chief agent for France; see Emil Guers, *Vie de Pyt* (Toulouse, 1850), 112, 136, 297. Pierre Mejanel, similarly one of the earliest agents of the Society and Pyt's predecessor as chief agent for France, was eventually carried by his longstanding restorationist leanings into the Catholic Apostolic movement which spread to France after 1832; see Alice Wemyss, *Le Reveil 1790-1849* (Toulouse, 1977), 103, and Stunt, *From Awakening to Secession* (2000), *passim.*

writings. The printing of these by the Bible Societies and their distribution by the colporteurs of the Continental Society was not so much an endorsement of the disputed writings as an action recognizing that nominal Catholics would be reluctant to accept any Bible from which they were absent. The arrangement seemed to work well and Scripture distribution went forward.[29]

Yet by 1826, acting in a private capacity, persons so prominent in the Continental Society as Henry Drummond, Hugh McNeile, rector of Albury, and Robert Haldane had entered into controversy with the British and Foreign Bible Society in this matter. They joined with others to charge that the Bible Society, in printing Bibles which included the apocryphal writings, had departed from its original mandate to print only the Holy Scriptures without note or comment.[30] The controversy divided the Bible Society and rival Bible societies began in both London and Edinburgh. Drummond, McNeile, Haldane and their supporters apparently made some headway with this cause within the Continental Society, for by 1826 the society was cautioning its agents to 'promote as much as possible the circulation of the Scriptures *exclusive* of the Apocrypha'.[31] But confusion was in the wind. At the 1827 May meeting, Hugh McNeile, representing the committee of the Society, found it necessary to openly combat the rumour that the Continental Society 'was opposed to the Bible Society'.[32] McNeile gallantly admitted that the quarrel with the Bible Society had been that of himself and Henry Drummond, not that of the mission society itself. He rejoiced that the Bible Society itself had reviewed and reversed its earlier decision to print Bibles including the Apocrypha. But here was an admission that two societies which had formerly operated fraternally were perceived to be at odds. That perception, however formed, was an ill wind for the younger society.

---

[29] *Report* (1821), 19; *Proceedings* (1822), 38, 39. The Society agent in the High Alps, Felix Neff, found it impossible in 1822 to distribute Bibles without the Apocrypha; see Ami Bost, *Letters and Biography of F. Neff* (London, 1855), 251.

[30] Hugh McNeile was, from 1824, a prominent member of the Continental Society's committee of management. Robert Haldane, though resident in Scotland, continued to be the Society's largest benefactor after Henry Drummond; see *Proceedings* (1824), preface and records of donations 1821-32. The controversy targeted not only the inclusion of the Apocrypha, but the welcome given by the B.F.B.S. to members who did not affirm the Trinity.

[31] *Proceedings* (1826), 16.

[32] *Proceedings* (1827), 115.

## *III. Controversy over Edward Irving*

Similarly, the Society suffered loss of the public's confidence through the increasing notoriety beginning in 1827, of prominent committee member Edward Irving, always closely associated with Henry Drummond.[33] From that year onward Irving, minister of London's Regent Square Church of Scotland, began to be associated with controversy over the relationship of Christ's human nature to sin. In time, he was charged and found guilty of heresy in the matter. But before that matter could be fully resolved, Irving was also, from 1830, the centre of a movement seeking the restoration of the charismatic gifts of the apostolic age. The London congregation he served became the site to which persons claiming the gifts gravitated.[34] Now this double-barrelled controversy placed the Continental Society in a very embarrassing situation for he had been featured as anniversary preacher and had served as member of the executive. In consequence, Irving was denied his role in the management of the society after 1829;[35] yet the matter had gone on too long. The public once more had reason to question the integrity of a mission society in which such persons played prominent roles; support sagged.[36]

---

[33] Irving had been active in the Society since as early as 1823 and was on the committee of management in 1828 and 1829.

[34] The standard account is provided in A. L. Drummond, *Edward !ruing and His Circle* (London, [1937]). Irving's popular ministry had drawn crowds which could no longer be accommodated at Hatton Garden. A new edifice, Regent Square, was the scene of his ministry from 1827.

[35] This inference is drawn from the omission of Irving's name from the *Proceedings* after that year and the claim of agent Henri Pyt, that he was promptly removed from the committee 'as soon as he propagated his errors'; see Guers, *Vie de Pyt* (1850), 296.

[36] Between 1829 and 1832, *Proceedings* are unavailable, but in that period donations had fallen from £2440 to £1909. The crisis brought upon the Society was plainly felt among its Francophone agents. Henri Pyt, from 1832 the central agent of the Society in France, observed on the basis of a trip to Britain in that year that 'the Society was quickly abandoned both by the supporters of Irving and by those who were opposed to the continued involvement in the Society of his comrade, Drummond'; see Guers, *Vie de Pyt* (1850), 296. Guers also records that this debacle in the Continental Society was shortly followed by efforts to direct evangelical itineration in France by an indigenous society based at Paris, the Societe Evangelique Fran<yaise. Dissolution of interdenominational goodwill was signalled by both the withdrawal of former Continental Society members in order to support the new Paris organization directly, and also by the formation of a Baptist Continental Society; see *The Evangelical Magazine* 12 n.s. (1834), 158.

### *IV. Controversy over Premillennialism*

But it is now time to take up the middle controversy of three; like the tumults of the apocrypha and Irvingite controversies, this also was a case of Society members whose agitation of questions outside the mission organization inevitably affected the affairs of the Society itself. I refer to the rise of strident premillennialism in the 1820s.

For the last half-century it has been commonly asserted that a strident historicist (as distinguished from futurist) premillennialism controlled the outlook of the Continental Society.[37] LeRoy Froom, that oft-quoted but undisguised Adventist apologist, insisted in 1946 that this Society had as its supreme motive 'heralding the impending judgement hour', and had as its 'real purpose' and 'unchanging keynote' the summoning of Europe to come out of 'Mystical Babylon'.[38] In more recent times, Froom's judgement has been followed by the better-esteemed Ernest Sandeen, who gave it as his opinion that the Continental Society was 'very quickly dominated by millenarian concerns'.[39] Froom, to his credit, had surveyed eight annual *Proceedings* of the Society in the 1819-1836 period before making his assertions.[40] Yet there are very good reasons for disputing his characterizations. It is not exaggerating the matter to suggest that in his partisan zeal, he investigated the Society only so far as was necessary to fuel his contention that premillennialism was in the ascendant.[41] What is of great significance for us is not simply

---

[37] Historicist premillennialism holds that the Biblical prophecies pertaining to last things and the return of Christ have been in process of fulfilment across the centuries of Christian history. There are, naturally, differences of opinion as to where the Christian church stands in the process of fulfilment at any given time. Futurist premillennialism, which arose in the 1820s, held that the bulk of biblical prophecies are as yet unfulfilled and await fulfilment at some indefinite future point.

[38] L. E. Froom, *The Prophetic Faith of Our Fathers* (Washington, DC, 1946), iii. 441-46.

[39] Ernest Sandeen, *The Roots of Fundamentalism: British and American Millenarianism 1800-1930* (Grand Rapids, 1978), 17. Sandeen names Froom's *Prophetic Faith* (1946) as the basis for this judgment, yet Sandeen had surveyed no printed *Records* or *Proceedings* of the Society, whereas Froom had.

[40] The present writer has located fourteen annual *Proceedings* of the Society and its successors, the European Missionary Society and the Foreign Aid Society.

[41] Indeed, so great was Froom's concern to press his millennial hypothesis, that he contended that the Evangelical Revival of the preceding century was itself the consequence of the superseding of the 'desolating flood' of older postmillennialism by the 'counteracting antidote' of premillennialism. From

what Froom found in those materials, but what he overlooked. In fact, two viewpoints clashed within the Continental Society. What is at stake here, I would stress, is not simply the truth about a modest-sized mission society in the 1820s, but more importantly, the accurate characterization of evangelical thought in pre-Victorian Britain. Was the 'wind' of premillennialism truly so ascendant as Froom suggested? The evidence suggests otherwise.[42]

It will be my aim, in what follows, to show that the Continental Society mirrored then-contemporary disagreements in British evangelical Christianity over the relationship of the present world-order to the events surrounding Christ's return; that the pan-evangelical supporters of the Society, overlapping so substantially with the constituencies of the existing missionary, tract and Bible societies, largely reflected the still-prevalent older optimistic eschatology which had undergirded them; that it was supremely the steady efforts of the Society's eo-founding patron, Henry Drummond, which ensured that a circle of self-conscious premillennialists, nurtured in Drummond's enclave for prophetic study known as the Albury Conferences, progressively assumed places of influence in the Continental Society and used its annual meetings as a springboard for their views; and that it was the inner-Society discord resulting from this clash of divergent views over the relation of the present world-order to the events surrounding Christ's return which ensured the steady decline of its reputation without, the dissolving of pan-evangelical goodwill within, and eventual inability to cope with the sharp crisis provoked by the strange doctrines of Edward Irving. In short, this quarrel more than any other doomed this society.

### The Continental Society: A Mirror of the Outlook of British Evangelical Christianity

The ministers and laymen who supported the Continental Society should be seen as a representative section of those British evangelical Christians who observed the revolutionary era in France

---

this vigorous counteraction had flowed religious awakening and the birth of the missionary societies; Froom, *Prophetic Faith* (1946), iii. 265.

[42] One may consult with profit the survey of this period provided by David Bebbington, *Evangelicalism in Modern Britain: A History from the 1730s to the 1980s* (London, 1989), chapter 3; Iain H. Murray, The *Puritan Hope: Revival and the Interpretation of Prophecy* (London, 1971), chapter 9; Ian S. Rennie, 'Nineteenth Century Roots of Prophetic Interpretation', in Carl E. Armerding and W. Ward Gasque (eds), *Dreams, Visions, and Oracles:* The *Layman's Guide to Biblical Prophecy* (Grand Rapids, 1977); and Sandeen, *Roots of Fundamentalism* (1978), *passim.*

(1789-1815) with a mixture of expectation and apprehension. The sense of expectation was attributable to the fact that the decades immediately preceding this revolution had been decades of heightened spiritual awareness – the era we call the Evangelical Revival. The Christian optimism engendered by this era of Christian advance had itself strengthened the launch of the missionary, tract and Bible societies of which we have made mention.[43] In the early decades of the nineteenth century the implications of this movement for society were still being worked out in campaigns against slavery, degrading prison conditions and the like. The difficulty however (and this is what gave root to the apprehension) lay in determining whether the events of the revolution in France furthered or retarded the world-changing purposes of God which the preceding revival had seemed to display.

There was plainly a cleavage on this question between persons loyal to the national churches of England and Scotland and those who were nonconformist.[44] The latter saw in the granting of complete religious liberty to French Protestants and the extension to them of a government subsidy comparable to that awarded Catholicism, a harbinger of their own possible deliverance from the handicaps imposed by the terms of the Act of Toleration a century before. English Independents, Presbyterians, Baptists and Methodists could neither vote nor sit in Parliament as the nineteenth century dawned; their chapels could only be erected by the obtaining of a licence and their marriages registered only when solemnized by an Anglican rector. They regretted the wanton bloodshed of the revolutionary era, the subsequent era of de-Christianization (which temporarily closed all churches) and the spread of French military dominance into surrounding nations; yet they concluded that on the whole, the revolutionary era was tending to further the purposes of God in opening up France to the influences of the Gospel. Thus the London Missionary Society was surveying France as early as 1802 so as to take advantage of the changed climate there.[45] The progress of the

---

[43] On this subject, one may consult with profit the essay of Stephen Orchard, 'Evangelical Eschatology and the Missionary Awakening', *JRH* 22:2 (1998), 132-151.

[44] The literature describing this era is extensive. See Stephen Pricket, *England and the French Revolution* (London, 1989); V. Kiernan, 'Evangelicalism and the French Revolution', *PP* 1 (1952), 44-56; Deryck W. Lovegrove, 'English Evangelical Dissent and the European Conflict 1789-1815', in W. J. Sheils (ed.), *Persecution and Toleration: Studies in Church History,* 20 (Oxford, 1983), 263-71.

[45] We have alluded to this activity above at footnote 3, above. The early L.M.S. activity following the Peace of Amiens (1802) is described in the

kingdom of Christ on earth had, on the whole, been assisted by this era as by the preceding.

Supporters of the national churches of Britain, however much they may have recognized the advance of the purposes of God in their nation's spiritual awakening prior to the revolution, found reason to be dismayed by the patterns of events which the revolution displayed. The arrest and eventual execution of the French king, the confiscation of church lands in order to stave off government bankruptcy, and the general lawlessness of the period we know as the 'reign of terror' all served to illustrate the anarchy into which Britain might descend if revolution came to her shores. As for Napoleon, he was judged to be 'Satan personified and his legions'.[46] Of great significance for us is the fact that this attitude towards the revolutionary events, lodged deeply in the minds of supporters of the national churches of Britain, inclined very many to view post-war events at home as just so many examples of a hellish revolutionary tendency at work in Britain. It was not simply evangelicals in the national churches, but fellow churchmen of other theological outlooks who viewed the Catholic Emancipation Bill (1829), the Reform Bill (1832) and the rise of working class agitation as disturbing evidences of the spread of European leaven.[47] To such

---

biographies of two persons commissioned by that society to conduct the survey; see James Hay and Henry Belfrage, *Memoir of Alexander Waugh D.D.* (Edinburgh, 1839), 164; James Bennett, *Memoir of the Life of David Bogue* (London, 1827), 227; and Stewart, 'Restoring the Reformation' (1991), 110-116.

[46] The perspective of various evangelical ministers in the Anglican establishment on such questions is available through the recorded dialogues preserved in J. H. Pratt (ed.), *The Thought of the Evangelical Leaders: Notes of the Discussions of the Eclectic Society, London 1798-1814* (London, 1856). Thus, in 1801, with the Peace of Amiens being negotiated, this society met on 26 October and discussed the question 'What have been the signal interpositions of Providence in favour of Britain during the late war?' The judgment of the members present was that Britain had been miraculously rescued 'from the principles of the French Revolution, which threatened to bring ruin on all constitutional governments'. In such troubles 'God had interposed and fought for England' (235). The remark regarding Napoleon was that of the Rev. John Venn, recorded in the Eclectic meeting for 21 May 1804 (331).

[47] The tendency to view domestic upheaval as related to apocalyptic prophecy was most commonly, but not exclusively, found in evangelicalism. A growing body of literature illustrates that Tractarians like E. B. Pusey, and J. H. Newman viewed these domestic developments in an apocalyptic framework; see, for instance, Sheridan Gilley, 'Newman and Prophecy', *JURCHS* 3:5 (1985), 160-188; David N. Hempton, 'Evangelicalism and Eschatology', *JEH*

minds, the revolutionary era and its aftershocks were symptoms of the decay of society and of the impending day of judgement.

Representatives of both the optimistic and apprehensive outlooks would be heard in the meetings of the Continental Society. But with these differences of perspective acknowledged, there were certain things about which the pan-evangelicals could agree. As it had been generally accepted since Reformation times that the Pope fitted the description of the Antichrist described in the New Testament, it was felt to be a grave lapse of judgement for the Government of Britain to have provided a haven for Catholic clergy who fled France after 1792. Conversely, there was satisfaction expressed at the way in which the young commander, Napoleon, had humiliated the Pope by stripping away some of his territories and wealth in 1797. There was a kind of consternation mixed with satisfaction at the British role at the Council of Vienna (1815); British supporters of the national churches may have rejoiced at the restoration of the monarchy to France – yet they also observed with alarm, as did nonconformists, the consequent rapid re-cementing of the old relationship between the Bourbon monarchy and the papacy. Yet for all that, there was a growing consciousness that Britain's preservation and triumph in the military conflict with France had delineated for her a role as God's instrument in leading the world for years to come.[48] The pan-evangelical membership of the Society reflected the still-prevalent older, more optimistic eschatology which had undergirded the earlier pan-Evangelical Societies.

An upsurge in the more apprehensive premillennial thinking about the Christian future can be traced from 1806, the year when G. S. Faber published his *Dissertations on the Prophesies.* His treatise was followed in rapid succession by the offerings of four other writers: William Cunninghame's *Dissertations on the Seals and*

---

31:2 (1980), 179-184; David Newsome, *The Parting of Friends* (London, 1966); W. H. Oliver, *Prophets and Millennialists: The Uses of Biblical Prophecy in England from the 1790s to the 1840s* (London, 1978); and S. L. Ollard, *A Short History of the Oxford Movement* (London, 1963).

[48] 'There is a public stand for God here. Britain is a grand medium of diffusing truth', stated the Anglican Basil Wood in the 21 May 1804 meeting of the Eclectic Society, where the discussion ranged around the subject, 'By what arguments shall we plead with God to deliver us from the French?'; see Pratt (ed.), *The Thought of the Evangelical Leaders* (1856), 330. Just such sentiments would issue from the pen of a Nonconformist writer in 1818, for in the *Eclectic Review* of that year one could read this sentiment: 'It is to her commercial character that England is, under Providence, mainly indebted for that high distinction which it is her noblest prerogative to enjoy, as the Evangelist of nations'; see *Eclectic Review* 27 (1818), 2.

*Trumpets* (1813), J. H. Frere's *Combined View of the Prophecies of Daniel, Esdras, and St. John* (1815), Lewis Way's *Letters* and John Bayford's *Messiah's Kingdom* (1816).[49] Interestingly, three of this number, Cunninghame, Way and Bayford would all be prominent supporters of the Continental Society. But it would be a serious error to suppose that the affiliation of the three to the Society was indicative of any particular support by it for their views.

In point of fact, as one examines just how broad was the circle of supporting members in the Continental Society, one is struck by the paradox of how few pronounced premillennialists can be identified there and yet (here is the paradox!) how very often they seized the initiative in the May meetings.[50] Cunninghame and Way, for instance, often took opportunity to illumine the assembled members on the ruin of European Christianity, the apostasy represented in the Papacy, and the like. But from the rank and file of the executive

---

[49] Froom, *Prophetic Faith* (1946), iii. 265. Froom indicates that the early decades of the new century witnessed the publication of four hundred such prophetic works.

[50] The numerical paucity of identifiable premillennialists in the Society is quite striking, especially in the early years. Even when relying on the efforts of Froom, who surely made it his business to highlight the activity of known supporters of the cause, the results are striking. In 1819, the Society executive (comprising President and Committee) consisted of twenty-six persons. Of these only two (Henry Drummond and John Bayford) emerge as pronounced premillennialists. In 1820 and 1821, of twenty-seven persons, only four (Drummond, Bayford, Lewis Way, and 'J. A. Wolfe') are of this stripe. In the following year, the proportion is unchanged though 'J. A. Wolfe', which we presume to be Joseph Wolff, the peripatetic missionary to the East, has given his place to C. S. Hawtrey, editor of the *Jewish Expositor*. Only by 1824 is there a sizeable influx of emergent premillennialists into the executive; in that year appear three premillennialist additions: Hugh McNeile, Spencer Perceval Jr., M.P., and Alexander Haldane, nephew to Robert, the eo-founding patron. (That Alexander Haldane should himself be numbered as a premillennialist in 1824 is quite open to question; I assume this here on the slender ground of his eventual attendance of at least one of the Albury Conferences which commenced in December 1826.) The proportion rises to nine of twenty-seven persons in the executive in 1826 with the addition of Edward Irving and Gerard Noel, and eleven of twenty-seven in 1827 when the Hon. John James Strutt (later Baron Rayleigh) assumed the presidency and Viscount Mandeville joined the circle of vice-presidents. It must be added that persons of non-premillennial views also continued to join the executive. See the *Reports* and *Proceedings* for these years. The reasons for the verbosity of the views of what was only a fraction of the executive and membership will be explored in the following section.

and membership such speeches were regularly answered by persons taking a very different view. Several examples will serve to illustrate this.

In the annual meeting of 1822, the Rev. Lewis Way, Society vice-president, director of the London Society for the Propagation of Christianity among the Jews, and ardent premillennialist, was delegated to move the adoption of the Society's report. He utilized the occasion to dilate at some length on the religious state of Europe as he had observed it on a recent tour:

> There is a time for all things: and I think this is the very time marked out by prophecy and determined by the circumstances of Europe when this society ought to commence a scriptural crusade under that sacred communion...to call (its inhabitants) out of the mystical Babylon. This is the foundation on which this society ought to rest and if continued on this foundation, stand it must...There is just no religion on the Continent at all! I don't mean to exclude the thousands who have not bowed the knee to Baal; God has his people there- but they are so few that I could not find them!

Way's verdict was that Christendom was now defunct because both the Catholic and Protestant churches had abandoned the Scriptures and Gospel. The ruin of Christendom was not temporary, but final; there was to be no large-scale reversal of this situation because this state of affairs was itself indicative of the near-end of the Christian era. Evangelisation must do what it could until the day of judgement fell. But such sentiments did not go unanswered. Mark Wilks, another Society member, had also seen Europe first-hand, but had drawn entirely different conclusions:

> The state of France is highly encouraging. There is a movement among the minds of men which is highly favourable to revealed truth. I shall neither therefore talk of the extent of infidelity nor of Catholic superstition, but tell you of the glorious appearance of divine goodness, truth and mercy in subduing infidelity with the Gospel...Certainly, if there are encouragements anywhere in the world to circulate the Scriptures, it is on the Continent and no portion of it excites more Christian feeling and hope than France...France however criminal its character, however disastrous its history, France is still what has been called a great nation and holds in its hands the destinies of the nations around it. The state of France is highly encouraging! There is among Catholics a disposition, perhaps not seen since the Reformation, to receive the truth and examine the truth...Bible Societies are now formed in France. Forty auxiliaries are established...Almost all the large cities in France now possess ministers of the Gospel who all

preach the fall of man, the necessity of the sacrifice of Christ and the doctrine of salvation by faith.[51]

Such strikingly different characterizations of the state of Europe were to become regular features of the Society meetings. Apprehensive premillennialists were constantly ready to infer the nearness of the end from the decay of Christianity on the Continent, while representatives of the older and more optimistic view continually saw signs that their own Evangelical Revival of the century previous was being replicated across the Channel. In 1823, William Cunninghame of Lainshaw, Scotland, himself a premillennialist author, stood to lament the 'wreck of Europe in the past thirty years' and the 'almost Egyptian darkness which has brooded over the Continent of Europe'. Again, Mark Wilks reported a different Europe where 'we look at a revival of religion on the Continent and religion reviving in every part of France'.[52] The differing perspective was not about the decay and destruction wrought by Enlightenment followed by revolution; on this all the pan-evangelicals were agreed.[53] The sharply defined difference had to do with what this decay of Europe meant in the timetable of the ages.

The premillennialist voices in the Society would grow more strident and vocal (though not because of numerical dominance) as the decade wore on. But always there was rebuttal from the older missionary postmillennialism which lay behind the pan-evangelical societies. The most doughty champion of this older view within the Continental Society was John Pye Smith, Professor of Theology at Homerton College and a Society committee member during the whole decade. In response to the apprehensive comments of founding eo-patron, Henry Drummond, in which that now-committed premillennialist began to lampoon the over-confidence of those of the older view who viewed 'the present dispensation ending in the conversion of the world, rather than in judgements from God' and who believed that 'their (mission) Societies were to be the means of introducing this state of things', Smith rose to reply: 'When the kingdoms of this world should be declared to be the kingdoms of our Lord and of his Christ, it should be by an extraordinary blessing poured out on those common means of grace which this Society was

---

[51] The remarks by Way and Wilks are taken from *Proceedings* (1822), 9-17.
[52] *Proceedings* (1823), 83, 89.
[53] It is instructive to find the premillennialists Way and Irving in essential agreement with the postmillennialsts Alexander Waugh and John Pye Smith on this matter in *Proceedings* (1824), 33-38.

engaged in sending among the Continental nations.'[54] By 1829, the taking of such liberties had gone on too long. Pye Smith spoke for many when he defended the original pan-evangelical vision of the Society and protested against more tendentious premillennialist remarks:

> This Society was founded upon the great common principles in which all Christians agreed; therefore he deeply lamented that there had been an infusion of other opinions, which to say the least were doubtful and which put those who conscientiously felt otherwise into the unwelcome alternative of seeming either to acquiesce by their silence, or, of raising their voices...He begged to express his dissent from the dark and gloomy views which some of them took of the state and prospects of Christianity. On the contrary, there was considerable ground for hope and for rejoicing. Smith respectfully conceived that opinions which are not generally approved by serious and devoted Christians ought not to be introduced on these occasions. As one of the original members of that Society, he wished to enter his humble plea against the introduction of these sentiments.[55]

The Continental Society had been a bright example of pan-evangelicalism at its foundation. Those who kept alive this vision of the advance of Christ's kingdom during the 1820s had to row against the stream. But row they did. How can the change of emphasis in the Society be satisfactorily explained? Not simply by the re-emergence of premillennialism, for the number of actual adherents of this view within the Society was never predominant – only by the manoeuvrings of Henry Drummond.

## Henry Drumrnond: Society Co-Founder and Promoter of Premillennialism

Henry Drummond was almost certainly not a premillennialist in 1817 when he succeeded Robert Haldane as advisor to the young Genevan evangelicals; the same may be said of his views at the time the Continental Society was formally inaugurated in London in the autumn of 1818.[56] By his own admission, he was a rather late convert to the cause. In a speech to the Society in May 1828, he declared: 'When I first perceived that the present dispensation was

---

54 *Proceedings* (1828), 32-35.
55 *Proceedings* (1829), 29.
56 The same may be asserted also about eo-founder Robert Haldane, but with this difference - the latter seems *never* to have entertained premillennial ideas.

not to end in the conversion of the world, but in judgements from God, I thought it so clear that I wondered why I had never seen it before and I concluded that all my Scripture friends were previously aware of it.'[57] The known premillennialists first identified with the Society were John Bayford and Lewis Way, each of whom had published a book on the subject since 1815.[58] Way had made the first recognizably premillennial speech to be heard in the Society in 1822. It drew a rebuttal and dropped out of sight.[59]

Yet Drummond, who vied with Robert Haldane throughout the 1820s for the role of largest benefactor of the Society, was all the while undergoing the process of re-evaluation to which he alluded in 1828.[60] He was nominally (at least) a member of the Church of England and seems originally to have embraced the optimistic outlook on eschatology found among Anglican evangelical clergy of the era.[61] But in 1825, under the influence of Edward Irving's London preaching on the Second Advent of Christ, Drummond's conventional views underwent change.[62] Irving had himself come under the influence of J. Hatley Frere's writings upon his settling in London.[63] Having adopted the change of view, Drummond went to

---

[57] *Proceedings* (1828), 32.

[58] See page 138 above.

[59] That of Mark Wilks, 139 above, and footnote 51.

[60] Drummond and Haldane each regularly contributed between £290 and £300 per annum throughout the decade. Combined, this comprised between 20-25% of total income.

[61] Thus, for instance, when the Eclectic Society discussed the subject of the millennium on 7 June 1802, Thomas Scott, the Bible commentator, gave it as his opinion that 'More will in the end be saved than will perish. Diseases, wars, passions, will all be subdued'; see Pratt (ed.), *The Thought of the Evangelical Leaders* (1856), 257. Edward Bickersteth, steadfast supporter of both the Church Missionary Society and Continental Society, like Drummond, himself underwent a change of view around 1833. His biographer recorded that he had formerly upheld this same view, 'the view that was then popular...[he] looked forward to the gradual conversion of the world, by the spread of missions and a larger blessing on the ordinary means of grace'; see T. R. Birks, *Memoir of the Rev. Edward Bickersteth* (London, 1851), ii. 42.

[62] Irving had come to London in October 1822 as minister of the Caledonian Chapel, Hatton Garden. For his influence upon Drummond in 1825, see Drummond, *Edward Irving and His Circle* ([1937]), 127. Lewis (ed.), *Blackwell Dictionary of Evangelical Biography* (1995), s.v. 'Henry Drummond', attributes Drummond's change of outlook not to Irving, but to Lewis Way. On this hypothesis, Drummond's re-orientation will have pre-dated 1825.

[63] Drummond, *Irving and His Circle* ([1937]), 125.

work with his conventional vigour, doing at least two things to advance his new understanding of Christian eschatology.

First, in December 1826 he began to host at his home in Albury, Surrey the first of what became known as the Albury Conferences for the consideration of prophecy. The conference, which was repeated from 1827 through 1830 was attended by a group of not less than twenty persons selected either on the basis of their stature as premillennialists of renown, or because of some willingness to explore the viewpoint. As Sandeen has rightly pointed out, this conference was 'dominated by Anglicans, with scarcely three or four participants not affiliated with either the English or Scottish national churches'. The same writer correctly asserts that 'many of those attending ... had been previously associated in the work of the Continental Society.'[64] The practical outcome of these two facts was highly important, for the 'Albury consensus' (if it may be called that) came increasingly to be advocated in the annual meetings of the Continental Society by these very ministers and gentlemen affiliated to the national churches. The Albury consensus is reflected in a summation published by Drummond in 1829 stating those conclusions of these conferences on which all of the participants had been in agreement. They were:

1. This 'dispensation' or age will not end 'insensibly' but cataclysmically in judgment and destruction of the church in the same manner in which the Jewish dispensation ended.
2. The Jews will be restored to Palestine during the time of judgment.
3. The judgment to come will fall principally upon Christendom.
4. When the judgment is past, the millennium will begin.
5. The second advent of Christ will occur before the millennium.
6. The 1260 years of Daniel 7 and Revelation 13 ought to be measured

---

[64] Sandeen, The *Roots of Fundamentalism* (1978), 19, 20. For the full text of Drummond's summary see p. 101 above. Sandeen provides a very comprehensive listing of both repeat and occasional attenders. It is not clear on what basis Sandeen suggests the Albury-Continental overlap; he shows no direct familiarity with the *Reports* or *Proceedings*. Even if it is only a surmise, it is correct. My own examination of the *Reports* and *Proceedings* of the Society enable me to identify no less than ten of the twenty regular attendees at Albury as persons also found among the Society's supporters in the years 1826-1828. Of twenty-five occasional attendees, only three are readily recognizable as Society supporters. Lewis (ed.), *Blackwell Dictionary of Evangelical Biography* (1995), s.v. 'Henry Drummond', states that the conferences continued until 1830. In this case, Drummond's published *Dialogues* (see footnote 65) cannot have reflected the totality of the proceedings. See also Carter, *Anglican Evangelicals* (2001), 176-9.

from the reign of Justinian to the French Revolution. The vials of wrath (Revelation 16) are now being poured out and the second advent is imminent.[65]

Drummond's second stratagem, carried out simultaneously with the first, was to seek every opportunity to encourage the representation of this Albury circle within both the executive and the annual meetings of the Continental Society.[66] No doubt in his capacity of major benefactor and member of the executive it would have been quite simple in 1824 to secure the involvement of the Rev. Hugh McNeile as anniversary preacher and member of the executive committee. Drummond, in his capacity as wealthy landowner, had just previously secured the appointment of McNeile to the parish church at Albury near his own residence. McNeile was certainly already a premillennialist when Drummond adopted this viewpoint in 1825, was a consistent participant in and chairman of the Albury Conferences, and a forceful advocate of premillennialism in the annual meetings of the Society.[67] By some similar procedure, the preacher invited to address the annual meeting in the following year was none other than Edward Irving, then guiding Drummond through his change of outlook. By the meeting of 1826, Irving had joined the executive committee, as had Gerard Noel. [68] Both would be present at Albury in December. In 1827, a new Society president was announced; in place of Thomas Baring, who had filled the role since 1819, the Hon. John James Strutt (later Baron Rayleigh) would preside. Strutt had been at Albury as had been a new vice-president,

---

[65] Sandeen has provided the six points from Drummond's *Dialogues On Prophecy* (London, 1829); these preserved the discussions of the Albury conferences without disclosing the identities of those whose personal opinions were being recorded. Pseudonyms were used to represent participants; Sandeen, *Roots of Fundamentalism* (1978), 21, 22.

[66] Drummond, to his credit, seems never to have forgotten that pan-evangelical cooperation was vital to the success of the Society. He sought not so much to exclude other opinions from the Society as to utilize the Society as an important venue in which to propagate the Albury perspective. Thus, even when he took the floor in 1828 to recount the tale of his own change of prophetic perspective, he was careful – since a member of the executive – to make it plain that the opinions expressed were purely his own; *Proceedings* (1828), 31.

[67] McNeile, of Irish birth, would continue in his premillennialism but break with Drummond and Irving over the Charismatic and Christological controversies. Liverpool was the scene of his ministry after 1832.

[68] *Proceedings* (1825, 1826).

George Montagu, Lord Mandeville.[69] We do not maintain here that Drummond forced the inclusion of such persons in the Society executive, or even that the executive came largely to represent persons favourable to him; only that when Drummond, eo-founder and major benefactor, proposed the inclusion of a friend or associate, this was a proposal which was taken most seriously. With such a circle of Albury associates installed within the executive of the Society, it was only natural that this cadre would attempt to catch the ear of the Society. And attempt it they did; several examples will serve to illustrate this. We will find that in nearly every case, such an attempt provoked strong reaction and even disorder.

In the 1827 meeting, Edward Irving took opportunity to dilate upon the favourite Albury theme of the ruin of European Christendom. He asked, 'Are not hollow Protestantism and superstitious Popery environing the Continent on all sides, threatening eternal destruction to the souls of her inhabitants?' Yet it was difficult for Irving to continue; he paused to complain:

> I would beg leave to suggest that those around me might be better employed than endeavouring to drown out the sound of my voice in the acclamation of their own...It is not to be endured that on such occasions as these a speaker should stand up and be overawed by the approbation or disapprobation of those that surround him, the effect of which must be to confine him to facts, not allowing him to give vent to those feelings with which every Christian heart ought to abound.[70]

In the following year, Henry Drummond himself, having related to the meeting his own change of prophetic outlook went on to indicate some of the outworkings of this change of opinion for his general view of life and society.[71] He began to decry 'the growth of tolerance in modern life' and cited as an example of this the foundation in that very year of 'that infidel London university'. The records of the Society meeting indicate that these remarks brought 'loud hissing from the bottom of the room and cheering from the platform'.[72]

---

[69] *Proceedings* (1827). George Montagu, Lord Mandeville a society vice-president from 1828, was a commander in the Royal Navy. Regarding Strutt, see T. C. F. Stunt, 'Trying the Spirits: The Case of the Gloucestershire Clergyman', *JEH* 39:1(1988), 95-105.

[70] *Proceedings* (1827), 103.

[71] A change described at page 147, above.

[72] There had been agitation since 1825 for the creation of a London university free from the religious tests still in place in the older universities. As the tests effectively required that a student conform to Anglicanism, persons of nonconformist as well as non-religious views were barred from

Drummond protested this behaviour, as had Irving the previous year; neither seemed the least inclined to take responsibility for having created the stir. At least one defender of the new London University rose to protest Drummond's remarks and to appeal for greater decorum.

The zenith of this premillennialist attempt to make the Society meetings a pulpit for the Albury consensus followed in 1829. The *Proceedings* make plain that not only the President, the Hon. John James Strutt, but executive committee members C. S. Hawtrey and George Montagu, Lord Mandeville – all members of the Albury circle – came well prepared for more speechifying at the May 1829 meeting. Strutt, as president, led off with a statement which disclosed just how much the Albury premillennialism was wedded to the historicist approach to prophecy, which sought to find fulfilments of prophecy in then-contemporary events.[73] He proposed: 'The political aspect of affairs seems to confirm the opinion that the sixth seal is nearly expired and we see the kingdom which formed the image of gold, silver, brass and iron in Nebuchadnezzar's dream.'[74] C.S. Hawtrey followed up Strutt's remarks with an appeal to Zechariah 14; here he believed was a description of the dawning of the millennial day arriving by the cataclysmic return of the Lord. George Montagu, Lord Mandeville was next; he proposed a motion declaring the Papacy to be 'the Apocalyptic Babylon' from which the Continental Society was to be steadfastly urging Europeans to depart. He went on to decry 'the spirit of liberalism, so called, which pervaded their public assemblies, which reached the palace, and from which not even the Church was free...Liberalism was that pestilence which had been foretold in the book of Revelation.'[75]

John Pye Smith, professor in Homerton College and not a premillennialist, had agreed in advance to second Montagu's motion identifying the Papacy with the Antichrist; yet he told the meeting that he believed many of Montagu's additional sentiments were plainly erroneous. He did not think that such sentiments should be introduced in such a meeting. At this point, another Albury circle member, Hugh McNeile, chairman of the meeting, defended the right of Montagu to speak his mind 'since the Society had agreed that it was not responsible for the sentiments of any individual'. Smith, who

---

enrolling. Drummond and those of his outlook viewed this as the nation's embracing of atheism; *Proceedings* (1828), 33, 34, 39.
[73] See footnote 37 for a definition of these terms.
[74] Strutt was alluding to Daniel 2. His remarks are recorded m the *Proceedings* (1829), 23.
[75] *Proceedings* (1829), 28.

was not quite finished, completed his cautionary remarks 'to a combination of hisses, applause, and cries of chair!'[76] The strategy of the Albury circle had ensured only that the meetings of the Society would acquire the atmosphere of a circus. It was 1829, and the Society was now staggering under the triple blows of apocrypha, charismatic, and premillennial controversies, controversies in which the same outspoken personalities had recurrently been at work. Could this Society survive?

## The Decline of the Continental Society

Ominous warning signs had been ignored by the executive of the Continental Society since at least 1826. Rumoured in that year to be 'opposed to the Bible Society', it took three years until a restoration of cordial relationships could be reported.[77] From 1826 onward the Albury circle, led by Henry Drummond, had made a concerted effort to highlight premillennial views within the Society. And while that sustained campaign was in progress, Edward Irving first made public statements which began to involve him in Christological controversy; simultaneously, with Henry Drummond he began his advocacy of the restoration of the charismata.[78] We have seen that the tremors of these controversies reached Europe and made the work of the society agents more difficult. It is hard to avoid the conclusion that this mission Society had been imposed upon by those who claimed to be its friends.

By 1829-30 its once-promising prospects were severely damaged. From a noble launch, it had descended by degrees to being what the chairman of its 1827 meeting had termed a society

more or less spoken against. In one town the best friends of your society are found amongst the members of the Established Church, your Dissenting brothers being your opposers. In another, the situation

---

[76] *Proceedings* (1829), 31-34.

[77] *Proceedings* (1829), 10.

[78] To this series of developments, the executive of the Society seems to have been incapable of bringing any resolution other than to enunciate a policy 'that it is by its Report that the Society is to be judged and not by the opinions of any particular member'; *Proceedings* (1827), 116. But this was an evasion; the printed reports of the Society served to record and disseminate the questionable opinions of particular members uttered in the May meetings, as well as the decisions of the executive. Such weak resolve suggests strong internal differences within the executive.

is reversed, and in a third individuals of all classes are to be found for and against you.[79]

From this, it sank to become something tragi-comic. Henry Drummond, the enigmatic eo-founder, admitted to the meeting of 1829 that he could not dispute the daily newspaper's characterization of their organization as 'a Society whose annual meetings are the exhibitions of theological mountebanks'.[80] Here, at least, the noble vision of pan-evangelicalism had received several mortal wounds. The Continental Society would survive, but only to limp through the 1830s as a smaller, poorer organization. A change of name to European Missionary Society could not save it from financial calamity. It was finally absorbed into the all-Anglican Foreign Aid Society in 1841.

## Epilogue

Villains and heroes may be easily identified in this tale of the Continental Society. But to content oneself in doing so involves the failure to observe the weakness evident in both those we find it easy to admire and those we find it easy to dismiss. On closer examination, the pan-evangelical optimists were rather like the pan-evangelical pessimists. These were alike in their readiness to chart their location on the sea of Christian history in reliance on soundings taken from both the contemporary society and the use of key Scriptures. But in a century which was supplying both reasons for expectation of massive Christian advance through missions and evangelism as well as reasons for alarm over the secularisation of life and society it is hard not to conclude that the difference was made for these Christian believers by a perspective which they brought with them to the survey of their world.

The Christian pessimists were so gripped by a sense of the social decay that they witnessed, that they began to dabble in speculation over the year of Christ's return. Dates in the 1840s and 1860s were suggested. Yet all the while, persons of this perspective as well as others were praying, giving, commissioning and being commissioned in the outworkings of what Kenneth Scott Latourette has called 'the

---

[79] *Proceedings* (1827), 12.
[80] *Proceedings* (1829), 35. The *Concise Oxford Dictionary* defines 'mountebank' thus: 'itinerant quack who holds forth to an audience from platform'. It seems the press had got it right.

great century' of Christian missionary expansion.[81] Though, of course, dwellers in the nineteenth century could not immediately perceive the expansiveness of the Christian advance which was underway (it was only properly estimable in hindsight), it was nevertheless underway and they failed to sense it. And so, in hindsight all their speechifying about Europe's 'Egyptian darkness' was somehow beside the point.

As for the Christian optimists, they who so easily believed that the eighteenth century Evangelical Revival was finding its echo in Europe, India and the Pacific, they could not perhaps then see that in the mysterious operations of the Spirit of God propitious times can be replaced with barren times. The Gospel advances in Europe which in 1819 seemed to bring nearer the day when Christ would come in glory, would by 1919 give way to a post-war Europe infinitely more wrecked and wretched than the most apprehensive members of the Albury circle could have envisioned. The carnage of the 1914-18 war apart, it is a simple matter of record that the era of nineteenth-century evangelical awakening had ended for Europe as surely as it had in Britain.[82] Where then was the unabashed optimism that the kingdom of Christ would be brought forward 'by the pouring out of extraordinary blessing upon common means of grace'?[83] It is widely appreciated that the eschatology which fuelled the launch of the great pan-evangelical Societies of the early nineteenth century has fallen on very hard times in this one. As one century and millennium have given way to another, have we any less fallible method of reckoning the times and the nearness of Christ's return than they? If this would be the case, where is the proof?

---

[81] The title was given to the fourth volume of Kenneth Scott Latourette, *History of the Expansion of Christianity* (London, 1944).

[82] The verdict of August Gretillat who surveyed nineteenth century evangelical advances made in Francophone Europe was that this movement was a spent force by 1891. See his 'Movements of Theological Thought Among the French-Speaking Protestants From the Revival of 1820 to the End of 1891', *Presbyterian and Reformed Review* 3 (1892), 421-447.

[83] The words of John Pye Smith, spoken in the Society meeting of 1828; see *Proceedings* (1828), 35.

# CHAPTER 7

# Millennialism and the Interpretation of Prophecy in Ulster Presbyterianism, 1790-1850

Andrew Holmes

Presbyterianism came to Ireland with the arrival of Scottish settlers to Ulster in the early years of the seventeenth century.[1] Over the following decades they consolidated a separate ecclesiastical and political identity in the north east of Ireland through the establishment of congregations, presbyteries and a General Synod in 1690. This coherence was challenged in the eighteenth century as Presbyterianism fractured along social and doctrinal lines. In the 1720s the largest Presbyterian group, the Synod of Ulster, experienced internal controversy over subscription to the Westminster Confession of Faith that led to the formation of the non-subscribing Presbytery of Antrim. Though this presbytery remained small, liberal theological views, partly influenced by the Scottish Enlightenment and known as 'New Light', became prominent within the Synod as the century progressed. Theological conservatism was maintained by the 'Old Light' party within the Synod and without by Scottish Seceders, who arrived in Ulster in the 1740s and became the growth sector of Presbyterianism before 1820. There was also a significant, yet numerically small, Covenanter

[1] Peter Brooke, *Ulster Presbyterianism: The historical perspective, 1610-1970* (Dublin, 1987) and R. F. G. Holmes, *Our Irish Presbyterian Heritage* (Belfast, 1985). The research for this paper was carried out while the author was in receipt of an Arts and Humanities Research Board postgraduate studentship and I thank them for their financial assistance. I should also like to thank Dr Crawford Gribben, Dr Allan Blackstock and Dr David Hayton for guidance in the completion of this chapter. Any errors of fact or interpretation are the sole responsibility of the author.

presence in Ulster, which established a permanent presbytery in 1792. These orthodox and rational Presbyterian traditions were challenged and modified by evangelicalism in the first decades of the nineteenth century. In 1829 the orthodox-evangelical majority in the Synod of Ulster forced out the descendants of the New Light party as many of them held Arian beliefs. Over the course of the following decades, evangelicalism became the dominant voice within Ulster Presbyterianism. This dominance led in 1840 to the formation of the General Assembly of the Presbyterian Church in Ireland, and, more spectacularly, to the 1859 revival.

The period from 1790 to 1850 was one of momentous change and upheaval throughout the western world. In Ireland the formation of the United Irish society in 1791 marked the beginning of a decade of political and sectarian upheaval that was to be pivotal in the development of modern Irish society. Ulster Presbyterians were at the forefront of this political radicalism in the 1790s. All but one of the original United Irishmen were Presbyterians, including two who were themselves sons of the manse.[2] The shared experience of exclusion from an Anglican confessional state and the impact of the French Revolution provided the context in which Presbyterians and Catholics could unite in order to challenge the political regime. Though the 1798 rebellion was an uncoordinated disaster, an estimated sixty-three Presbyterian ministers were implicated in an uprising that aimed to overthrow British rule and establish Irish independence.[3] By the First Home Rule Crisis in 1886-7, however, the overwhelming majority of Ulster Presbyterians were committed to the Union with Great Britain (enacted in 1801) and fearful of the ascendancy their one-time Catholic allies would have in an Irish Home Rule parliament.[4] It is nevertheless important to appreciate that though Presbyterians became unionists, it did not follow that they became political conservatives. Many remained ardent political liberals and supported a wide range of reform measures, including tenant right.

The study of eschatology and the interpretation of prophecy amongst Ulster Presbyterians has often begun and ended with their

[2] I. R. McBride, *Scripture Politics: Ulster Presbyterians and Irish Radicalism in the late Eighteenth Century* (Oxford, 1998).
[3] McBride, *Scripture Politics* (1998), 232-6.
[4] R. F. G. Holmes, 'United Irishmen and Unionists: Irish Presbyterians, 1791 and 1886', in W. J. Sheils and Diana Wood (eds), The *Churches Ireland and the Irish,* Studies in Church History 25 (Oxford, 1989), 171-89.

political mobilisation in 1798.[5] In the standard account, the events of 1789 in France, the clamour for political reform, the subsequent violence of the rebellion and government suppression charged the atmosphere with apocalyptic expectancy. Historians informed by models derived from sociology and political science see millenarian ideas as providing a convenient medium for secular radicals to politicise the lower orders who naturally viewed the world as continually open to divine intervention. Scholars have largely ignored the continued importance of eschatology to Ulster Presbyterians in the nineteenth century, as those ideas did not inspire popular protest as in the preceding century. More generally, David Miller has argued that 'the capacity to believe in the possibility of supernatural intervention in the external world' had all but disappeared in Ulster by the early nineteenth century.[6] He argues that evangelicalism, with its emphasis upon personal conversion, led to the transferral of God's activity from the wider world to within the individual believer. Miller believes that this illustrates a general drift within Ulster Presbyterianism from 'prophetic Calvinism' to conversionist evangelicalism because of the modernisation of Irish society.[7] One of the aims of this chapter is to argue that biblical prophecy and the 'prophetic' interpretation of God's activity in the world were as important in the nineteenth century as they had been in the 1790s. Furthermore, the millennial views that characterised Presbyterianism after 1800 fuelled an interest in mission that was profoundly influenced by modernity.[8] The explicit object of millennialism in that period was religious, as Presbyterians, fired by the crusading zeal of evangelicalism, sought to convert sinners. This desire had important social and political implications that had a profound impact upon Presbyterian self-perception and their relationships with their Anglican and Catholic neighbours.

In order to examine these issues, this chapter will be divided into

---

[5] D. W. Miller, 'Presbyterianism and "modernisation" in Ulster', *PP* 80 (1978), 66-90; Myrtle Hill, *The Time of the End: Millenarian beliefs in Ulster* (Belfast, 2001).

[6] Miller, 'Presbyterianism and "modernisation" in Ulster' (1978), 84-5.

[7] Miller has modified his opinion by suggesting that Presbyterians continued to see God's activity in the world, but only in cataclysmic events such as the Irish famine of the 1840s. This does not substantially alter his previous views; see D. W. Miller, 'Irish Presbyterians and the great famine', in Jacqueline Hill and Calm Lennon (eds), *Luxury and austerity: Historical Studies 21* (Dublin, 1999), 175.

[8] Brian Stanley (ed.), *Christian Missions and the Enlightenment* (Grand Rapids, MI, 2001).

five sections. Section one examines the role of prophecy in the 1790s and the reorientation of Presbyterianism in the early nineteenth century. The following two sections begin by outlining Presbyterian responses to Edward Irving and the premillennialism associated with him. It is clear that Ulster Presbyterians were postmillennial in outlook and that many of them continued to be intensely concerned with the application of biblical prophecy to contemporary events. This interest, as section four explains, was predicated upon basic protestant assumptions concerning biblical authority, providence, the place of the papacy in God's plans, and forms of personal and corporate piety. The chapter will conclude by suggesting a number of reasons why premillennialism did not develop within Ulster Presbyterianism in the first half of the nineteenth century. The use of terminology in this chapter may not be as precise as some would wish. The primary aim is to outline the eschatological views of those Presbyterians who referred in their published work to the thousand-year reign of Christ mentioned in Revelation 20. The terms millennia!, millenarian, eschatology and prophecy are used interchangeably to illustrate the general point that prophetic speculation remained a central component of the Presbyterian worldview in the first half of the nineteenth century.

## The Reorientation of Ulster Presbyterianism, 1790-1830

The fall of the Bastille in 1789 and subsequent European events shook the *ancien regime* to its core and sent Christians to the prophetic books of the Bible in search of a way to make sense of what had happened. The Rev. Thomas Ledlie Birch, orthodox minister of Saintfield Synod of Ulster congregation, suggested in 1794 that 'blind indeed must those persons be, who do not at present observe some *mighty event* in the womb of providence, convulsing the earth with its struggles to be brought forth.'[9] The French Revolution was interpreted as either a fulfilment of the divine will or the triumph of Enlightenment reason and liberty.[10] Both religious and rational

---

[9] Thomas Ledlie Birch, *The Obligations upon Christians, and especially Ministers, to be Exemplary in their lives; Particularly at this important period, when the prophecies are seemingly about to be fulfilled in the fall of Antichrist, as an introduction to the flowing in of Jew and Gentile into the Christian church. A sermon preached before the very reverend General Synod of Ulster, at Lurgan, June 26th, 1793* (Belfast, 1794), 32.

[10] Robin Barnes, 'Images of hope and despair: Western apocalypticism, ea. 1500-1800', in Bernard McGinn, John J. Collins, and Stephen J. Stein (eds), *The Encyclopedia of Apocalypticism* (New York, 1998), ii. 177-9.

elements were present and variously mixed in Presbyterian responses to the 1790s. Consequently, millennia!ideas provided a common language and set of assumptions that could bind together different social groups within Ulster, not least middle-class political radicals and rural handloom weavers or farmers.[11]

For Presbyterian commentators, the fact that French Catholic peasants had rebelled against their own church was a sure sign that the papal Antichrist was about to crumble. This provided the space necessary for a Presbyterian-Catholic political alliance to develop in Ulster, informed by their shared experience of political and social exclusion within the Anglican confessional state.[12] Presbyterians of all opinions agreed that the political and religious tyranny exemplified in Catholicism and to a lesser extent in prelacy, was facing its imminent downfall. Yet, emphases differed between Presbyterians. Covenanters gleefully predicted not only the imminent fall of the papacy but also the British monarchy, which they argued had reneged upon the Covenants of the 1640s by establishing an Erastian churchY For New Light Presbyterians, Antichrist and popery were conceived in abstract terms as any sort of political or spiritual tyranny. This could mean the superstitious practices of Catholics, the church-state relationship since Constantine, or, in their own context, the imposition of man-made statements of faith upon the conscience of the individual.[14]

According to one scholar, 'The millennium provided a common language and set of images and concepts in which people could express both individual and collective needs...but it remained a mode of expression, a means of communication, rather than an end with an agreed meaning and programme.'[15] In Ulster, bourgeois radicals used the expectancy of the imminent return of Christ, and

---

[11] James Donnelly, 'Propagating the cause of the United Irishmen', *Studies* 69 (1980), 5-23, especially 15-21; N. J. Curtin, *The United Irishmen: Popular Politics and Dublin 1791-1798* (Oxford, 1998); McBride, *Scripture Politics* (1998), 195-201.

[12] I. R. McBride, 'Presbyterians in the Penal Era', *Bullan* 1 (1994), 73-86.

[13] McBride, *Scripture Politics* (1998), 201.

[14] McBride, *Scripture Politics* (1998), 197-9. For an example of New Light thinking see William Steel Dickson, *Three Sermons on the Subject of Scripture Politics* (Belfast, 1793). For the wider interest of rational dissenters in prophecy see Iain McCalman, 'New Jerusalems: Prophecy, dissent and radical culture in England, 1786-1830', in Knud Haakonssen (ed.), *Enlightenment and Religion: Rational Dissent in Eighteenth-century Britain* (Cambridge, 1996), 312-35.

[15] J. F. C. Harrison, *The Second Coming: Popular Millenarianism, 1780-1850* (London, 1979), 6.

the prospect of worldly improvement during the millennium, to urge the rural population into rebellion. In that regard, prophecy had important political and social implications, particularly its promise of a world turned upside down.[16] The radicals' newspaper, the *Northern Star*, published letters written by Birch predicting the overthrow of civil and religious tyranny and the inexorable advance of liberty and knowledge.[17] Reprints of works by Robert Fleming, John Owen and James Bicheno, under the aegis of the Covenanter, the Rev. William Stavely, were published in Belfast in 1795 and advertised in the same newspaper.[18] Provincial presses such as Monaghan and Strabane reproduced prophetic material, while the Rev. Josias Wilson of Donegore published extracts from the prophecies of Richard Brothers.[19] The prophecies of the seventeenth-century Covenanter Alexander Peden proved to be extremely popular in Presbyterian areas, while those of Thomas Rhymer were distributed amongst Catholics. The irony was that by distributing such blatantly sectarian material, the United Irishmen were undermining their own non-sectarian principles.[20] Yet, eschatology and sectarianism were attractive to certain elements within the Ulster countryside before the 1790s and would remain so in the following decades.[21]

When the rebellion finally came in the summer of 1798, an estimated 30,000 people were killed in an uncoordinated series of engagements.[22] The violent suppression of the rebellion by government troops and news of the massacre of Protestants by Catholics in Wexford had a profound impact upon Ulster Presbyterians. The failure of political radicalism in 1798 acted as an accelerator to the growth of evangelicalism within Presbyterianism. In 1799 the Rev. Benjamin McDowell, the most prominent evangelical in the Synod of Ulster, urged upon his fellow members of the General Evangelical Society the need to propagate the gospel in order to save souls,

---

[16] Hill, *Time of the End* (2001), 21-3.

[17] Donnelly, 'Propagating the cause' (1980), 16-17.

[18] Donnelly, 'Propagating the cause' (1980), 17.

[19] J. R. R Adams, *The Printed Word and the Common Man: Popular Culture in Ulster, 1700-1900* (Belfast, 1987), 86-90.

[20] Miller, 'Presbyterianism and "modernisation" in illster' (1978), 82-3.

[21] For example, ongoing research by Allan Blackstock has uncovered a continued sense of apocalyptic expectancy in Irish popular loyalism in the first half of the nineteenth century. I am grateful to Dr Blackstock for a number of informative conversations on this topic. See also Sean Farrell, *Rituals and Riots: Sectarian Violence and Political Culture in Ulster, 1784-1886* (Lexington, KY, 2000), 115-6.

[22] R. F. Foster, *Modern Ireland, 1600-1972* (London, 1989), 278-82.

combat infidelity and resist violent republicanism: 'Impelled by the importance of the object, encouraged by the aspects of providence, and relying upon the promised aid of omnipotence...let us awake to greater exertions in this too long neglected work, and may the Lord smile success upon our humble endeavours, for his name and mercies sake.'[23] It took time before the various Presbyterian bodies took up this evangelical battle cry. The first indigenous Presbyterian home mission appeared in 1818 and the first foreign missionaries were sent out in 1840.

This did not mean that some of the synods did not reflect the mood of the times. In 1811 the Associate (Burgher) Synod of Ireland gave thanks to God for the emergence of interdenominational missionary societies and hoped 'that the happy times promised are drawing near, when the mountain of the Lord's house shall be established in the top of the mountains and exalted above the hills'.[24]

Individual Presbyterian ministers became involved in voluntary religious societies and shared the optimistic, postmillennial view of the great evangelical missionary organisations of the time.[25] In doing so a desire developed for unity amongst evangelicals both at home and abroad. The Rev. John Lowry wrote in 1816, 'The *Plant of Renown* has taken root in our land; let the rose, the shamrock and the thistle, entwine around it, and diffuse its fruit and fragrance to far-distant climes.'[26] Similarly another Secession minister declared, 'Is not the church of Christ one? Although she hath many members, and these members have many names; yet, if in union with Christ the head, they are all members one of another. They are all

---

[23] Benjamin McDowell, *The Standing Orders of Christ to the Messengers of his Grace, of every Church, and in every Age; Considered, and applied to the present time, in a Sermon preached in St Mary's Abbey meeting-house, on Sunday the 21st of July, 1799, from Isaiah LXII. 10, at the request of the General Evangelical Society; and now published at their desire* (Dublin, 1799), 38.

[24] *Reasons for Humiliation and Thanksgiving, Drawn up by Mr Millar, according to Appointment, were Read, Corrected and Approved of by the Associate Synod of Ireland, extracted by John Rogers, clerk of the Associate Synod* (1811), 4.

[25] R. F. G. Holmes, 'The triumph of evangelicalism in the Synod of IDster in the early nineteenth century', in W. D. Patton (ed.), *Ebb and Flow: Essays in Church History in honour of R. Finlay G. Holmes* (Belfast, 2002), 9-19; Brian Stanley, 'The future in the past: Eschatological vision in British and American protestant missionary history', *TB* 51 (2000), 101-20.

[26] John Lowry, *Sermon Preached before the Associate Synod of Presbyterians, in Ireland, July 1816* (Belfast, 1816), 24.

brethren.'[27] The missionary excitement of the early nineteenth century created a sense of expectancy amongst some that the millennium was about to dawn.[28] The Rev. Samuel Edgar, Secession minister at Ballynahinch and founder member of the Down Missionary Society, believed that history involved both periods of religious decline and revival.[29] In a reference to the over-exuberance of some evangelicals, he did 'not wish to rave as some have done, about a commenced millennium; nor do we think the world will be perfect when that happy period shall arrive'.[30] Nevertheless, he did believe that the times in which he lived were marked by religious and moral progress, particularly the extension of missionary activity. According to Edgar, God's plan 'from the beginning of time, seems to have been a gradual communication of more and more knowledge, and consequently moral improvement'.[31]

As reflected by Edgar's emphasis upon progress, the missionary movement was motivated both consciously and unconsciously by the mood of the Enlightenment.[32] This was reflected in their desire to draw 'heathen' societies into the modern world by encouraging civilised behaviour and denouncing inhuman practices. Ulster Presbyterians variously assailed infanticide, the burning of widows on Indian funeral pyres, and black slavery.[33] They also sought to spread the gospel by the rational means of education, literacy, social reform and Bible reading.[34] It is little wonder that the dawning of

---

[27] James Rentoul, *The Angelic Anthem, applied to the Present Times, in Two Sermons* (Strabane, 1815), 66.

[28] David Stuart, *The Claims of the Poor Children of Ireland on Christians, Stated and Enforced: A Sermon...Preached in the new Meeting-house, Mary's Abbey, on Sabbath, the 9th of April, 1820, in aid of the Funds of Mary's Abbey Sabbath and Weekday Evening Schools* (Dublin, 1820), 33-9.

[29] Samuel Edgar, *The Times, a Sermon, Preached at the ordination of the Rev Thomas Heron, Fourtowns, Donoughmore* (Belfast, 1814), 51-8.

[30] Edgar, *The Times* (1814), 51. For an example of over-exuberance, see the report of the Tyrone Missionary Society, 24 May 1816, in *Hibernian Evangelical Magazine*, 18 (1816), 296-7.

[31] Edgar, *The Times* (1814), 50.

[32] For a general introduction, see, Stanley (ed.), *Christian Missions and the Enlightenment* (2001).

[33] For example, Samuel Edgar, *A Sermon; Preached before the Down Missionary Society, at Rathfriland* (Belfast, 1815), 11-17.

[34] For specific examples from Ulster see Samuel Hanna, *Love to Christ: An incitement to Ministerial and Missionary exertions. A sermon, preached before the London Missionary Society, at Surrey Chapel, on Wednesday morning, May 8, 1822* (2nd ed., Belfast, 1822); James Morgan, *A Scriptural Statement of the Nature of the Obligations of Christian Missions to the*

the millennium was seen in optimistic terms and that its preparation and extension would be achieved through worldly means
animated by God's power. In 1826 the Rev. Samuel Butler saw signs
of the approaching millennium in an increased interest taken in the
arts and sciences, opportunities for travel, the rise of the American
and British empires, the weakening of black slavery, and missionary
successes in Australia and India. Given these developments, he
believed, 'Advance is now the Christians motto, for the time. Let
there be no desertion, no retrograde movements.'[35] This optimism
and interest was not confined to ministers but was reflected by the
laity in the rapid establishment of missionary auxiliaries and
religious societies across Ulster.[36] In 1835, William Ferguson of
Belfast edited and published *The Religious Advocate, and Christian
Monitor: a weekly fund of Christian instruction.* The second of the
eight subjects to be covered was the 'most authentic and correct
review of the prophecy relating to the spread and accomplishment of
universal righteousness, and the consummation of all things, as
contained in Daniel's prophecy and the Book of the Revelations'.[37]

    The 1814 sermon in which Edgar promoted his optimistic views
was savagely reviewed in the politically liberal *Belfast Monthly
Magazine* for its inherent conservatism and perpetuation of abuses
within the political and religious establishment.[38] In many respects,
this was a legitimate conclusion, as evangelicalism seemed to be
equated with political and religious conservatism in Ulster. The
failure of 1798 had 'focused the attention on the potential of
[evangelicalism's] moral creed and its anti-catholicism to act as
compelling antidotes to civil and political unrest'.[39] Millennialism
had provided radicals with the means of mobilising the masses for
political ends in the 1790s. In the nineteenth century, evangelicals
believed that the preaching the gospel and the living out of its
implications would bring about the millennium. As with Butler,
Edgar suggested that contemporary developments provided reasons

---

*Heathen World. A Sermon Preached to the Lisburn Presbyterian
Congregation, on the 17th September 1826* (Belfast, 1826).

[35] Samuel Butler, *Death and Life in many Views; Or, a Series of Fifty-two
Discourses* (Londonderry, 1826), 358-60.

[36] David Hempton and Myrtle Hill, *Evangelical Protestantism in Ulster
Society, 1740-1890* (London, 1992), 47-51.

[37] The *Religious Advocate, and Christian Monitor: A weekly fund of
Christian instruction* (Belfast, 1835), 1.

[38] *Belfast Monthly Magazine* 12 (1814), 365-71.

[39] David Hempton, *Religion and Political Culture in Great Britain and
Ireland from the Glorious Revolution to the Decline of Empire* (Cambridge,
1996), 95.

to be hopeful. As evidence of progress and divine favour, he pointed to an improvement in living conditions, an increased supply of money, Britain's greatness at sea and in commerce, their God-given victories in the French wars, and the British constitution.[40] Yet, as will be shown, the impact of prophecy upon political opinion was never predictable, as its meaning depended upon the individual involved, the context in which it was articulated and the end to which it was directed.

## Presbyterian Response to the Advent of Premillennialism

The optimism of the missionary movement, and the 'worldly evangelicalism' it represented, was seriously challenged in the early nineteenth century by the premillennialism of a group of radical evangelicals of whom Edward Irving was the most prominentY The evangelical debate about prophecy in the 1820s 'was...between the optimistic postmillennialists, safely anchored in the present and inspired by a vision of the millennium which was an ameliorated continuation of the existing world, and those premillennialists whose despair of contemporary society encouraged them to posit an almost complete caesura between the present and the transfigured future'.[42] This radical variant of evangelicalism grew up within the established churches in the 1820s 'thanks to economic alarms, Catholic Emancipation, the crisis over parliamentary reform, and other 'signs' of an impending divine initiative'.[43] Broadly speaking, Irving was a historicist premillennialist, that is, he maintained the prophecies contained in the prophetic books of Scripture were being fulfilled in contemporary events.[44] As he believed that the moral life of the religious and secular world was rapidly degenerating, only the imminent, personal return of Christ could reverse the decline. Christ's appearance would herald the millennium, at which time Satan would be bound for a thousand years. Christ would then personally reign with his saints on earth before Satan was let loose for a last rampage that would end in his destruction and the final

---

[40] Edgar, *The Times* (1814), 34-5.

[41] T. C. F. Stunt, *From Awakening to Secession: Radical Evangelicals in Switzerland and Britain, 1815-35* (Edinburgh, 2000).

[42] Grayson Carter, *Anglican Evangelicals: Protestant Secession from the via media, c. 1800-c. 1850* (Oxford, 2001), 157.

[43] Boyd Hilton, 'The role of providence in evangelical social thought', in Derek Beales and Geoffery Best (eds), *History, Society and the Churches: Essays in honour of Owen Chadwick* (Cambridge, 1985), 222-3.

[44] D. W. Bebbington, *Evangelicalism in Modern Britain: A history from the 1730s to the 1980s* (1989; revised London, 1995), 81-5.

judgement. The futurist position, by contrast, held that the events predicted from Revelation 4 onwards referred to the end of the age that was yet to come. The pessimism of both types of premillennialism offered a radical critique of the methods and ethos of the major evangelical missionary societies. For its adherents, 'worldly evangelicalism' had imbibed the ways of the world too greedily and had turned its back upon the primitive simplicity of the New Testament church. Such was the impact of Irving's premillennial vision that one historian has identified him as at least partly responsible for England not becoming evangelical.[45]

Irving visited Ulster in the autumn of 1830 and preached in a number of Presbyterian meetinghouses. A series of charity sermons delivered at May Street in Belfast attracted considerable attention from the local press. The *Belfast News-Letter* thought Irving was a sincere and passionate man, but doubted his orthodoxy regarding the person of Christ and as for 'his doctrine of the *personal reign* of the redeemer upon earth, we dissent *in toto*'.[46] Other journalists questioned his popularity and pointed as evidence of this to the small amounts collected at the meetingsY All agreed that Irving was a remarkable, earnest preacher, but when reports of speaking in tongues arrived from London the following year, prejudices were sharpened and Irving was denounced as delusional.[48] His trial and eventual dismissal by the Scottish General Assembly was greeted with satisfaction by all the local papers. Theologically liberal Presbyterians agreed that Irving was a fanatic but they also saw him as a kindred spirit who had been persecuted for holding opinions contrary to the man-made Westminster Confession of Faith.[49]

The advent of premillennialism provoked Ulster Presbyterians to make their own postmillennial views known. They began by affirming the reality of the millennium, a future period of blessing for the church that would occur before the Second Coming. In 1833 the Seceder periodical, the *Christian Freeman,* stated that 'the scriptures declare that mankind shall yet attain to a universality, and to height of knowledge, wisdom, piety, virtue, and happiness, to which the earth has been a stranger since the fall.'[50] Ulster

---

[45] Sheridan Gilley, 'Edward Irving: Prophet of the millennium', in Jane Garnett and Colin Matthew (eds), *Revival and Religion since 1700: Essays for John Walsh* (London, 1993), 95-110.

[46] *Belfast News-Letter [BNL],* 21 September 1830.

[47] *Northern Whig [NW],* 23 September 1830.

[48] For example, *BNL,* 8 May 1832; *NW,* 31 October and 7 November 1831.

[49] *Bible Christian [BC],* 6 (1835), 97-111.

[50] *Christian Freeman* [CF], 1 (1833), 146.

Presbyterians, however, dissented completely from Irving's view that Christ's return was imminent and that his reign on earth would be physical. Christ's reign in the millennium would be by the power of the Holy Spirit through his saints and would be 'one of righteousness and peace and love' and of conversions.[51] Again, the *Christian Freeman* summed up the Presbyterian consensus in 1836:

> We...hold, with the great body of the church in all ages, that Christ's reign on earth, during the thousand years, will not be a visible bodily reign, but a reign of grace – a reign in the person of his saints – a reign such as he is now exercising by his spiritual presence in his church, and in the hearts of believers, only amazingly heightened above what it is now; a reign by his Spirit in the hearts of men, stirring them up to a vast productiveness in grace and good works; a great moral reign of truth and righteousness.[52]

The general view was that the one thousand years should not be interpreted literally but as a definite period of time that would be brought to an end on the day of judgement by the return of Christ.[53]

Postmillennialists believed there were numerous obstacles to overcome before the dawning of the millennium and many writers, including Thomas Chalmers, maintained they could only be removed through cataclysmic events and divine judgements.[54] The Rev. John Brown of Aghadowey, County Londonderry, declared that 'Before that period, alas! the inhabitants of the earth are destined to pass through a severe ordeal, and true Christians are required to sustain a severe conflict with the abettors of the Man of Sin.'[55] These ordeals or obstacles included Satan, Islam, the ingathering of the Jews, political despotism, corrupt churches, infidelity, and in some quarters, liberalism and the cruelty of nominal Christianity.[56] Yet, God had promised to build and extend His church. A number of

---

[51] Charles Morrison, *The Question, Will Christ's Reign during the Millennium be Personal? Answered from Scripture* (Edinburgh, 1839), 112-4; *Covenanter* *[Cov]* 2 (1832), 349-59, 397-406; *Orthodox Presbyterian* [OP], n.s., 2 (1839), 219.

[52] *CF* 4 (1836), 150.

[53] Morrison, *The Question* (1839), 10-12. Samuel Butler believed that the millennium would last 360,000 years; Butler, *Death and Life* (1826), 361-9.

[54] Thomas Chalmers, 'On the miraculous and internal evidences of the Christian revelation, and the authority of its records', in *The Collected Works of Thomas Chalmers* (Glasgow, 1835-42), iii. 371-4.

[55] John Brown, *Christian Freedom: A Sermon, preached, in reference to the appointment of Cardinal Wiseman, preached in the Presbyterian church of Aghadowey, on the first Sabbath of October, 1850* (Londonderry, 1851), 18.

[56] For example, *CF* 1 (1833), 146-8, 178-9.

writers used the biblical prophecy in Isaiah concerning 'the mountain of the Lord's house' (Isaiah 2:2-4) to illustrate this.[57] Part of this extension involved the purification and renewal of the church, which seemed to be confirmed by the ongoing reforms within the Synod of Ulster in the 1830s.[58] Much of this reform was directed towards promoting religious revival through the identification and proper use of the means of grace. The Rev. James Carlile declared,

> There is power in the ordinary means of conversion, the ministration of the truth of God by his people, accompanied by the outpouring of the Spirit of God, to effect greater things than the world has yet witnessed. And all that is implied in a millennial prosperity may be accomplished by them, and yet the honour be reserved to Christ himself at his coming to destroy Satan and all evil, to restore all things, and to introduce his people, not to a temporary, but to an eternal state of glory and felicity in his presence.[59]

Preaching was particularly important in overcoming these obstacles. Charles Morrison suggested that it 'will be the means, in the hand of the Spirit, of converting every individual, whether Jew or Gentile, *that is to be* converted'.[60] The laity were also urged to get involved in spreading the Kingdom through a variety of activities, including teaching in a Sunday school, distributing tracts and Bibles, or praying in private for revival.[61] Presbyterians did not believe that the personal appearance of Christ was needed to bring about the millennium. The faithful use of the ordinary means of grace, the involvement of all believers and the continued spread of education would achieve that end. In that regard, their vision was a profoundly worldly one.

Postmillennial optimism provided the impetus for the establishment of both home and foreign missionary societies in the 1830s and 1840s. Some believed that they had been given a strategic role in the

[57] John Paul, *The Mountain of the Lord's House: A sermon preached at Rathfriland, Sabbath evening, June 16, 1839...and published at the request of the committee of the Rathfriland Sabbath-School Union* (Belfast, 1839); James Carlile, *'The Mountain of the Lord's House.' A discourse delivered before the General Assembly of the Presbyterian Church in Ireland, on Tuesday, July 7, 1846* (Belfast, 1846).
[58] John Brown, *The Christian Ambassador. A sermon, preached before the General Synod of Ulster, at Cookstown, upon the last Tuesday of June, 1833* (Belfast, 1833).
[59] James Carlile, *The First and Second Advents, with a View of the Millennium* (Edinburgh, 1848), 30-1.
[60] Morrison, *The Question* (1839), 116.
[61] For example, Paul, *Lord's House* (1839), 36; *OP*, n.s., 2 (1838), 222.

conversion of the Catholic population of Ireland, though they depended upon the financial and moral support of British evangelicals to realise their aims.[62] The Rev. John Brown, for example, made a number of fundraising trips to Scotland. He told a Glasgow audience in 1838, 'To neglect Ireland at this critical juncture will display a want of confidence in God, and inattention to the indications of God's will – to the lessons taught us by passing events.'[63] The foundation of a Jewish missionary society in 1841 also demonstrated interest in the conversion of the Jews. The place of the restoration of Israel in biblical prophecy undoubtedly played an important role in the formation of this society despite disagreements about the character of a Jewish homeland during the millennium and their role in the future conversion of the world.[64]

An important aspect of missionary activity was its inter-denominational character and desire for evangelical unity. This unity provided both a means of spreading the gospel and a dynamic for developing transatlantic co-operation. It is significant that post-millennialists like Brown, Carlile and Morrison were connected with attempts to forge international evangelical solidarity during the 1840s. Brown was a member of the Evangelical Alliance and all three were members of a committee set up by the General Assembly to correspond with evangelical churches in other parts of the world, including Australia, France, Germany and the United States.[65] The Rev. John Coulter believed that Christians had 'reason to expect, not only that the unity of the spirit, but that visible and external unity will prevail, to a very great extent, in the church at the latter day.

---

[62] [William Gibson], *The Position of the Church of Ireland and the Duty of Presbyterians in reference to it, at the present crisis* (Belfast, 1835), 75-8. The evidence for Gibson's authorship comes from a hand-written note on the title page of a copy of this pamphlet held in Union Theological College, Belfast. For British links see Hempton and Hill, *Evangelical Protestantism in Ulster Society* (1992), pp 47-61.

[63] John Brown, *Meroz: A sermon showing the duty of Scottish Christians to Ireland at the present crisis. Preached in Hope Street Gaelic church, on the 18th November* (Glasgow, 1838), 14.

[64] *Second Annual Report of the Home and Foreign Missions of the General Assembly of the Presbyterian Church in Ireland* (Belfast, 1842), 30; David Hamilton, *State and Prospects of Israel: A sermon preached in May Street church, on the 15th November, 1842, at the designation of the Rev William Graham, first missionary to the Jews from the General Assembly of the Presbyterian Church in Ireland* (Belfast, 1843); Carlile, *Mountain* (1846), 32-3.

[65] *Minutes of the General Assembly of the Presbyterian Church in Ireland, 1840-1850* [hereafter, *MGA]* (1844), 326; *MGA* (1845), 417.

The light and love of the millennium will break down barriers, which we now deem hopeless.'[66] In 1840 Coulter was to have the unity he longed for when the Seceders and the Synod of Ulster united to form the General Assembly.

## Reading the Signs of the Times: The 1830s and 1840s

All varieties of Presbyterian opinion believed the 1830s and 1840s were decades of momentous change, although different groups and traditions were interested in different events for different reasons. In 1832 the *Orthodox Presbyterian* declared, 'We live, perhaps, with one exception, in the most eventful period of the history of man – in an age when mighty moral movements are taking place in our own lands, and in the nations around us.'[67] Perhaps inevitably, this sense of expectancy led to the interpretation of developments through the prism of prophecy. By doing so, many Presbyterians hoped to explain events and situate themselves in the purposes of God. According to one commentator, though the study of prophecy had been devalued by certain people, the times demanded 'that the prophetic declarations, especially of the "latter day glory" – now at hand – should at this moment have a very large measure of the attention, and study and prayerful consideration of every genuine disciple of the Lord Jesus Christ'.[68]

The events of the 1790-1850 period certainly provided enough evidence for a prophetic interpretation of the times. In 1836 *The Christian Freeman* declared:

> The amazing fulfilment of prophecy in the events of the French Revolution- the overthrow of the antiquated despotisms of continental Europe – the obvious pouring out of divine judgement on the ancient seats of Papal superstition – the decline of the Turkish empire, with a variety of other occurrences – have powerfully called the minds of the multitudes, in the later days, to the study of the book of Revelation.[69]

Commentators identified the troubles experienced by the papacy with the judgements described by the seventh trumpet and the associated vials of Revelation 11:14-19. The *Covenanter* was even

---

[66] John Coulter, *Will the Two Synods ever Unite? The Rev John Coulter's address to the student's united prayer meeting, Belfast College, on the prospect of union between the General and Secession Synods* (Belfast, 1839), 23.

[67] *OP* 4 (1832), 74.

[68] *OP* 3 (1832), 390.

[69] *CF* 4 (1836), 419.

more specific when it asserted in 1833 that the sounding of the third woe trumpet mentioned in the same passage covered the times they were living in.[70] It was widely believed by Irish and British evangelicals that this period would end in 1866-67 with the commencement of the millennium, possibly heralded by the overthrow of the papacy.[71]

Other developments, including the various European wars, revolutions and diplomatic tensions, along with cholera epidemics and the Irish famine of the 1840s, were interpreted by those interested as 'signs of the times'. Doctrinal innovations were also considered as signs, including, for Covenanters at least, premillennialism:

> To this taste for unwarranted novelties, we may ascribe the revival of the vagaries of the fifth monarchy men, under the name of modern *millenarianism* – the absurd and self-contradictory dogma of *universal pardon* – and, worst of all, that compound of Nestorianism and Socinianism which maintains the *fallen humanity* of an incarnate saviour.[72]

Furthermore, threats to established churches caused concern amongst Presbyterians despite the fact that Presbyterianism was not the established church in Ireland. There were signs that voluntary opinion was gaining ground in the 1830s and some Seceders believed that established churches would cease to exist with the advent of the millennium.[73] In general, however, Presbyterians upheld both the state endowment of true religion and the spiritual independence of the church from the state. This position was informed by adherence to their doctrinal standards, the efforts of the Rev. Henry Cooke to promote protestant unity against Catholic nationalism, and their state endowment via the *regium donum*.[74] Adherence to these principles fuelled their opposition to the further funding of Maynooth College and their unanimous support for the Free Church in 1843.[75]

At the same time, there was a feeling amongst many Presby-

---

[70] *Cov* 3 (1833), 370-2.

[71] Bebbington, *Evangelicalism in Modern Britain* (1989), 83-4; Butler, *Death and Life* (1826), 337-8, 341-3; *CF* 1 (1833), 146.

[72] *Cov*, n.s., 2 (1835), 14.

[73] Brooke, *Ulster Presbyterianism* (1987), 158-63; *CF* 1 (1833), 151; *CF* 2 (1834), 256-7.

[74] R. F. G. Holmes, *Henry Cooke* (Belfast, 1981).

[75] *MGA* (1843), 220-1; William Gibson, *The Flock in the Wilderness; Or, the secession of eighteen hundred and forty-three* (Belfast, 1843); *idem, Maynooth. A protest against its endowment* (Belfast, 1843).

terians that the Church of Ireland was a venial and cumbersome institution that had hindered the spread of the gospel in Ireland.[76] Despite Cooke's best efforts, antipathy towards the established church was heightened when the legality of Presbyterian marriages was called into question in the early 1840s. Politically liberal Presbyterians were also increasingly active in denouncing the power of Anglican landlords through their involvement in the tenant right movement in the 1840s and 1850s.[77] Presbyterians also expressed concern about the spread of Puseyite and anti-evangelical sentiments amongst the Anglican parish clergy and the episcopal bench.[78] The Rev. A P. Goudy claimed that owing to these developments, the Church of Ireland 'must be content to be called the betrayer, instead of the bulwark of protestantism'.[79] The unease created by the growth of Tractarianism was exacerbated by the religious and political mobilisation of Catholics from the 1820s. Presbyterianism had been ambivalent about Catholic emancipation in 1829, though the hotter protestants amongst them were in no doubt about the dangerous import of the measure.[80] The 'Causes of fasting' published by the Reformed Presbyterian synod in 1830 testified 'against the admission of the votaries of popery into high places in the British empire, on account of their tyranny'. The document went on to question whether given the foretold destruction of Antichrist in the Bible, it was right to pray for, and offer allegiance to, the adherents of Catholicism who were now permitted to take high office within the British government.[81] As the 1830s and 1840s progressed, the O'Connellite campaign for repeal of the union, the question of increasing the endowment given to Maynooth, the

---

[76] For example, [D.G. Browne], The *First Blast of the Trumpet against the Monstrous Coalition between Presbytery and Prelacy* (Londonderry, 1834); *idem*, The *Second Blast of the Trumpet against the Monstrous Union of Prelacy and Presbytery* (Londonderry, 1835). Again, the evidence for Browne's authorship comes from a hand-written note on the title page of a copy of this pamphlet held in Union Theological College, Belfast.

[77] Frank Wright, *Two Lands on one Soil; Ulster politics before Home Rule* (Dublin, 1996), 165-207.

[78] Clark Houston, *Letters on the Present Position, Enemies, Prospects, and Duties of Presbyterians* (Londonderry, 1843); [Gibson], *Position of the Church of Ireland* (1835), 50-6.

[79] A. P. Goudy, *Zion's Good; Or, the position and duty of the Irish Presbyterian Church, at the present time: a sermon preached before the Synod of Derry and Omagh, at its annual meeting, in Omagh, on Tuesday, the 16th of May, 1848, and published at its request* (Derry, 1848), 21.

[80] Holmes, *Henry Cooke* (1981), 63-6.

[81] These were reprinted in *Cov* 3 (1836), 18-21.

noted increase in the number of protestant-catholic marriages in Ulster, and the papal aggression of Cardinal Wiseman, intensified anti-Catholic feeling and the sense of approaching upheaval.[82]

The perceived threat to true religion was heightened by what political conservatives believed was a pernicious spirit of liberalism. This mixture of ideas, it was argued, encouraged both Catholicism and atheism. Writers commented upon the unholy alliance of Catholics, Unitarians and infidels, striving to promote liberal principles by supporting, amongst other things, emancipation, voluntaryism, the establishment of the University of London, and Irish municipal reform.[83] Liberality of principle was particularly evident in the scheme of National Education for Ireland implemented in the 1830s. One writer believed that it was a divine judgement 'on Ireland's lukewarm, ungodly, protestant people'.[84] Most Presbyterians objected to the system as it weakened scriptural education by employing books of Scripture extracts and restricting time spent reading the Bible within school hours.[85] Presbyterians were divided, however, over how to articulate their grievances. In 1833 the Synod of Ulster agreed to a series of principles on which they would co-operate with the National Board. Unfortunately for the Synod, relations with the government degenerated over the following year and in 1834 Cooke proposed a hard-line motion against the Board that passed by only six votes. Before 1840, when the government gave in to Presbyterians demands, at least forty ministers had dealt with the Board on the basis of the 1833 propositions.[86] This is an important point for it highlights, again, the fact that Presbyterians were divided into politically liberal and conservative camps. Liberals such as James Carlile, John Paul and the Rev. H. W. Rodgers of Kilrea supported the scheme and were generally more restrained than conservatives in the interpretation of prophecy. On the other hand, conservatives like the Rev. W. K. McKay, and to a lesser extent Cooke, were strongly anti-Catholic in their public pronouncements and more likely to describe events in

---

[82] *OP*, n.s., 2 (1839), 73-9; *MGA* (1845), 414-5; Gibson, *Maynooth* (1843); [W.D. Killen], *Doctor Montgomery and the Pope; Or, the credulous and the creedless* (Belfast, 1851); Brown, *Christian freedom* (1851).

[83] *Cov*, n.s., 3 (1836), 49-56, 241-8; *Cov*, n.s., 4 (1837), 1-10; *OP* 4 (1832), 81-8, 112-21, 153-65.

[84] David Hamilton, *A Sermon on National Education* (Belfast, 1834), 21. Henry Cooke, *National Education. A sermon preached in the Presbyterian church May Street, Belfast, upon, the 15th January, 1832* (Belfast, 1832).

[85] Holmes, *Henry Cooke* (1981), pp 94-104.

[86] D. H. Akenson, *The Irish Education Experiment: The National System of Education in the nineteenth century* (London, 1970), 177.

apocalyptic language.[87] They were also noticeably more political in their response, though it should be pointed out that Carlile was a commissioner for the Board in the 1830s. McKay and his colleague, the Rev. George McClelland, were disciplined by the Synod in 1834 for organising public demonstrations against the scheme and for inciting violence against ministers who had supported it.[88]

The cumulative effect of these pressures led Edward Irving and Henry Drummond to view the United Kingdom as an apostate nation.[89] There was a general feeling amongst conservative Presbyterians in Ulster that 'Everything protestant seems threatened with proscription or extirpation, and nothing seems safe, or in favour with the world, but hypocrisy, liberalism, and popery.'[90] The *Covenanter* argued that by introducing the National Education, 'British rulers have recklessly and wickedly innovated on various principles which are fundamental to the peace, prosperity, and we may add, the very existence of a well-constructed protestant state.'[91] The Rev. William Gibson, minister of Coronary congregation, County Cavan, offered the most notable charge of national apostasy from an Ulster Presbyterian. Gibson argued in 1847 that government concessions to Catholics and their unjust treatment of Presbyterians and Protestants proved 'that the British Empire is still a horn in the great beast' as foretold in Revelation 11.[92] He identified the seventh trumpet and the seven golden vials of Revelation with the destruction of the papal Antichrist in 1866 or 1868 and warned that Britain would also fall because of its apostasy.[93] At the same time, Gibson acknowledged the 'wonderful revival of religion in these lands' and suggested that the approaching troubles would purify both God's church and the nation, the latter acting as a model 'for the remnant of other nations'. As soon as that occurred and the nations were subdued, 'then will Jesus reign in the gracious manner in which it is promised to him and his church in the glorious

---

[87] Henry Cooke, *Speeches of the Rev Dr Cooke, and the Rev. Hugh McNeile, at the Protestant Meeting at Manchester, on Thursday, September, 26, 1839* (Belfast, 1839); W. K. McKay, The *Mystero-hermoneusis: Being an explanation of the prophetic symbols of the apocalypse. Vol. I* (Belfast, 1836).

[88] Akenson, *Irish Education Experiment* (1970), 179-82.

[89] W. H. Oliver, *Prophets and Millennialists:* The *uses of biblical prophecy in England from the 1790s to the 1840s* (Auckland, 1978), 108-10.

[90] *OP* 3 (1832), 115.

[91] *Cov*, n.s., 2 (1835), 192; also *Cov*, n.s., 3 (1836), 11-21.

[92] William Gibson, The *Fall of Antichrist, and especially the Prospects of the British Empire, in Connexion with the Death, Resurrection, and Exaltation of the 'Two Witnesses'- Rev. XI* (Monaghan, 1847), 12-13.

[93] Gibson, The *Fall of Antichrist* (1847), 16-29.

millennium'.[94] Gibson used apocalyptic language but he was not a premillennialist. Though judgements and cataclysmic events would occur before the millennium, it would not be inaugurated by the personal appearance and subsequent reign of Christ on earth.

According to the resolutions of the Irish General Assembly, the majority of Presbyterians in the 1840s still believed that the days of popery were numbered.[95] James Carlile, writing in 1848, refused to take any part 'in the dark and gloomy apprehensions which the present course of events, and the stream of prophecy, suggests to the minds of men'.[96] He saw signs of the weakening of Catholicism in the worldwide distribution of the Bible, the overthrow of monarchies supporting the papacy in the 1848 revolutions, and the revival of the spirit of the Christian martyrs in the Canton de Vaud and the Scottish Free Church.[97] Similarly, the Rev. John Brown of Aghadowey, who had constantly predicted the immanent fall of the papacy through the 1830s and 1840s, declared in 1849 that though the British state had offered too many concessions to Catholicism, 'we rejoice that the schoolmaster is at work, the Bible is open, and God will hear our prayers and hasten the time when earth and heaven shall exult, saying, "Babylon the great is fallen, is fallen."'[98] The devastating Irish famine of the 1840s, and the early success of the Presbyterian Connacht mission, led some to believe that Catholicism would soon become a spent force in Ireland.[99] Disagreements remained about the specific interpretation of events and whether believers should be pessimistic or optimistic about current developments. Nevertheless, they agreed that by living and proclaiming an active evangelical faith, the fate of 'the man of sin' was secured, not only because of its wickedness, but because the will of God had been revealed in the prophecies of Scripture.

## Explaining the Appeal of Prophecy

Given the views of premillennialists, it may seem strange that optimistic and modern postmillennialists continued to have an active

---

[94] Gibson, *The Fall of Antichrist* (1847), 14-15.

[95] *MGA* (1846), 485; *MGA* (1848), 680; *MGA* (1849), 771; *MGA* (1850), 836.

[96] Carlile, *First and Second Advents* (1848), 29.

[97] Carlile, *First and Second Advents* (1848), 29-30.

[98] John Brown, *'Thy Kingdom Come.' A sermon, preached at Magherafelt, on the 29th May, 1849, at the opening of the synod of Ballymena and Coleraine* (Coleraine, 1849), 11-12.

[99] Brown, *Thy Kingdom Come* (1849), 24-7; E. M. Dill, *The Mystery Solved: Or, Ireland's miseries; The grand cause, and cure* (Edinburgh, 1852), 277-94; D. W. Miller, 'Irish Presbyterians and the great famine' (1999), 173-5.

interest in scripture prophecy and its application to contemporary events. In a recent survey of apocalyptic thought in mainstream American Protestantism, J. H. Moorhead has suggested that the answer to this apparent paradox 'involves the complex interaction of protestant beliefs about the nature of biblical predictions, the notion of multiple fulfilments of apocalyptic prophecy throughout history, and the sense of the religious life of each person as a recapitulation in miniature of the Apocalypse'.[100] Taking Moorhead's insights as a framework, this section will explain the continued interest in the interpretation of prophecy amongst Ulster Presbyterians by examining their beliefs concerning the authority of scripture, God's providence and the shape of history, and their personal and communal devotions.

Orthodox, New Light, Unitarian and evangelical writers upheld the supreme authority of scripture, though their exegesis differed in response to the particular features of their theology, whether the place of reason or confessional tradition. Consequently, the existence of a period of spiritual blessing in the millennium had to be explained because it was part of God's revelation to humanity.[101] John Brown acknowledged that though Revelation 20 had been used as the basis of the 'wildest theories', he maintained that 'the lowest view that could be taken of these prophecies' indicated a far-reaching dissemination of the gospel and widespread blessedness.[102] Scholars have pointed out that premillennialists interpreted the Bible, especially prophecy, in a much more literal sense than moderate evangelicals.[103] Literalism often led to an esoteric interpretation of prophecy, as the framework of exegesis was not a theological tradition or canonical context, but often the personal views of the individual, who had a preconceived notion as to how a particular text should be read. Charles Morrison recognised this when he criticised the work of the premillennialist writer William Cunninghame in 1839. Morrison argued that the personal reign of Christ so dominated the premillennialist worldview that 'whether a literal interpretation of a passage would favour this hypothesis, a literal interpretation must be given to it; but when a literal interpretation would prove fatal to their theory, it must be at once discarded, and

---

[100] J. H. Moorhead, 'Apocalypticism in mainstream Protestantism, 1800 to the present', in McGinn *et al.* (eds), The *Encyclopedia of Apocalypticism* (1998), iii. 79.

[101] Compare Dickson, *Sermons* (1793), 63-6; Butler, *Death and Life* (1826), 335-9; *CF* 4 (1836), 149-50.

[102] Brown, *Thy Kingdom Come* (1849), 8.

[103] Bebbington, *Evangelicalism in Modern Britain* (1989), 86-8.

some other mode of interpretation adopted.'[104] The response of moderates like Morrison and Carlile was to place the interpretation of prophecy within the whole canon of Scripture, to recognise much of its symbolic character, and to interpret it where possible by applying passages to past events.[105] For Carlile in particular, the application of prophecy to specific contemporary events was fraught with danger. Any interpretation, he argued, should be considered 'merely as possible or probable conjectures in regard to times and places, and even in regard to the precise nature of the good or evil indicated in them'.[106]

There were indications during this period that a more literal approach to Scripture was developing in Ulster. The works on inspiration by Alexander Carson and Robert Haldane, seen as exemplars of biblical inerrancy and verbal inspiration, were well reviewed by the *Orthodox Presbyterian*.[107] The interpretation of prophecy continued to be applied with confidence to specific contemporary events, especially, though by no means exclusively, by political and theological conservatives. Debate would continue as to the meaning of particular prophecies, however, as Presbyterians from different theological, prophetic and political perspectives agreed on the authority of scripture. As Samuel Davidson suggested in a review of one of Brown's sermons,

> unfulfilled prophecy admits to a great variety of interpretations, all of which may be very plausibly defended, though they be not such as were intended by the Spirit. We ought to be very prayerful, lest we be permitted to go astray in this extended field of scriptural investigation.[108]

The shared conviction that the Bible was the word of God and that every part of scriptural revelation was useful for some purpose may explain the popularity in Ulster of the Free Church premillennialist, the Rev. Alexander Keith. His concern with the past fulfilment of biblical prophecy may have made him more congenial to Ulster Presbyterian postmillennialists. His works, particularly *The study of prophecy indicated by the signs of the times* (1832), were well reviewed in the periodical press and became common in Presbyterian

---

[104] Morrison, *The Question* (1839), 100.
[105] Morrison, *The Question* (1839), 33-5; Carlile, *First and Second Advents* (1848), *passim;* BC 3 (1832), 399-407, 449-56.
[106] Carlile, *First and Second Advents* (1848), 19.
[107] *OP* 2 (1830), 68-72; Bebbington, *Evangelicalism* m *Modern Britain* (1989), 86-90.
[108] *OP*, n.s., 1 (1838), 178.

congregational libraries.[109]

From their reading of Scripture and their confessional tradition, Presbyterians believed that God was sovereign, involving himself in the affairs of the world and directing them for the good of His people. In 1834 the *Covenanter* laid down two principles to be followed when observing the signs of the times: '1. Divine providence is administered by the Mediator; and, 2. All its movements are directed and controlled by him in subserviency to the interests of the church.'[110] Every incident, no matter how small, had meaning in His providential purposes and believers were to learn from God's activity, repent where necessary and thereafter live holy lives. God's people were exhorted to interpret and obey the signs of the times, whether they were international events or personal hardships and struggles:

> Since God often conveys to us lessons of duty, not merely by his revealed word, and by the works of nature, but also by the dispensations of his providence, and as every period of time brings with it a special duty, it becomes us not merely to mark the aspect of the sky to form conjectures about the revolutions of nature, but also so to discern the times and the seasons that we attend to the duties arising from our present circumstances, lest he command his curse upon us, as the angel said 'Curse ye Meroz'Y[1]

In general, the Bible provided the framework for viewing the shape and direction of history: 'For the sake of time past, the Christian studies the Scriptures, as the only authentic record of God and his providence; for the sake of time present, he studies the Scriptures, in which alone he can discover the rule of duty and the secret spiritual enjoyment; and for the sake of the future, he studies the Scriptures, because in them alone he finds the words of eternal life in the testimony of our Lord and Saviour.'[112] In particular, the prophecies contained in Daniel and Revelation furnished a means for Presbyterians to interpret contemporary events. As Moorhead states, the vials, trumpets, beasts, earthquakes and other symbols, were not

---

[109] *Cov* 2 (1832), 392-4, 424-7; *OP* 3 (1832), 389-93; *Catalogue of the Presbyterian Congregational Library, Carrickfergus. Established 1831* ([1831]).
[11] *Cov,* n.s., **1**(1834), 146-7.
[111] Brown, *Meroz* (1838), 7-8.
[112] *OP* 3 (1832), 109. This interest in the passage of time complemented the veneration of history and tradition by Romanticism. In that context, it is significant that the 1830s saw the publication of the first volume of J. S. Reid's monumental *History of the Presbyterian Church in Ireland* (Edinburgh, 1834).

reserved for some future fulfilment, but 'constituted the fabric of all history'.[113] According to Brown, 'under these symbols are veiled God's purposes of mercy and trial to his church, until she shall be raised to a high station of glory and prosperity'.[114] The interpretation of the statue and the four kingdoms mentioned in Daniel 2 and 7 provided a general biblical framework by which to trace and assess the growth of Catholicism in its various political and religious manifestations. This task was given added urgency after 1829 with the increase of anti-Catholic feeling in Britain and Ireland when it seemed that the government was conciliating Catholics at every turn.[115] On at least one occasion, premillennialist writers were berated for identifying 'the man of sin' with general infidelity rather than specifically with the papacy.[116]

The continued interest in prophecy was further stimulated by the corporate and individual devotions of Presbyterianism. Individual conversion, striving for personal holiness, experiencing doubts, fears and hardships, all contributed to an interest in eschatology. The themes of salvation, death, judgement, hell and heaven were common to Christians of all traditions and were heightened by the earnest call of evangelicals to 'flee from the wrath to come' by turning to Christ. For moderate postmillennialists, daily devotions and the pursuit of holiness realised the millennial reign of divine grace and the Holy Spirit within the individual. Charles Morrison argued that instead of expecting the personal reign of Christ on earth, 'Let us look for its establishment in the soul, by the power of divine grace; and let us seek to show, by a holy walk, and Christian conversation, that it has, in deed, and in truth, been set up *'within'* us.'[117] James Carlile maintained that the practice of family worship produced a 'millennial family'.[118] Public worship also had eschatological significance, particularly the Lord's Supper. According to the Secession minister of Carnone, the Rev. William Dickey, at the communion table the believer 'anticipates the moment when he shall drink the new wine in the kingdom of his heavenly father'.[119]

---

[113] Moorhead, 'Apocalypticism' (1998), 80.

[114] Brown, *Thy Kingdom Come* (1849), 10.

[115] McKay, *Mystero-hermoneusis* (1836); Hempton and Hill, *Evangelical Protestantism in Ulster Society* (1992).

[116] *CF* 4 (1836), 157.

[117] Morrison, *The Question* (1839), 102.

[118] Carlile, *Mountain of the Lord's House* (1846), 20.

[119] William Dickey, *The Marriage of the Lamb; Or the joy occasioned by the future conversion of the Jews. A sermon preached in the Seceding meeting-house of Gamone, October 15, 1826, immediately before the dispensation of the Lord's Supper* (Strabane, 1827), 38. More generally, see Leigh Eric

Evangelicalism may have been concerned with the soul of the individual, but communal acts of worship created a sense of community that cannot by ignored.

The interpretation of scripture, the tracing of God's providential hand in current events, and the devotional life of the individual and community, encouraged Presbyterians to consider the course of history and its ultimate end. Prophecy situated them in the divine plan, giving them hope and confidence in the midst of otherwise bewildering events. Eschatology instilled in believers the certain hope that the devil and his minions, particularly the papacy, would be destroyed and that Christ and his saints would be united in heaven for eternity. Before then, the achievement of millennia!glory on earth provided hope that sin and darkness would not ultimately triumph. Contrary to those who emphasise the 'this-worldly' aspect of millennia! beliefs in the 1790s, nineteenth-century postmillennialists also saw improvement in temporal terms, though they differed in the means of achieving it. It was not the imminent return of Christ but the diligent use of the means of grace that would bring about the millennium. They believed the study of prophecy prepared God's people for all eventualities and gave them hope for the future. As James Carlile remarked, believers studied prophecy that they 'may be able to look forward with confidence to the end of the world's eventful history in the coming of the Lord Jesus Christ to effect the restitution of all things'.[120]

## Conclusion: Postmillennial Consensus

According to David Hempton, early premillennialists shared some of the following characteristics:

> biblical literalism, social and ecclesiastical pessimism, Calvinism, anti-catholicism, anti-radicalism, anti-rationalism and support for the Established Churches. It was as much a matter of temperament as a matter of theology.[121]

Premillennial ideas did not develop in small, apocalyptic sects, but amongst well-educated clergymen in the established churches. In addition, the impact of Romanticism with its emphasis upon the individual, the natural world, and the imagination prepared the nineteenth-century religious mind for the adoption of a more vivid

Schmidt, *Holy Fairs: Scottish communions and American revivals in the early modern period* (Princeton, NJ, 1989), 166-8.
[120] Carlile, *First and Second Advents* (1848), 19.
[121] David Hempton, 'Evangelicalism and eschatology', *JEH* 31 (1980), 191.

depiction of the end times.[122] All these characteristics existed to a greater or lesser degree in Ulster Presbyterianism and it is surprising that they did not promote the growth of premillennialism as they had done elsewhere. It could be argued that Presbyterian pesslmlsm should have been more acute given that the overwhelming majority of the Irish population was Catholic.

One characteristic that was absent from the writings of Ulster Presbyterians was the intense pessimism and contempt that Irving and his acolytes had for moderate evangelicalism. Though many Presbyterians, especially political conservatives, had a gloomy view of contemporary events, they believed that the world would improve if the means of grace were used and God executed His judgements through His providential rule. This conviction was also informed by the optimism of the Enlightenment that progress could be achieved through the correct use of rational means, particularly education. Ulster Presbyterianism was not an established church either. They had a strong sense of provincial identity based upon a concentration of numbers, economic influence, and the constant annoyance at the undeserved political and social supremacy of their Anglican neighbours.[123] Moreover, many Presbyterian ministers and tenant farmers in the nineteenth century were political liberals. Included in this group were the ministers James Carlile, John Paul and John Brown. Some of the most radical advocates of tenant right were Presbyterian ministers whose opinions on land reform were denounced by Cooke as 'perfect communist interpretations'.[124] It is much easier to understand the postmillennialism of these men in the context of their reformist political beliefs and jealousy of Anglican privilege. The strong political anti-Catholicism of writers such as Cooke accounts for their more apocalyptic and pessimistic inter-pretation of both prophecy and contemporary events. Yet Presby-terian provincial chauvinism and the optimism generated by internal religious reform, militated against the despondency into which Irving and others slipped.

As Ulster Presbyterians became more immersed in evangelical activity, they were not prepared to criticise methods they believed were bringing about a spiritual reawakening in their own congre-gations. The mood of optimism evident in the 1830s was tempered by realism that reform was only in its infancy. In order to combat the decades of spiritual neglect, Presbyterians did not pray for the

---

[122] Bebbington, *Evangelicalism in Modern Britain* (1989), 75-104.
[123] J. R. B. McMinn, 'Presbyterianism and politics in Ulster, 1871-1906', *Studia Hibernica* 21 (1981), 127-46.
[124] Holmes, *Henry Cooke* (1981), 177.

immediate return of Christ, but for revival and a reawakening of zeal amongst ministers and laity. On a number of occasions, especially around 1859, writers linked the prospect of revival with the dawning of the millennium.[125] Furthermore, the sense of Protestant unity created through interdenominational religious societies was directly threatened by premillennialism. Brown castigated both Irving and J. N. Darby for encouraging schism within evangelicalism. He commented in 1849, 'I think it right to add that the pride and scorn with which its [premillennial] adherents, affect to look down on others, together with its tendency to paralyse missionary exertion and upset the fixed order of Christ's Kingdom, should lead us to view it with suspicion and distrust.'[126] The growth of the Brethren in Ulster after 1859 prompted Presbyterian writers to question both their orthodoxy and impact upon protestant unity.[127]

Ulster Presbyterians did not adopt premillennialism because it threatened the means by which they sought to revive their church and secure their place within a worldwide evangelical network. The millennialism of Presbyterianism after 1798 was explicitly religious and aimed at drawing people to Christ through the preaching of the gospel. This did not mean that the interpretation of prophecy was limited to theological and religious debate. The use of prophecy had as important political and social implications in the nineteenth century as in the 1790s, not least by strengthening links between British and Irish evangelicals that may have also reinforced unionist sympathies. Ultimately, biblical prophecy and the hope of the millennium provided a set of theological categories that could be used by believers to articulate their religious and political concerns and to provide hope in a rapidly changing society. Nineteenth-century Ulster Presbyterian millennialism is unjustly ignored because it did not politicise the masses. An examination of the neglected evidence indicates its continued importance in shaping the beliefs and perceptions of Ulster Presbyterians in the 'modern' nineteenth century.

---

[125] *OP* 7 (1835), 61-2; *Revivals and the Millennial Advent Foretold by the Prophets and Apostles. By a revivalist believer* (Belfast, 1859).

[126] Brown, *Thy Kingdom Come* (1849), 18.

[127] Crawford Gribben, "The worst sect that a Christian man can meet': Opposition to the Plymouth Brethren in Ireland and Scotland, 1859-1900', *SSR* 3 (2002), 34-53.

CHAPTER 8

# Andrew Bonar and the
# Scottish Presbyterian Millennium

Crawford Gribben

In 1859, as the evangelical revival which had emerged in the United
States began to break over northern Ireland and southern Scotland,
Protestant church leaders rushed to offer an initial assessment of
this remarkable 'year of grace'.[1] For the most part, the heirs of the
Reformed tradition were profoundly enthusiastic. The Rev. James
McCosh, formerly a minister of the Free Church of Scotland and
future president of Princeton College, endorsed its progress
throughout Ulster: 'the work has reached nearly every district of the
Counties Antrim and Down...it has reached many places in Derry,
Tyrone, Monaghan, and Armagh, and some places even in Donegal
and Cavan...thousands and tens of thousands have been convinced
or converted.'[2] But for many, an enthusiasm for revival came as part
of a much larger theological package. Many of McCosh's peers in the
Irish Presbyterian church hailed the revival as the precursor of a
much greater work of God, understanding its remarkable progress as

---

[1] For the impact of the revival, see I. A. Muirhead, 'The revival as a
dimension of Scottish church history', *RSCHS* 20 (1980), 179-96; Kathryn
Teresa Long, *The Revival of 1857-58: Interpreting an American Religious
Awakening* (Oxford, 1998); Janice Holmes, *Religious Revivals in Britain and
Ireland, 1859-1905* (Dublin, 2000); Crawford Gribben, 'The worst sect a
Christian man can meet: Opposition to the Plymouth Brethren in Ireland
and Scotland, 1859-1900', *SSR* 3:2 (2002), 34-53; and Kenneth S. Jeffrey,
*When the Lord Walked the Land: The 1858-62 Revival in the North-east of
Scotland,* Studies in Evangelical History and Thought (Carlisle, 2002).
[2] James McCosh, *The Ulster Revival and its Physiological Accidents: A Paper
Read Before the Evangelical Alliance, September 22, 1859* (Belfast, 1859), 10-
11. On McCosh and Princeton, see David B. Calhoun, *Princeton Seminary:
The Majestic Testimony, 1869-1929* (Edinburgh, 1996), 7.

an   apocalyptic  intervention   heralding   the    promise   of   the
millennium.[3] These patterns of events, the Rev. John Weir expected,
pointed onwards 'to  the  glories of  the  millennia!age',  [4] and would
recur  'by  periodic, special, and  abundant  visitations  of  heavenly
influence, until  Christianity  shall become  the  dominant power  in  the
world'.[5] Others   understood   the   revival  to   have    cosmological
implications, according to another clerical commentator, who noted
'some  strange  appearances  in  the  heavens, such  as comets and  other
phenomena', and  enthused, 'thank  God,  the  days  of  the  millennia!
advent  are   ushering  in.'[6]  In  Ireland,  Presbyterian  leaders  were
endorsing  the  revival because  it  seemed  to  anticipate  –  if not  to
inaugurate-the  millennium itself.

The  Scots tended  to  match  their  enthusiasm  without  necessarily
endorsing  the  distinctive  expectation  of  their  eschatological  hope.
One  of  the  leading  ministers  of  the  Free  Church,  for  example,
hurried  across  to  Ulster  and  returned  with  enthusiastic  news  of  the
revival's impact.[7] The  revival had  made  a major impact upon  his  own
denomination:  forty-two  of  the   church's  sixty-six  presbyteries
reported  'decided  revivals'  during  the    period.[8]  But    as  events
progressed, it became clear  that  he  did  not  share  the  optimistic,
postmillennial  view  that  characterised  so  many  of  the  Irish
ministers. Instead,  the  Rev.  Andrew  Bonar  marked  the  'year  of
grace' by  publishing  a  robustly  premillennial  commentary  on  the
Psalms. He  wrote  with  a  strange  sense  of  foreboding about  the
uncertain  future  of  conservative  Protestantism  in  'Britain,  the
retreat  of  God's  hidden  ones'. Paralleling  the  national  election  of
ancient Israel  and  the  modern British  state,  he  discerned among  the
signs  of  the   times  a   vast  international   conspiracy designed  to
undermine  the   traditional  faith  of  the    Anglo-Saxon  Protestant
establishment:

> it seems  probable  that He who knew  men's  hearts saw  more  than  once
> this same  hatred to Israel taking  the  form of a combined conspiracy of

---

[3] See Iain H. Murray, *The Puritan Hope: Revival and the Interpretation of Prophecy* (Edinburgh, 1971), *passim.*
[4] John Weir, *The Ulster Awakening: Its Origin, Progress, and Fruit: With Notes of a Tour of Personal Observation and Inquiry* (London, 1860), 9.
[5] Weir, *The Ulster Awakening* (1860), 7.
[6] [Anon], *Revivals and the Millennial Advent Foretold by the Prophets and the Apostles* (Belfast, 1859), 5.
[7] *DSCHT,* s.v. 'Bonar, Andrew'. This event is not recorded in the published *Diary.* See Jeffrey, *When the Lord walked the land* (2002), 259.
[8] Muirhead, 'The revival as a dimension of Scottish church history' (1980), 184.

all the nations round. Even thus has it been more than once in regard to Britain, the retreat of God's hidden ones; and even thus, were the vail lifted up, might it be found to be true to this hour of the foes of Protestant truth. And yet more shall the Latter Days bring to view a combination of kings and people against the Lamb and his faithful few – a combination which shall meet with extinction on the plains of Megiddo.[9]

Expecting persecution rather than millennial bliss, it was not the first time that Bonar's distinctly apocalyptic temper put him out of step with the sympathies of his age.

## Bonar's Background

Andrew Bonar was born on 29 May 1810, the seventh son of an Edinburgh lawyer. With his two brothers Horatius and John, he was part of a famous trio of ministers who exercised profound influence upon the piety of the Free Church movement and the hymnody of a wider evangelicalism throughout the nineteenth century.[10] Following arts and theological studies in Edinburgh, Andrew Bonar was inducted into the ministry of the Church of Scotland, becoming assistant to John Purves at Jedburgh, in 1835, and to the young Robert Smith Candlish at St George's, Edinburgh, in 1836. In 1838, he was called to the parish of Collace, where he exercised devoted pastoral care and from which he took part in the celebrated 'mission of inquiry' to Palestine, along with his close friend Robert Murray McCheyne, in 1839. Profoundly moved by McCheyne's untimely death at the age of twenty-nine, he edited his friend's memoirs into one of the most popular pietistic textbooks of Victorian evangel-icalism. The reception of McCheyne's hagiography laid the found-ation for Bonar's extensive literary career, which included projects as diverse as editing the letters of Samuel Rutherford and writing a systematic repudiation of the postmillennial position which the Covenanting theologian had espoused. In 1843, when one third of the ministers and one half of the laity in the Church of Scotland withdrew to form the Free Church, Bonar identified with the evangelical secession, and preached in a tent until a Free Church building was constructed in the parish.[11] He continued with the

[9] Andrew Bonar, *Christ and his Church in the Psalms* (London, 1859), 247.

[10] For Horatius Bonar, see [Anon.], *Horatius Bonar, D.D.: A Memorial* (London, 1890).

[11] Donald M. Lewis (ed.), *Blackwell Dictionary of Evangelical Biography* (Oxford, 1995), s.v., 'Bonar, Andrew'. For a recent survey of Disruption scholarship, see Donald J. Withrington, 'The Disruption: A century and a

support of his Collace congregation until his call to Finnieston,
Glasgow, in 1856. Amid the social deprivation of Finnieston he again
oversaw the construction of a new church building – its Hebrew
motto of 'he that winneth souls is wise' (Proverbs 11:30) indicating
his sustained interest in Jewish missions- and used the church as a
base for his enthusiastic participation in the Moody and Sankey
missions of 1873-5.[12] By then established as an evangelical
statesman, his ecclesiastical responsibilities were matched by public
honours. In April 1874 he was awarded an Edinburgh D.D., and in
1878 he was appointed Moderator of the Free Church General
Assembly, in which position he used his influence to support the
faltering conservative party. Twelve years later, in the General
Assembly of 1890, he led the unsuccessful conservative protest
against Marcus Dods, who had been appointed as Professor of New
Testament Criticism and Exegesis at New College, Edinburgh, one
year earlier, but whose liberal views on biblical inspiration were
provoking the ire of the conservatives. As he lay dying, two years
later in December 1892, Bonar was preoccupied with the thought of
his congregation's forthcoming collection for Jewish missions; but

> he closed his eyes and fell asleep so quietly that those round his bed
> hardly knew when life was gone. A look of inexpressible peace, almost
> of delighted surprise, rested on his face, as if he had suddenly and
> unexpectedly found himself in the presence of his much-loved Lord and
> Master, with whom he had been walking all his years on earth, and
> who now 'received him into glory.'[13]

In 1893, when his daughter Marjory published his *Diary*, Bonar, who
had shaped the legend of McCheyne, was elevated into evangelical
sainthood for himself.

It is ironic that Bonar's literary canonisation should have
consolidated his prominence in the Scottish evangelical mainstream,
for Bonar was not a likely candidate for fame. If his diary can be
trusted, his early years of ministry evidenced a continual struggle
with the system of eschatology then dominating the Scottish
Presbyterian establishment. With its adherence to the Westminster
Confession of Faith (1647), mainstream Scottish Presbyterianism

half of historical interpretation', *RSCHS* 25:1 (1993), 118-153. See also
Angus Calder, 'The Disruption in Fiction', in Stewart J. Brown and Michael
Fry (eds), *Scotland in the Age of the Disruption* (Edinburgh, 1993), 113-132.
[12] Kenneth R. Ross, 'Calvinists in Controversy: John Kennedy, Horatius
Bonar and the Moody Mission of 1873-74', *SBET 9:1* (1991), 51-63.
[13] Marjory Bonar (ed.), *Andrew A. Bonar: Diary and Life* (1893; rpt.
Edinburgh, 1960), 387.

tended to adhere to an optimistic, if rather undefined, millennia! position, which, as the nineteenth century progressed, was increasingly identified as postmillennialism.[14] Bonar, influenced by a culture far removed from Protestant scholasticism, does not ever seem to have shared the salient structures of that position. Millennia!themes are central to Bonar's thinking throughout his career, but his was a variant of the vigorous premillennialism growing throughout the early nineteenth-century revival of primitivistic Calvinism.[15] Thus a strong interest in premillennialism seems to precede his conversion to evangelical faith, colours his sense of call to the ministry, and pervades the formative years of his theological training.

In May 1829, for example, his diary recorded the impact of the most famous premillennialist (and most notorious heretic) of the early nineteenth century, the Rev. Edward Irving.[16] Irving had travelled from London to Edinburgh hoping to capitalise upon the success of his lectures on the Apocalypse exactly one year before. In 1829, he lectured on the same subject, despite the growing theological suspicions of the Edinburgh clergy, and made a profound impression upon some of his auditors.[17] Bonar had been 'hearing Mr. Irving's lectures all the week, and am persuaded now that his views of the Coming of Christ are truth. The views of the glory of Christ opened up in his lectures have been very impressive to me.' On 1 January 1830, struggling with his sense of call to ministry, he recorded that 'I have thought reputation much, but I see that, to one who believes the Word of God regarding the last days, such desire is folly.'[18] Exactly one year later, on 1 January 1831, he noted that 'wars and rumours of wars prepare us for things coming upon the

---

[14] **It** is anachronistic to apply the terms 'premillennial' and 'postmillennial' to the eschatological positions of the seventeenth century, for the *OED* suggests the terms were only coined in the nineteenth century. For the debate about the eschatological position of the Westminster Confession of Faith, see Crawford Gribben, 'The eschatology of the puritan confessions', *SBET20:1* (2000), 51-78.

[15] D. W. Bebbington, *Evangelicalism in Modern Britain: A History from the 1730s to the 1980s* (London, 1989), 77-86.

[16] For Irving, see Gordon Strachan, *The Pentecostal Theology of Edward !ruing* (London, 1973); Arnold Dallimore, *The Life of Edward !ruing: Forerunner of the Charismatic Movement* (Edinburgh, 1983); Graham W. P. McFarlane, *Christ and the Spirit: The Doctrine of the Incarnation according to Edward !ruing* (Carlisle, 1996); Calumba Graham Clegg, *Gathered Under the Apostles: A Study of the Catholic Apostolic Church* (Oxford, 1992).

[17] Dallimore, *Life of Edward !ruing* (1983), 85-97.

[18] Bonar (ed.), *Andrew A. Bonar* (1960), 9.

earth. It may be, also, the sudden appearing of the Lord Jesus Christ. The nations are waking.'[19] By October of that year, Bonar's premillennialism was emphatic: 'more and more convinced that the time of Christ's Coming is before the thousand years; often grieved by hearing opposition to this.'[20] On 21 January 1832 he discoursed upon the first resurrection and the reign of Christ in a paper he presented to the Exegetical Society at the University of Edinburgh.[21] By March he was grieving over his colleagues' lack of enthusiasm for foreign mission, and felt dissuaded from personal involvement in the missionary task only by his brother Horatius, who 'spoke about the need for labourers and ministers at home, and the witness for Christ's Second Coming borne by few in this land. That may be part of our work.'[22]

If the defence of premillennialism was indeed central to Bonar's sense of his own life and work, it was a powerful indication of the extent to which conservative and evangelical Scottish Presbyterians were actively involved in re-shaping the theology of the Westminster Confession- and an indication of how early this process of revision began. The received historiography of nineteenth-century Scottish Calvinism has regularly called attention to the Free Church's role in the initial dissemination of German 'higher criticism' and scientific materialism within the British Isles, but has tended to signal the process of confessional revision as an interest of 'liberals' within the church.[23] It is liberals who are most often blamed for the fact that the church that began in the revivalistic scenes of the 1843 Disruption should within its first fifty years become the most important conduit of liberal Biblical criticism within the English-speaking world. Thus the celebrated trials of William Robertson Smith, the young Free Church professor whose contributions to the *Encyclopaedia Britannica* proved so disturbing to conservatives and so influential upon radicals such as Professor Charles Briggs and Sir James Frazer, only indicated the extent to which theological liberalism had come to be tolerated within the institutions of his church. Similarly, the controversial Declaratory Act of 1892 signalled an official permission for Free Church students to qualify their own confessional subscription in a manner similar to that of

---

[19] Bonar (ed.), *Andrew A. Bonar* (1960), 15.
[20] Bonar (ed.), *Andrew A. Bonar* (1960), 5, 17.
[21] Bonar (ed.), *Andrew A. Bonar* (1960), 19.
[22] Bonar (ed.), *Andrew A. Bonar* (1960), 20.
[23] D. W. Bebbington, 'Henry Drummond, evangelicalism and science', *RSCHS* 28 (1998), 132-38; Iain D. Campbell, "Fact not dogma': George Adam Smith, evangelicalism and Biblical criticism', *SBET* 18:1 (2000), 3.

other mainstream denominations. These trends converged in the year of the church's jubilee, signalling the dramatic conclusion to its changing theological consensus. The anniversary was marked not only by the Assembly's reception of accolades from sister communions around the world, but also by a 'Second Disruption', as a significant proportion of the Free Church's Highland population, after years of contesting this growing liberalism, left to form the Free Presbyterian Church.[24]

But Bonar's intellectual development challenges the late date that historians have often proposed for the beginnings of this 'Great Confessional Controversy'.[25] It challenges too B. B. Warfield's belief, articulated in an 1889 article in the *Presbyterian Review,* that 'widespread agitation regarding the relation of the churches to the Westminster Standards' was a feature only of 'the last few years'.[26] It is true that the 1880s and early 1890s mark the conclusion of the agitation for revision, but this was only the end of a process that had its origins in the early intellectual development of some of the foremost leaders in the Disruption movement. In Scotland, Bonar's experience demonstrates how unhelpful it is to see this process of confessional qualification either as a distinctly recent or as a distinctly liberal trend. The origins of this confessional revisionism should be traced to the very inception of the Free Church, and to the ecclesiastical environment that was shaping the youthful Bonar.

In recent years, there has been some recognition of the theological ambivalence of the early Free Church. Various scholars have discussed the extent to which the foundational theologians of the Free Church movement – men like James Bannerman, William Cunningham and Robert Candlish – were responsible for their students' growing confessional ambiguity. R. A. Riesen's *Criticism and Faith in late Victorian Scotland* (1985) argued that the seeds of the later controversy were sown in the latent liberalism of the 'Free Church Fathers', and particularly in their diverging doctrines of Scripture. Others, like Nicholas R. Needham in *The Doctrine of Holy Scripture in the Free Church Fathers* (1991), have replied by arguing that Riesen's thesis proves too much: 'I am unable to detect any

---

24 James Lachlan MacLeod, The *Second Disruption:* The *Free Church in Victorian Scotland and the Origins of the Free Presbyterian Church* (East Linton, 2000), *passim.*
25 A. C. Cheyne, 'The place of the Confession throughout three centuries', in A. I. C. Heron (ed.), The *Westminster Confession in the Church Today* (Edinburgh, 1982), 125.
26 B. B. Warfield, 'The Presbyterian Churches and the Westminster Confession', *Presbyterian Review* 10:40 (1889), 646.

serious departure in the views of Chalmers, Cunningham, Bannerman, Candlish and Duncan from what intelligent spokesmen of Protestant orthodoxy have always held on the matter of Scripture.'[27] Perhaps, therefore, attention should be focused elsewhere. The tensions in Andrew Bonar's youthful commitment to premillennialism, for example, confirm Riesen's belief that the origins of the later debates can be traced to the influence of the Free Church Fathers; but they do also confirm Needham's belief that they need not be traced to the Free Church Father's doctrine of Scripture. Bonar's experience seems to suggest that it was in their elaborations of eschatology, rather than the doctrine of Scripture, that Free Church evangelicals first responded to the pinch of confessional restriction.

Bonar's youthful enthusiasm for eschatology was very much a part and parcel of the Romantic tenor of his age.[28] He had been influenced by Irving, as we have seen, who had in turn been influenced by Coleridge and had been hailed somewhat Byronically as 'that misguided son of genius'.[29] Irving's eschatological enthusiasms would have been sustained in Bonar's imagination by the ministerial training course upon which he had embarked. In Edinburgh, listening to the lectures of Thomas Chalmers, 'possibly the most influential Scot of the nineteenth century', Bonar gained personal experience of the tightly knit nexus of Scottish millennia! Presbyterians, for Chalmers and Irving were well known to one another.[30] Both were socially-concerned advocates of a primitivistic ecclesiology; both were among the most celebrated preachers within Scottish Presbyterianism; and both were firmly millennia!. Irving had been Chalmers' assistant at St John's Church, Glasgow, where he had described his mentor in 1822 as 'the most eloquent of men' who had 'diverged further than any of his age from the approved course of preaching, and launched a bold adventure of his own into the ocean of religious speculation, bringing off prouder triumphs to

---

27 Nicholas R. Needham, *The Doctrine of Holy Scripture in the Free Church Fathers* (Edinburgh, 1991), 151.

28 For growth in ecclesiastical and theological primitivism during the Romantic period, see Deryck Lovegrove, 'The Mirage of Authenticity: Scottish Independents and the Reconstruction of a New Testament Order of Worship, 1799-1808', in R. N. Swanson (ed.), *Continuity and Change in Christian Worship,* Studies in Church History 35 (London, 1999), 261-274; and Gribben, 'The worst sect a Christian man can meet' (2002).

29 William Reid, *Plymouth Brethrenism Unveiled and Refuted* (Edinburgh, 1875), 296.

30 T. M. Devine, *The Scottish Nation 1700-2000* (London, 1999), 364.

his Redeemer than any ancient pilot of them all'.[31] Irving's judgement emphasises the extent to which Chalmers' vast theological intellect defies either easy categorisation or uncomplicated adherence to the Westminster Confession.[32] Although historians rarely note its importance, it is crucial to identify eschatological speculation as one important locus of Chalmers' confessional ambivalence. His published statements, with characteristic ambiguity, seem to suggest a distinctively apocalyptic philosophy of history combined with a firm postmillennialism.[33] Listening to Chalmers, whatever his uncertainties, Bonar was being taught by one of the most significant apocalyptic thinkers of his day.

Bonar's growing interest in millennial themes was further encouraged by his contacts with the Rev. John Purves, a noted premillennialist. In July 1835, 'John Purves and I had an interesting and profitable conversation on the Second Advent, and the exaltation of Christ.'[34] By September, 'especially after two sermons of John Purves on the subject, have felt more truly than before the desirableness of the Coming of our Lord.'[35] By September 1836, Bonar could note that Purves had been preaching 'God's truth regarding Christ's Coming'.[36] The influence of Purves was so extensive that Bonar submitted to him his sense of call to an assistantship with Candlish in November 1836:

> my intercourse with Mr. Candlish would be perhaps useful in many things; and my preaching to his people gives such large opportunity of usefulness among the intellectual classes, and among many of my old school-fellows, who are anxious for my coming. I feel that I might help in the study of prophecy, especially if Horace goes away. I feel that if John Purves were to advise my going, I would be quite satisfied, and believe it the leading of Providence.[37]

31 Edward Irving, 'Farewell Discourse at St. John's, Glasgow', in *The Collected Writings of Edward !ruing*, ed. G. Carlyle (London, 1865), iii. 346, 350-1.

32 John Roxborogh, *Thomas Chalmers: Enthusiast for Mission: The Christian Good of Scotland and the Rise of the Missionary Movement* (Carlisle, 1999), xiii; MacLeod, *The Second Disruption* (2000), 187.

33 Thomas Chalmers, 'The Second Coming of Christ', in *The Works of Thomas Chalmers* (Glasgow, n.d.), x. 170; and Chalmers, 'On the Miraculous and Internal Evidences of the Christian Revelation and the Authority of its Records', in *Works* (n.d.), iii. 372-4.

34 Bonar (ed.), *Andrew A. Bonar* (1960), 31.

35 Bonar (ed.), *Andrew A. Bonar* (1960), 35.

36 Bonar (ed.), *Andrew A. Bonar* (1960), 42.

37 Bonar (ed.), *Andrew A. Bonar* (1960), 44.

Despite his association with one of the leading Free Churchmen-for 'Candlish was second only to Thomas Chalmers in his prestige' in the new denomination[38] – Bonar discovered that his adherence to premillennialism was acting as a barrier to his being situated in a pastoral charge. In his diary entry for 9 September 1837, he noted being 'cast down by the circumstance of my being kept out of several appointments on account of my millenarianism chiefly'.[39] Even the congregation of St. Peter's Dundee, where the saintly Robert Murray McCheyne had ministered until his death in 1843, would reject their late minister's close friend on that basis: 'many of the electors could not bear my views of Christ's Advent.'[40] But perhaps they received news of Bonar's eschatological beliefs with some degree of surprise. Despite their close friendship and literary co-operation, overt premillennialism had not been a feature of Bonar's public interactions with McCheyne.

## The Mission to the Jews (1839)

The negotiated centre of Bonar and McCheyne's shared millennialism was clearly outlined in the *Narrative of a Mission of Inquiry to the Jews from the Church of Scotland in 1839* (1842). This book was a written account of what was perhaps the most influential missionary journey undertaken by representatives of the Scottish churches in the nineteenth centuryУ The initial impetus for the expedition had been given by Robert Candlish, who encouraged McCheyne to consider travelling to Palestine for the sake of his troubled health. McCheyne and Bonar organised their journey along with Dr Alexander Keith (1791-1880), an older man who had gained a reputation as a leading exponent of premillennialism. His *Evidence of the Truth of the Christian Religion from the Literal Fulfilment of Prophecy* (1828) would go through almost forty editions during his own lifetime, reaching the thirty-sixth edition in 1849, and would be widely applauded: 'We cannot fail to have our confidence in the literality of the still unfulfilled word of prophecy greatly strengthened, by the perusal of such a volume of evidence on the past.'[42] Less popular, if no less influential, the *Narrative* was

---

[38] J. R. Wolffe, 'Candlish, Robert Smith', in *DSCHT* (1993), 134.

[39] Bonar (ed.), *Andrew A. Bonar* (1960), 55.

[40] Bonar (ed.), *Andrew A. Bonar* (1960), 103.

[41] Don Chambers, 'Prelude to the last things: The Church of Scotland's mission to the Jews', *RSCHS* 19:1 (1975), 43-58.

[42] *Blackwell Dictionary of Evangelical Biography,* s.v. 'Keith, Alexander'; review of Keith's *Evidence* in *Quarterly Journal of Prophecy* 1:2 (1849), 192.

prepared after Bonar and McCheyne had returned from their 'mission of inquiry' and had embarked on deputations throughout Scotland to promote their findings.

Reflecting the shared conclusions of both authors, the *Narrative* offered a vaguely millennia!perspective but refused to endorse any particular millennia! detail. Throughout its pages, there are no references to the millennium, and no citations of Revelation 20. It seems that shared authorial responsibilities were moderating Bonar's intense apocalyptic excitement. Thus the *Narrative* evidences a conservative and Confessional view of the identity of the antichrist. Landing at Boulogne, Bonar and McCheyne's first impressions of France were not positive: 'Popery is strong here, and to meet with so many ensigns of the "Man of Sin" on our first arrival, did not make France the more agreeable to us.'[43] Later in the journey, in Malta, the authors noted that 'Popery is their curse; churches and priests abound; and our government has hitherto done too much to countenance the Man of Sin in Malta.'[44] One sure marker for the prevalence of antichristian evil was the scant respect paid to the Scottish Sabbath: 'a Sabbath of holy rest is a thing unknown in the dominions of the Man of Sin.'[45]

But if the *Narrative* takes a seventeenth-century view of the 'man of sin', its evaluation of major European cultural centres owes more to the apocalyptic Protestants of the late eighteenth century. 'No city seems more to resemble Sodom,' the authors agreed of the French capitaU[6] Footnoting Revelation 11:8 ('And their dead bodies shall lie in the street of the great city, which spiritually is called Sodom and Egypt, where also our Lord was crucified'), they noted that 'Paris is supposed by many to be "the street of the great city," referred to in the book of Revelation.'[47] In Genoa, Bonar and McCheyne continued their fiercely allegorical apocalyptic exegesis; there, the rich were 'as intent on pleasure, as if the day of Babylon's doom was afar off.[48] And, as was appropriate for the city whose condemnation was gained for its trading in 'slaves, and souls of men' (Revelation 18:13), Babylon's sin was explained to be inherent in the political dangers of Roman Catholic hegemony. Invoking a staple of Protestant polemic,

---

[43] Andrew A. Bonar and Robert Murray McCheyne, *Narrative of a Mission of Inquiry to the Jews from the Church of Scotland in 1839,* second edition (Edinburgh, 1842), i. 4.

[44] Bonar and McCheyne, *Narrative* (1842), i. 47-8.

[45] Bonar and McCheyne, *Narrative* (1842), ii. 280.

[46] Bonar and McCheyne, *Narrative* (1842), i. 10.

[47] Bonar and McCheyne, *Narrative* (1842), i. 11.

[48] Bonar and McCheyne, *Narrative* (1842), i. 23.

the authors argued that the dangers of 'Popery' lay in its incipient threat to liberty: 'No country has freedom like our own, because no land on earth has had the truth of God so fully preached, and so widely embraced.'[49] The civic benefit of the Reformation, they felt, was pronounced upon their return to Prussia: 'we felt that we breathed a freer air as soon as we knew we were beyond the dominions of the Man of sin.'[50]

Like much travel literature of the period, the authors interpreted their experiences through analogies that their readers would recognise. At times this is humorous – such as Mount Carmel's disappointing size in comparison with Lochnagar – but the method worked consistently to involve the general ecclesiastical concerns of Scottish evangelicals with the particular issue of Jewish evangelism.[51] In Egypt, on 16 May 1839, the travellers thought of home: 'It was the morning of the day on which our General Assembly was to meet in Edinburgh, an Assembly in which the important question of the Spiritual Independence of our Church, and the privilege of its Christian people, were likely to be keenly discussed.'[52] The ecclesiastical struggle the authors anticipated was interpreted through the lens of predictive prophecy. Receiving news of an important development on the pathway to the Disruption, Bonar and McCheyne surmised that the news 'seemed to intimate a time of coming trial to the Church of Scotland. The time seemed to be come when judgment must begin at the house of God in Scotland; and we called to mind the clear intimations of prophecy, that "there shall be a time of trouble such as never was since there was a nation," at the very time when Israel shall be delivered.'[53] Beyond the imminent judgement, however, Scotland's links with Israel also brought hope. Meditating on their first sight of Jerusalem, the authors concluded that they were 'not aware that any clergyman of the Church of Scotland was ever privileged to visit the Holy City before, and now that the four of us had been brought thus far by the good hand of our God upon us, we trusted that it might be a token for good, and perhaps the dawn of a brighter day for our beloved Church, a day of generous self-denied exertion in behalf of scattered Israel and a perishing world.'[54] In their eschatological worldview, the purity of the Church of Scotland was bound up with the struggle for the

---

49 Bonar and McCheyne, *Narrative* (1842), ii. 293.
50 Bonar and McCheyne, *Narrative* (1842), ii. 307.
51 Bonar and McCheyne, *Narrative* (1842), i. 306.
52 Bonar and McCheyne, *Narrative* (1842), i. 71.
53 Bonar and McCheyne, *Narrative* (1842), i. 251.
54 Bonar and McCheyne, *Narrative* (1842), i. 170.

independence of its church courts and its taking seriously its responsibility for Jewish evangelism.

The times were certainly propitious. Bonar and McCheyne frequently noted the apocalyptic expectations of the Jews: 'The hope of Messiah's coming is strong in the hearts of many Jews here. Many believed that it would be in the year 1840, as that was the end of a period fixed in the book ofZohar.'[55] This belief was shared by Jews in Constantinople,[56] Jews in Seret (in Austrian Poland),[57] and in Moldavia: 'Some of them expressed their belief that Messiah would come in the year 1840, and others think it is to be in the seventh-thousand year of the world, and then a time of Sabbaths is to follow.'[58] The Jewish community was in danger of such ferment, the *Narrative* recorded, that a Polish Rabbi had been warning them off expecting a Messiah in 1840, for fear that their eventual discouragement would lead many of the hopeful to abandon their faith.[59]

Bonar and McCheyne, nevertheless, stated their firm belief in the literal hermeneutic which the Jews adopted to reach these conclusions. Its method was so fundamental, they believed, that it ought to be incorporated into the training of every missionary. Of course missionaries should have linguistic competence in Hebrew (which ought to be acquired with a Spanish accent), Arabic, Spanish, German and Italian. But a missionary should also be 'well-grounded in prophecy, and he should be one who fully and thoroughly adopts the principles of literal interpretation, both in order to give him hope and perseverance, and in order to fit him for reasoning with Jews.'[60] The *Narrative* later approvingly quotes one converted Jew from London, then engaged in Jewish evangelism in Israel: 'The Jews feel their dispersion to be literal; and therefore if you explain unfulfilled prophecy by saying it is spiritual, they reckon you a kind of infidel.'[61] This emphasis upon a literal hermeneutic is foundational to the discussions of the *Narrative*, and perhaps explains why the missionary team was as much engaged in the evaluation of their eschatological hermeneutic as they were in direct evangelism. As at Gaza, the missionaries tested what they saw by the expectations of what they should see if their principles of literal interpretation were

---

55 Bonar and McCheyne, *Narrative* (1842), i. 174.
56 Bonar and McCheyne, *Narrative* (1842), ii. 135.
57 Bonar and McCheyne, *Narrative* (1842), ii. 237.
58 Bonar and McCheyne, *Narrative* (1842), ii. 210.
59 Bonar and McCheyne, *Narrative* (1842), ii. 201.
60 Bonar and McCheyne, *Narrative* (1842), i. 258-9.
61 Bonar and McCheyne, *Narrative* (1842), i. 328.

correct: 'It appeared at first as if there had been no fulfilment of those distinct predictions...But when we had completed our investigation, we found that not one word had fallen to the ground.'[62] Bonar and McCheyne may have disagreed on their understanding of the millennium, but they seem to have shared with Keith the literal hermeneutic of the millennial approach.

It was with some degree of surprise, therefore, that Bonar and McCheyne noted that not all of the Christians whom they encountered were prepared to share this view. In Smyrna, for example, they discovered that:

> Every thing indicates that the strength of the empire is gone, and that the time is at hand when "the waters of the great river Euphrates shall be dried up." [Revelation 16:12] This state of things has contributed very much to direct the attention of English Christians in Turkey to the study of prophecy, and to make them watch every new sign of "the way of the kings of the east being prepared," [Revelation 16:12] and the glorious events that are to follow. Few, however, of our American brethren there have been led to take any deep interest in these views.[63]

But this was to the Americans' loss, for 'these views' were appearing to be ever more fundamental not only to the resurgence of Jewish evangelism, but also to the renewal of the missionaries' sending churches. While McCheyne was away from his Dundee pulpit, revival had broken out under his pastoral replacement, William Chalmers Burns, as well as in Burns' father's church in Kilsyth. This religious awakening brought spectacular renewal to the jaded Scottish evangelicals, and represented, Bonar and McCheyne believed, the blessing that God had in store for those who prayed and worked for the peace of Jerusalem: 'God had done this in the very year when the Church of Scotland had stretched out her hand to seek the welfare of Israel, and to speak peace to all her seed.'[64] There could therefore be renewal in the Scottish church, troubled though it was by ecclesiastical discontent – but it would be a renewal that would come when Scottish Presbyterians played their part in restoring to Israel the gospel blessings they had spurned.[65]

## The Disruption and the Death of McCheyne (1843)

As Bonar and McCheyne saw their *Narrative* through to publication,

---

[62] Bonar and McCheyne, *Narrative* (1842), i. 134-5.
[63] Bonar and McCheyne, *Narrative* (1842), ii. 118.
[64] Bonar and McCheyne, *Narrative* (1842), ii. 356.
[65] Chambers, 'Prelude to the last things' (1975), 51.

events heralding secession from the Scottish church seemed to be gathering speed. The theological trends that had been causing such concern to Scottish evangelicals seemed to be coming to a focus. The evangelical establishment was rocked by two significant events. In March 1843, as typhus raged through his parish, McCheyne's fragile hold upon life was extinguished. Two months later, in May, Chalmers led the Scottish evangelicals out of the establishment. The Disruption was to be one of the most dramatic events to occur in nineteenth-century Scotland.[66]

In the tumultuous first year of the new church's life, Bonar responded to the events of 1843 not by a polemical defence of the evangelical secession, but by editing the *Memoirs and Remains of R. M. McCheyne* (1844), a volume that established his friend's reputation as the patron saint of Victorian evangelicals and appropriated his reputation for the Free Church movement. The volume was singularly successful in ensuring that, with the exception of Chalmers, 'probably no figure in Scottish ecclesiastical life during the nineteenth century bequeathed a legacy more widespread and enduring' than did McCheyne.[67] Thus the *Memoirs and Remains* present their subject as a typical Romantic hero, writing poetry, taking an interest in the struggle for Greek nationalism, and being 'naturally of a feeling and sentimental disposition'.[68] The volume's presentation of McCheyne's millennialism was also quite in keeping with its presentation of his personality and worldview. Most of the establishment ministers who had adopted millennialism had joined the Free Church's cause.[69] As a Calvinist and millennia!Romantic, McCheyne was becoming the patron saint of the Free Church movement.

Bonar's selections from his friends 'remains' illustrate the extent to which both Chalmers and Irving were crucial to McCheyne's developing millennia! commitment. The charges of heresy that surrounded Irving did not eclipse McCheyne's respect for him; in a diary entry for 9 November 1834, he noted his response to news of Irving's death: 'I look back upon him with awe, as on the saints and martyrs of old. A holy man in spite of all his delusions and errors. He is now with his God and Saviour, whom he wronged so much, yet, I

---

[66] Withrington, 'The Disruption' (1993), 119-120.

[67] *Blackwell Dictionary of Evangelical Biography,* s.v. 'McCheyne, Robert Murray'.

[68] Andrew Bonar, *Memoirs and Remains of Robert Murray McCheyne* (1844; second edition, 1892; rpt. Edinburgh, 1966), 4-5, 16.

[69] Ernest Sandeen, *The Roots of Fundamentalism: British and American Millenarianism, 1800-1930* (Chicago, 1970), 40.

am persuaded, loved so sincerely.'[70] Editing the memoirs, Bonar builds on that respect for Irving to emphasise McCheyne's involvement in the unfulfilled prophecy study-group that Bonar had established at universityo[71] (Of the members, Bonar noted, John Cochrane and Waiter Wood were both overtly committed to the premillennial faith;[72] of his brother Horatius, he noted that premillennialism was a 'grand characteristic of his ministry'.[73]) Again and again the memoir indicates McCheyne's interest in eschatological themes – he meditates upon the second coming before his third communion and expects that it may occur imminently;[74] he preaches on the second coming on 14 October 1838, and felt its power 'more than ever before, how the sudden coming of the Saviour constrains to a holy walk separate from sin'.[75] But although they debated several varieties of millennialism, Bonar could not get McCheyne to agree with his own point of viewo[76] McCheyne was sympathetic, noting in 1839 that the 'horror' of 'some good people in Glasgow at the millenarian views is very great, while at the same time their objections appear very weak'o[77] But where Bonar and McCheyne could agree, they shared a strong sense of the importance of Jewish missions and the centrality of the land of Israel in unfulfilled prophecy: McCheyne expected the Messiah to return to the literal land of Israel.[78] They seem also to have shared the Westminster Confession's identification of the Pope as the Man of Sin,[79] as the earlier *Narrative* emphasised, and both lived with a strong sense of apocalyptic imminence: 'The time is short; eternity is near; yea, the coming of Christ the second time is at hand.'[80] Thus those letters of McCheyne included in the memoir anticipate the second coming,[81] identify Revelation's 'kings of the east' as converted Jews (as he and Bonar had done at Smyrna),[82] and identify Roman Catholicism as the 'Babylon' doomed in Biblical prophecyo[83] His

---

[70] Bonar, *Robert Murray McCheyne* (1892), 270
[71] Bonar, *Robert Murray McCheyne* (1892), 300
[72] Bonar, *Robert Murray McCheyne* (1892), 180, 1850
[73] Bonar, *Robert Murray McCheyne* (1892), 1780
[74] Bonar, *Robert Murray McCheyne* (1892), 81.
[75] Bonar, *Robert Murray McCheyne* (1892), 820
[76] Bonar, *Robert Murray McCheyne* (1892), 840
[77] Bonar, *Robert Murray McCheyne* (1892), 1240
[78] Bonar, *Robert Murray McCheyne* (1892), 87, 960
[79] Bonar, *Robert Murray McCheyne* (1892), 1100
[80] Bonar, *Robert Murray McCheyne* (1892), 1330
[81] Bonar, *Robert Murray McCheyne* (1892), 210, 211, 213, 224,
[82] Bonar, *Robert Murray McCheyne* (1892), 2130
[83] Bonar, *Robert Murray McCheyne* (1892), 253, 261.

contemporary reputation was such that an Irish correspondent was able to inquire of him how best to study prophecy.[84]

But with McCheyne's untimely death, the Scottish evangelicals lost one of their most promising young leaders. In early January 1844, looking back over the tumultuous events of the previous twelve months, Bonar noted in his diary that 1843 'will be a marked year in eternity. I often feel that Christ's Coming is nearer and nearer.'[85] It was this strong sense of the imminent end of all things that coloured his portrayal of the life of McCheyne and his response to the early days of the Free Church movement.

## Charting the Free Church's Course

Facing an uncertain future, the apologists of the young Free Church launched a virile publicity campaign in which they sought to justify and explain the sacrifices of the ministers and laity who had left the establishment. The twin themes of revival and eschatology recur throughout their material. In 1845 Horatius Bonar, editing for republication John Gillies' *Historical Collections Relating to Remarkable Periods of the Success of the Gospel* (1754), wrote the early experiences of the new denomination into the canon of Scottish revivalism, 'not the history of the sleeping many, but of the waking few'.[86] A conclusion appended to Gillies' original work charted the impact of the religious revival that had accompanied the Disruption. Horatius Bonar noted that 'in Scotland there have been some very remarkable awakenings during the last half century. At Moulin, in 1798 and 1800; in the island of Skye, in 1812 and 1814; in the island of Lewis, in 1824 and 1835 — the Spirit of God seems to have been largely poured down.'[87] Extended space is given to the unusual events of Kilsyth in 1839, and further brief accounts are offered by a number of Disruption ministers including John Milne, John Purves, Robert Murray McCheyne, and Andrew Bonar. According to its apologists, the Free Church was a movement born in revival.

But while the apologists agreed on the importance of revival, they could not hide the Free Church's internal eschatological struggle. Building on his growing interest in Judaism, Andrew Bonar published *A Commentary on Leviticus* (1846), which interpreted the

---

[84] Bonar, *Robert Murray McCheyne* (1892), 292.

[85] Bonar (ed.), *Andrew A. Bonar* (1960), 111.

[86] Horatius Bonar, 'Editor's Preface', in John Gillies, *Historical Collections Relating to Remarkable Periods of the Success of the Gospel* (1754; rpt. Kelso, 1845), v.

[87] Gillies, *Historical Collections* (1845), 556.

Old Testament's ancient liturgical details through an evangelical and pre-millennial paradigm. With Bonar identified on the title page as the author of the *Narrative of a Mission of Inquiry to the Jews,* the commentary was explicitly aimed at convincing a Jewish readership of the propriety of regarding Jesus Christ as the Messiah, so that 'some of the house of Israel may here have their eye attracted to the Saviour'.[88] Bonar was clearly sustaining his argument by reference to the mission of inquiry, indicating that the fulfilment of prophecies relating to the Jewish nation was sufficient proof of the authenticity of the literal hermeneutic.[89] Again, Bonar demonstrated his eschatologically-influenced perception of a strong link between the conversion of the Jews and the revival of the Scottish church: 'the overflowing stream of the Holy Spirit (who shall be poured out at Jerusalem on the house of David first), winding its course over earth' would 'convey saving health to all nations'.[90] In his hermeneutic – which employed 'the obvious and common-sense principle' of literal interpretation[91] – he paradoxically drew upon the allegorical method of the epistle to the Hebrews, but admitted areas where millennialists and anti-millennialists were 'alike at sea', indicating that interpretive finality would be achieved only in the millennium itself, when Ezekiel's temple would be constructed as a vast symbol of the scheme of redemption.[92] Perhaps his readiness to anticipate a millennial temple owed something to the temple preparations he had witnessed on his 'mission of inquiry'. Certainly the commentary drew readers' attention to that expedition, and illustrates the extent to which Bonar drew upon the Jewish ideas of messianic hope that he had encountered.

Just as the Jews in Moldavia had suggested a paradigm of history founded upon the seven days of the week of creation, for example, so Bonar outlined human history in seven periods of one thousand years' duration: God 'allows the fallen world *its six days*– its 6,000 years – during which time no judgement is pronounced on it. He waits for the seventh day, when the priest, who has examined already into the case, shall come and see the "shut up" leper, and declare his doom.'[93] The typology of the Sabbath, he believed, regularly represents millennial rest: 'it will be on the morning of *the*

---

[88] Andrew A. Bonar, *A Commentary on the Book of Leviticus* (London, 1846), IV.
[89] Bonar, *Leviticus* (1846), v.
[90] Bonar, *Leviticus* (1846), vii.
[91] Bonar, *Leviticus* (1846), 19.
[92] Bonar, *Leviticus* (1846), viii, x.
[93] Bonar, *Leviticus* (1846), 206, 225-6.

*Sabbath,* the seventh thousand year of the earth, that He shall be set gloriously before his people in fresh fullness.'[94] This symbolism had been built into the pattern of chronology established in the world's first week: 'each *Sabbath-day* was a type of the coming rest to creation after its 6,000 years of woe.'[95] All would then have perfect understanding of the events the Bible had foretold: 'in those days of millennia!glory, much that is new shall be discovered; tenfold light will be cast on many a truth.'[96] But perhaps the most significant event that should occur in the millennium would be a dramatic confirmation of the propriety of the literal hermeneutic – Israel would return to her ancestral homeland and to a living relationship with her covenant God: '**It** is true, they may return *before* they repent; but the *land* is not theirs *until* they repent.'[97] Writing in 'the evening of the world's day', and with contemporary geo-politics increasingly confirming his pessimistic worldview, it was easy for Bonar to anticipate the Second Coming 'even before we have slept with our fathers, if it seem good in thy sight'.[98]

What is perhaps most remarkable about the Leviticus commentary is its evidence that Bonar, a mere three years after the Disruption, was already sitting lightly on the foundational issue in Free Church apologetics – the issue of Biblical church government. He was certainly renegotiating the ecclesiological controversy in denying both the Erastianism and the voluntaryism then concerning the Scottish churches. A church, he lamented, 'may be denying some great truth in theory or in practice. Thus, it may make light of the duty which kings and magistrates owe to Christ, as is done by some Churches.' Alternatively, it 'may be admitting some civil element into the management of its spiritual affairs, as is done in many Protestant Churches.'[99] But **if these** errors are avoided, he claimed, the form of church government that is chosen is 'not in any way the essence of the truth, but it is the fence around the truth. **It** is not the jewel, but it is the precious case that encloses the more precious jewel. Whatever form of worship is best fitted to effect this purpose is surely the best for our adoption.'[100] This ambivalence may explain his later preaching for the Plymouth Brethren assembly in Bristol, where he 'was received with great cordiality'. Invited by Henry

---

[94] Bonar, *Leviticus* (1846), 410.
[95] Bonar, *Leviticus* (1846), 419.
[96] Bonar, *Leviticus* (1846), 444.
[97] Bonar, *Leviticus* (1846), 465.
[98] Bonar, *Leviticus* (1846), 175-6.
[99] Bonar, *Leviticus* (1846), 64.
[100] Bonar, *Leviticus* (1846), 347.

Craik, who had been educated at St Andrews and had served on the committee of the St Andrews University Missionary Association which Chalmers patronised, Bonar was charting a course of personal fellowship that seems consistent with his premillennial interests but hardly consistent with the boundaries of the confessional Presbyterianism against which he was increasingly reacting.[101]

But others were much less inclined to either Bonar's ecclesiastical ambivalence or his enthusiasm for premillennialism. In 1846, the Glasgow Free Church minister David Brown, who had been assistant to Edward Irving until the outbreak of tongues-speaking in his London church, questioned his earlier premillennialism in a major work entitled *Christ's Second Coming: Will it be Premillennial?* His book was a theological sensation, the most thorough English-language defence of postmillennialism published to that date, and an ironic indication of the extent to which premillennialism was increasing in influence and was being popularised by the Bonars, as the repeated references to Horatius and 'my estimable friend' Andrew would indicate.[102] Brown's book certainly seems to have been part of a rush of millennial speculation. In 1849, an editorial in the first issue of the *Quarterly Journal of Prophecy* declared its purpose to 'awaken inquiry' into prophetical studies: 'The increase of inquirers, especially in Scotland, during the last five years, is most cheering', though, they admitted, 'many who are studying "things hoped for," are by no means firmly established' in the premillennial faith.[103] Much was at stake; Brown's vigorous polemic could not go unanswered. Andrew Bonar replied with *Redemption Drawing Nigh* (1847), and Horatius provided three article-length refutations in the *Presbyterian Review* as well as a book-length critique. These arguments were followed up by Andrew Bonar's matured thoughts on what he regarded as the doctrinal foundation of confessional postmillennialism – the largely uncontested identity of the 'man of sin'. In a dramatic reversal of his earlier position, Bonar listed in *The Development of Antichrist* (1853) a number of reasons why he could no longer believe that the 'man of sin' was the Pope. It was an overt attack upon the Westminster Confession – and one, significantly, that never explicitly named the confession as its target.

---

[101] Stuart Piggin and John Roxborogh, *The St. Andrews Seven* (Edinburgh, 1985), 51; Bonar (ed.), *Andrew A. Bonar* (1960), 116, 249.

[102] David Brown, *Christ's Second Coming: Will it be Premillennial?* (1846; 1882 ed., rpt. Edmonton, 1990), 91.

[103] 'Preface', *Quarterly Journal of Prophecy* 1 (1849), iv.

## The Westminster Confession and
## *The Development of Antichrist* (1853)

Perhaps this silence indicates Bonar's sense that Presbyterians were highly aware of the Confession's status while being insufficiently aware of its contents. It does seem that the Confession was being cited in the eschatological debate. The *Quarterly Journal of Prophecy* – with Horatius as its editor – cited 'some of the soundest and most eminent divines of the Westminster Assembly' as premillennialists.[104] Diplomacy was certainly required, for Bonar was attempting to challenge a formidable doctrinal consensus. For over two centuries, the institutions of Scottish Presbyterianism had spoken with one voice on the identity of the true church's eschatological enemy, the antichrist, the 'man of sin'. The subordinate standard of the Presbyterian churches clearly identified the antichrist as the Pope (Westminster Confession of Faith 25:6). With the rise of premillennialism, however, many interpreters were increasingly moving away from the principle of historicism, in which Revelation was believed to represent the drama of the totality of church history, to futurism, in which Revelation was believed to apply mostly to the events at the conclusion of world history.[105] It became increasingly difficult to integrate an historicist view of the antichrist with a futurist view of the rest of the book. Wider trends in the evangelical interpretation of Revelation were militating against the continuing identification of the traditional enemy of Protestants.

Writing his account of *The Development of Antichrist,* Bonar explicitly signalled the historical context of the 'Pope as antichrist' idea. He documented the opinions of the Church Fathers to evidence his claim that 'the idea of a personal Antichrist with a short supremacy at the close of this dispensation is no novelty...it was in fact the universal early belief, men then taking Scripture words to mean what they really said.'[106] Instead, it was reserved 'for a later generation, who had fallen under the cruelties of papal oppression, to fancy it to be the unequalled trouble and predicted apostasy of the last times, and even to alter the literal meaning of words to make it so'.[107] Bonar believed that these 'fanciful and metaphorical interpreters' – among whom, presumably, he included the West-

---

[104] *Quarterly Journal of Prophecy* 1:2 (1849), 199-200.
[105] D.N. Hempton, 'Evangelicalism and Eschatology', *JEH* 31 (1980), 179-94.
[106] Andrew Bonar, *The Development of Antichrist* (1853; rpr. Chelmsford, n.d.), 54.
[107] Bonar, *Antichrist* (n.d.), 15.

minster divines – had obscured the clear teaching of Scripture.[108] The historic development of Protestant eschatology emphasised their difficulty: 'the whole way by which they have come, is strewed with abandoned assertions.'[109]

Ironically, however, Bonar based a great deal of his Biblicist opposition to the confessional view upon contemporary events rather than Biblical exegesis. He repeatedly claimed that one of the major reasons why the Pope could not be antichrist was simply because the Papacy had become too weak.[110] Neither, he believed, did the seventeenth-century opinion of the Westminster Confession take account of contemporary threats to the elect of God in the rise of Islam, the growing influence of Voltaire, and the military danger of Napoleon.[111] To define the antichrist as the Pope, therefore, was to ignore too many of the apocalyptic threats of the modern world. Thus he pointed to the impact of political media in the new urban centres. The 'weekly issue of impure and irreligious publications in the Metropolis' cast doubt on the imminent golden age the postmillennialists seemed to be expecting; 'no thinking man does believe this, or that the pope can be either the only or even the greatest Antichrist we are to see.'[112]

These political publications, and the democratic ideas they advocated, gave great concern to many evangelical leaders. Some premillennialists linked the growth of popular republicanism to the future tyranny of antichrist.[113] In similar fashion, Bonar understood the growth of secular democracy to represent one of the most serious dangers facing Victorian evangelicals. In his Edinburgh lectures of 1828, Irving had railed against Parliament's considering the repeal of the Test Act, which was designed to annul previous restrictions on political involvement.[114] Bonar seemed to echo Irving's fears. To thoughtlessly expand the franchise was to let 'the greatest questions be decided by expediency, or (what is nearly the same thing) the wisdom of the majorities, with a sneer at every attempt to appeal to Scripture for guidance'; to do away with the demand that public officials should be members of established churches was to 'frame laws by which the Roman Catholic may legislate and hold office in our Protestant community, and the Jew, too, sit in parliaments, care

---

108 Bonar, *Antichrist* (n.d.), 8.
109 Bonar, *Antichrist* (n.d.), 98.
110 Bonar, *Antichrist* (n.d.), 16-7.
111 Bonar, *Antichrist* (n.d.), 20.
112 Bonar, *Antichrist* (n.d.), 95.
113 *Quarterly Journal of Prophecy* 2 (1850), 302-3.
114 Dallimore, *Life of Edward Irving* (1983), 86.

having been taken that his conscientious belief of our Saviour being an impostor should meet with nothing to offend it on entering there'.[115] Evangelical concerns about the impact of popular democracy were not only directed at the electoral preferences of the newly enfranchised classes, but also at the formerly marginalized interest groups who might profit by their votes. Bonar seems therefore to prove David Hempton's claim that 'Pre-millennialism, at least in the early stages of its growth, attracted men with several of the following characteristics – biblical literalism, social and ecclesiastical pessimism, Calvinism, anti-Catholicism, anti-radicalism, anti-rationalism and support for the Established Churches.'[116]

But Bonar's fear of Jews in Parliament should not be understood as anti-Semitism, however; Bonar continued to find the Jewish people at the centre of unfulfilled prophecy. By 1853, he was certain that the evangelisation of the world (though not its conversion, of which he despaired) would be completed before the Jews would return to centre stage in the unfolding of providence.[117] In a major revision to his earlier writings, Bonar argued that the Jewish people would return to Israel *before* the millennium, and in unbelief.[118] Their return to the land would begin the cataclysmic final seven years of world history, and would occur at the same time as the revelation of the antichrist and the final apostasy in the Gentile churches. Under the wrath of God, they would rebuild the Temple (preparations for which were already being made in the United States), re-establish the sacrificial system, and enter a time of unparalleled tribulation.[119] And, in 1853, these events could not be thought of as far off: 'the tendency of all things is toward 'the apostasy' and the revelation of the man of sin.'[120]

*The Development of the Antichrist* certainly suggested that the apostasy of the Gentile churches was near at hand. In fact, Bonar argued, the growing influence of liberal German theology was grounded in the basic problem of the Scottish churches – the allegorical hermeneutic they had constructed in order to shore up their postmillennial consensus. In his belief, the hermeneutic of postmillennialism was simply inconsistent with a high view of Scripture.[121] Its allegorical method was shared with German

[115] Bonar, *Antichrist* (n.d.), 22.
[116] Hempton, 'Evangelicalism and Eschatology' (1980), 191.
[117] Bonar, *Antichrist* (n.d.), 57.
[118] Bonar, *Antichrist* (n.d.), 31, 34.
[119] Bonar, *Antichrist* (n.d.), 35, 38, 40.
[120] Bonar, *Antichrist* (n.d.), 71.
[121] Bonar, *Antichrist* (n.d.), 93.

liberalism and was consequently damned by this association.[122] So long as the postmillennialists controlled the ecclesiastical establishment, Bonar implied, they were tacitly paving the way for the triumph of the theology they contested. Surveying the situation of Free Church evangelicals ten years after the Disruption, Bonar could only expect 'a darker day than has appeared'.[123] But the roots of the liberalism he so feared, and the postmillennialism that seemed to justify it, lay, Bonar believed, in the Westminster Confession of Faith. The foundational document of Scottish Presbyterianism, and the eschatological consensus based upon it, had paved the way for the eclipse of the evangelical ideal; the Free Church cause had been betrayed by the contents of its evangelical constitution. Bonar's study of *The Development of the Antichrist* was offering a radical re-interpretation of Scottish ecclesiastical life. One reviewer noted, 'It has not convinced us, but we have read it with much pleasure.'[124]

This polite but distant reception did not obscure the seriousness of the situation. With postmillennialists controlling many of the church's institutions, Bonar needed recourse to argument. But he did not defend the church's confusion on the basis of the free play of ideas; instead, he pointed to the influence of Satan, who, if he could not eclipse the church's interest in prophecy, would do what he could to confuse it.[125] To combat this form of demonic attack, and to expand his circle of ecclesiastical influence, it was vital that Bonar should return to an urban congregation. Within three years, in 1856, he had been called to the urban pastorate of Finnieston, and had declared his intention to go with one stated ambition: 'I desire to bear witness to Christ's Coming in the city of Glasgow.'[126] His priorities made it already clear why he would be out-of-step with the celebration of the revival in 1859. Its appropriation by postmillennial historians meant that the revival of true religion was being celebrated in terms that would lead, irreversibly, to its decline. It was a concern to maintain premillennial orthodoxy and Biblical inerrancy that forced Andrew Bonar to abandon the Westminster Confession of Faith.

### Postscript: The Triumph of Premillennialism

But if Bonar was out of step with the prevailing optimism of 1859, he would recover his equilibrium fifteen years later. In November 1873

---

[122] Bonar, *Antichrist* (n.d.), 98.
[123] Bonar, *Antichrist* (n.d.), 99.
[124] *Quarterly Journal of Prophecy* 5 (1853), 198.
[125] Bonar, *Antichrist* (n.d.), 4.
[126] Bonar (ed.), *Andrew A. Bonar* (1960), 174.

the American revivalist Dwight L. Moody arrived in Scotland with Ira D. Sankey. Their series of mass crusades in Edinburgh, Glasgow and other towns on the west of Scotland attracted unparalleled numbers and the criticism of those conservative clergy who objected to Sankey's innovative use of hymns, his musical accompaniment of public worship, and Moody's apparent doctrinal deviations. Resisting the objections of leaders of the Highland Free Church, Horatius Bonar took a leading role in defending the Americans from conservative attacks, and Andrew Bonar, too, publicly endorsed Moody's message.[127] In Finnieston Free Church, during scenes of revival, Moody preached on the subject of the Second Coming.[128] Moody returned Bonar's invitation, and in August 1881 Bonar was speaking at his Northfield Conference.[129] The American trip interrupted Bonar's climactic series of forty monthly lectures on prophetic themes. These lectures, delivered in the Finnieston church between 1879 and 1883, seemed to Bonar 'the finishing of my works'.[130] But there was more to come.

Nearly thirty years after the 1859 revival, in November 1886, Bonar wrote a 'letter of regret' to the organisers of the International Prophetic Conference in Chicago. Sharing their 'cherished hope of the pre-millennial coming of the Lord', Bonar demonstrated his continued eschatological interest: 'during all my ministry (now nearly forty-eight years) I can not recollect of any occasion on which I brought to a close the services of a communion Sabbath without reminding my flock of what was implied in "till he comes".'[131] But Bonar's inability to attend the Chicago conference did not preclude him from organising one of his own. In October 1888, when Bonar hosted a three-day conference of prophetic studies in the Free Church General Assembly hall in Edinburgh. It was an iconic occasion. At last, in the institutional centre of the Free Church, he was able celebrate the premillennialism that had so determined his ecclesiastical career. At least, he could claim, the legacy of Chalmers was his: 'Our Professor in the Divinity Hall was Dr. Chalmers, and we sometimes told him our thoughts on these subjects, and the opposition shown to us....I am glad to say that before he died he

---

[127] Ross, 'Calvinists in Controversy' (1991), 51-63.
[128] Bonar (ed.), *Andrew A. Bonar* (1960), 294.
[129] Bonar (ed.), *Andrew A. Bonar* (1960), 330.
[130] Bonar (ed.), *Andrew A. Bonar* (1960), 323, 338, 521.
[131] *Prophetic Studies of the International Prophetic Conference (Chicago, November 1886)* (Chicago, 1886), 41. I owe this reference to the generosity of the Rev. Dr Barry Horner.

ranged himself with the Premillennialists.'[132] Bonar's comments observed the emerging pan-denominational fellowship of premillennial evangelicals: 'Fifty years ago, those of us that held this truth were very few and much despised. But these three days have been days when, from all sections of the Church of Christ, there have been brethren brought together.'[133] With its novel basis for unity, Bonar's conference was constructing in Scotland the kind of evangelical ecumenism that he had witnessed at Moody's Northfield conferences. Based upon a shared commitment to premillennialism and the Biblical inerrancy that underpinned its literal hermeneutic, Bonar had moved from his early obscurity, caused by his commitment to the premillennial faith, to take a leading role in the emergence of a British fundamentalism.[134] Within fifty years, the premillennialism that had frustrated Bonar's early career, and signalled his distance from confessional orthodoxy, had come to characterise his crowning achievement.

---

[132] Andrew A. Bonar, *Sheaves After Harvest: A Group of Addresses by Dr. Andrew Bonar, Edited by his Daughters* (London, n.d.), 44. I owe this reference to Bonar scholar Jayne Newbold. The claim that Chalmers tended towards premillennialism was repeated in *Quarterly Journal of Prophecy* 1 (1849), 70, and *Quarterly Journal of Prophecy* 3 (1851), 416.

[133] Bonar (ed.), *Andrew A. Bonar* (1960), 359.

[134] The American prophetic conferences are discussed in Sandeen, *Roots of Fundamentalism* (1970), 132-161.

# Index

# Studies in Evangelical History and Thought
*(All titles uniform with this volume)*
Dates in bold are of projected publication

Clyde Binfield
**The Country a Little Thickened and Congested?**
*Nonconformity in Eastern England 1840-1885*
Studies of Victorian religion and society often concentrate on cities, suburbs, and industrialisation. This study provides a contrast. Victorian Eastern England-Essex, Suffolk, Norfolk, Cambridgeshire, and Huntingdonshire-was rural, traditional, relatively unchanging. That is nonetheless a caricature which discounts the industry in Norwich and Ipswich (as well as in Haverhill, Stowmarket, and Leiston) and ignores the impact of London on Essex, of railways throughout the region, and of an ancient but changing university (Cambridge) on the county town which housed it. It also entirely ignores the political implications of such changes in a region noted for the variety of its religious Dissent since the seventeenth century. This book explores Victorian Eastern England and its Nonconformity. It brings to a wider readership a pioneering thesis which has made a major contribution to a fresh evolution of English religion and society.
*2005 1 1-84227-216-0 1approx. 274pp*

John Brencher
**Martyn Lloyd-Jones (1899-1981) and Twentieth-Century Evangelicalism**
This study critically demonstrates the significance of the life and ministry of Martyn Lloyd-Jones for post-war British evangelicalism and demonstrates that his preaching was his greatest influence on twentieth-century Christianity. The factors which shaped his view of the church are examined, as is the way his reformed evangelicalism led to a separatist ecclesiology which divided evangelicals.
*2002 1 1-84227-051-6 1xvi + 268pp*

Jonathan D. Burnham
**A Story of Conflict**
*The Controversial Relationship between Benjamin Wills Newton
and John Nelson Darby*
Burnham explores the controversial relationship between the two principal leaders of the early Brethren movement. In many ways Newton and Darby were products of their times, and this study of their relationship provides insight not only into the dynamics of early Brethrenism, but also into the progress of nineteenth-century English and Irish evangelicalism.
*2004 1 1-84227-191-1 1xxiv + 268pp*

J.N. Ian Dickson
**Beyond Religious Discourse**
*Sermons, Preaching and Evangelical Protestants in*
*Nineteenth-Century Irish Society*
Drawing extensively on primary sources, this pioneer work in modem religious history explores the training of preachers, the construction of sermons and how Irish evangelicalism and the wider movement in Great Britain and the United States shaped the preaching event. Evangelical preaching and politics, sectarianism, denominations, education, class, social reform, gender, and revival are examined to advance the argument that evangelical sermons and preaching went significantly beyond religious discourse. The result is a book for those with interests in Irish history, culture and belief, popular religion and society, evangelicalism, preaching and communication.
*2005 1 1-84227-217-9 1 approx. 324pp*

Neil T.R. Dickson
**Brethren in Scotland 1838-2000**
*A Social Study of an Evangelical Movement*
The Brethren were remarkably pervasive throughout Scottish society. This study of the Open Brethren in Scotland places them in their social context and examines their growth, development and relationship to society.
*2003 1 1-84227-113-X lxxviii + 510pp*

Crawford Gribben and Timothy C.F. Stunt (eds)
**Prisoners of Hope?**
*Aspects of Evangelical Millennia/ism in Britain and Ireland, 1800-1880*
This volume of essays offers a comprehensive account of the impact of evangelical millennialism in nineteenth-century Britain and Ireland.
*2004 1 1-84227-224-1 lxiv + 208pp*

Khim Harris
**Evangelicals and Education** *Evangelical*
*Anglicans and Middle-Class Education in*
*Nineteenth-Century England*
This ground breaking study investigates the history of English public schools founded by nineteenth-century Evangelicals. It documents the rise of middle-class education and Evangelical societies such as the influential Church Association, and includes a useful biographical survey of prominent Evangelicals of the period.
*2004 1 1-84227-250-0 1 xviii + 422pp*

Mark Hopkins
**Nonconformity's Romantic Generation**
*Evangelical and Liberal Theologies in Victorian England*
A study of the theological development of key leaders of the Baptist and Congregational denominations at their period of greatest influence, including C.H. Spurgeon and R.W. Dale, and of the controversies in which those among them who embraced and rejected the liberal transformation of their evangelical heritage opposed each other.
*2004 1 1-84227-150-4lxvi + 284pp*

Don Horrocks
**Laws of the Spiritual Order** *Innovation and*
*Reconstruction in the Soteriology ofThomas*
*Erskine ofLinlathen*
Don Horrocks argues that Thomas Erskine's unique historical and theological significance as a soteriological innovator has been neglected. This timely reassessment reveals Erskine as a creative, radical theologian of central and enduring importance in Scottish nineteenth-century theology, perhaps equivalent in significance to that of S.T. Coleridge in England.
*200411-84227-192-XIxx + 362pp*

Kenneth S. Jeffrey
**When the Lord Walked the Land**
*The 1858-62 Revival in the North East of Scotland*
Previous studies of revivals have tended to approach religious movements from either a broad, national or a strictly local level. This study of the multifaceted nature of the 1859 revival as it appeared in three distinct social contexts within a single region reveals the heterogeneous nature of simultaneous religious movements in the same vicinity.
*2002 1 1-84227-057-5 1xxiv + 304pp*

John Kenneth Lander
**Itinerant Temples**
*Tent Methodism, 1814-1832*
Tent preaching began in 1814 and the Tent Methodist sect resulted from disputes with Bristol Wesleyan Methodists in 1820. The movement spread to parts of Gloucestershire, Wiltshire, London and Liverpool, among other places. Its demise started in 1826 after which one leader returned to the Wesleyans and others became ministers in the Congregational and Baptist denominations.
*2003 1 1-84227-151-2 lxx + 268pp*

Donald M. Lewis
**Lighten Their Darkness**
*The Evangelical Mission to Working-Class London, 1828-1860*
This is a comprehensive and compelling study of the Church and the complexities of nineteenth-century London. Challenging our understanding of the culture in working London at this time, Lewis presents a well-structured and illustrated work that contributes substantially to the study of evangelicalism and mission in nineteenth-century Britain.
*2001 1 1-84227-074-5 lxviii + 372pp*

Herbert McGonigle
**'Sufficient Saving Grace'**
*John Wesley's Evangelical Arminianism*
A thorough investigation of the theological roots of John Wesley's evangelical Arminianism and how these convictions were hammered out in controversies on predestination, limited atonement and the perseverance of the saints.
*2001 1 1-84227-045-1 lxvi + 350pp*

Lisa S. Nolland
**A Victorian Feminist Christian**
*Josephine Butler, the Prostitutes and God*
Josephine Butler was an unlikely candidate for taking up the cause of prostitutes, as she did, with a fierce and self-disregarding passion. This book explores the particular mix of perspectives and experiences that came together to envision and empower her remarkable achievements. It highlights the vital role of her spirituality and the tragic loss of her daughter.
*2004 1 1-84227-225-X 1 approx. 360pp*

Ian M. Randall
**Evangelical Experiences**
*A Study in the Spirituality of English Evangelicalism 1918-1939*
This book makes a detailed historical examination of evangelical spirituality between the First and Second World Wars. It shows how patterns of devotion led to tensions and divisions. In a wide-ranging study, Anglican, Wesleyan, Reformed and Pentecostal-charismatic spiritualities are analysed.
*1999 1 0-85364-919-7 1 xii + 310pp*

Ian M. Randall
**Spirituality and Social Change**
*The Contribution of F.B. Meyer (1847-1929)*
This is a fresh appraisal of F.B. Meyer (1847-1929), a leading Free Church minister. Having been deeply affected by holiness spirituality, Meyer became the Keswick Convention's foremost international speaker. He combined spirituality with effective evangelism and socio-political activity. This study shows Meyer's significant contribution to spiritual renewal and social change.
*2003 1 1-84227-195-4 1xx + 184pp*

James Robinson
**Pentecostal Origins (1907-c.1925): A Regional Study**
*Early Pentecostalism in Ulster within its British Context*
Harvey Cox describes Pentecostalism as 'the fascinating spiritual child of our time' that has the potential, at the global scale, to contribute to the 'reshaping of religion in the twenty-first century'. This study grounds such sentiments by examining at the local scale the origin, development and nature of Pentecostalism in the north of Ireland in its first twenty years. Illustrative, in a paradigmatic way, of how Pentecostalism became established within one region of the British Isles, it sets the story within the wider context of formative influences emanating from America, Europe and, in particular, other parts of the British Isles. As a synoptic regional study in Pentecostal history it is the first survey of its kind.
***2005** 1 1-84227-329-9 1approx. 424pp*

Geoffrey Robson
**Dark Satanic Mills?**
*Religion and Irreligion in Birmingham and the Black Country*
This book analyses and interprets the nature and extent of popular Christian belief and practice in Birmingham and the Black Country during the first half of the nineteenth century, with particular reference to the impact of cholera epidemics and evangelism on church extension programmes.
*2002 1 1-84227-102-4 1xiv + 294pp*

Roger Shuff
**Searching for the True Church**
*Brethren and Evangelicals in Mid-Twentieth-Century England*
Roger Shuff holds that the influence of the Brethren movement on wider evangelical life in England in the twentieth century is often underrated. This book records and accounts for the fact that Brethren reached the peak of their strength at the time when evangelicalism was at it lowest ebb, immediately before World War 11. However, the movement then moved into persistent decline as evangelicalism regained ground in the post war period. Accompanying this downward trend has been a sharp accentuation of the contrast between Brethren congregations who engage constructively with the non-Brethren scene and, at the other end of the spectrum, the isolationist group commonly referred to as 'Exclusive Brethren'.
*2005 1 1-84227-254-3 1 approx. 318pp*

James H.S. Steven
**Worship in the Spirit**
*Charismatic Worship in the Church of England*
This book explores the nature and function of worship in six Church of England churches influenced by the Charismatic Movement, focusing on congregational singing and public prayer ministry. The theological adequacy of such ritual is discussed in relation to pneumatological and christological understandings in Christian worship.
*2002 1 1-84227-103-2 lxvi + 238pp*

Peter K. Stevenson
**God in Our Nature**
*The Incarnational Theology of John McLeod Campbell*
This radical reassessment of Campbell's thought arises from a comprehensive study of his preaching and theology. Previous accounts have overlooked both his sermons and his Christology. This study examines the distinctive Christology evident in his sermons and shows that it sheds new light on Campbell's much debated views about atonement.
*2004 11-84227-218-7 lxxiv + 458pp*

Martin Wellings
**Evangelicals Embattled**
*Responses of Evangelicals in the Church of England to Ritualism, Darwinism and Theological Liberalism 1890-1930*
In the closing years of the nineteenth century and the first decades of the twentieth century Anglican Evangelicals faced a series of challenges. In responding to Anglo-Catholicism, liberal theology, Darwinism and biblical criticism, the unity and identity of the Evangelical school were severely tested.
*2003 1 1-84227-049-4 1 xviii + 352pp*

James Whisenant
A Fragile Unity
*Anti-Ritualism and the Division of Anglican Evangelicalism
in the Nineteenth Century*
This book deals with the ritualist controversy (approximately 1850-1900) from the perspective of its evangelical participants and considers the divisive effects it had on the party.
*2003 1 1-84227-105-9 lxvi + 530pp*

Haddon Willmer
Evangelicalism 1785-1835: An Essay (1962) and Reflections (2004)
Awarded the Hulsean Prize in the University of Cambridge in 1962, this interpretation of a classic period of English Evangelicalism, by a young church historian, is now supplemented by reflections on Evangelicalism from the vantage point of a retired Professor of Theology.
*2005 1 1-84227-219-5*

Linda Wilson
Constrained by Zeal
*Female Spirituality amongst Nonconformists 1825-1875*
*Constrained by Zeal* investigates the neglected area of Nonconformist female spirituality. Against the background of separate spheres, it analyses the experience of women from four denominations, and argues that the churches provided a 'third sphere' in which they could find opportunities for participation.
*2000 1 0-85364-972-3 lxvi + 294pp*

Paternoster
9 Holdom Avenue
Bletchley
Milton Keynes MK1 1QR
United Kingdom

Web: www.authenticmedia.co.uk/patemoster

November 2004

ND - #0094 - 270225 - C0 - 229/152/12 - PB - 9781842272244 - Gloss Lamination